How Children Learn to Write

How Children Learn to Write

How Children Learn to Write

Supporting and Developing Children's Writing in Schools

Dorothy Latham

**Paul Chapman
Publishing**

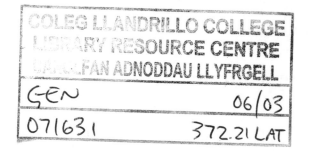
First published 2002

Paul Chapman Publishing
A SAGE Publications Company
6 Bonhill Street
London EC2A 4PU

SAGE Publications Inc
2455 Teller Road
Thousand Oaks, California 91320

SAGE Publications India Pvt Ltd
32, M-Block Market
Greater Kailash - I
New Delhi 110 048

Library of Congress Control Number: 2002105148

A catalogue record for this book is available from the
British Library

ISBN 0 7619 4781 7
ISBN 0 7619 4782 5 (pbk)

Typeset by Pantek Arts Ltd, Maidstone, Kent
Printed in Great Britain by Cromwell Press,
Trowbridge, Wiltshire

Contents

Acknowledgements   vii

Preface: About this Book – A Route Map   ix

Introduction: Writing and the Alphabet   xi

1 Early Brain Development, Laterality and Gender Differences   1

2 Early Speech, Language Acquisition and Related Theories   17

3 Language and Thinking, and Cultural and Social Influences on Language Use   31

4 Some Cognitive Functions in Literacy – How Working Memory Affects Reading and Writing   45

5 The Development of Secretarial Skills – Spelling, Handwriting and Presentation   59

6 Stages of Writing Development and their Evaluation   73

7 A Taxonomy of Writing Purposes and their Pertinence for Cross-Curricular Application   91

8 Basic Strategies for Extending and Enhancing Self-Generated Writing   113

9 Using Reading to Enhance Writing   131

10 Using Speaking and Listening and Drama to Stimulate Writing   147

Epilogue: Improving Writing – An Overview   159

Appendix   167

Glossary   177

Bibliography   187

Index of Authors and Sources   203

Subject Index   205

| Acknowledgements

In the course of my work I am often asked by headteachers and English co-ordinators how they can improve their schools' performances in writing. Teaching children to write is complex and not an easy task. This book sums up my professional knowledge and experience as an in-depth response to the problem, and I hope it will help individual students, serving teachers and whole school staffs. I write as an independent educationist and do not represent any official authority or body.

The book also owes some of its origins to the initiative of Miss M. Byrne, sometime Inspector for Early Years with Kent County Council's Education Department, when she produced a groundbreaking in-service package for Kent teachers entitled 'Becoming a Writer'. Later, overtaken and rendered out of date by new structures and information in the National Curriculum for England and the National Literacy Strategy, it nevertheless owned seminal status for my ideas at the start. Thanks are also due to Mike Aylen, Principal Adviser for Kent County Council's Education Department for his professional help and encouragement, and to a number of colleagues in both the education service and the inspection service. Among these must be mentioned Professor Stephen Clift, Margaret Alfrey and Teresa Grainger, all of Canterbury Christ Church University College, who gave me encouragement and support in pursuing my plan for the book. I must also thank Bob Cross, of Phoenix Educational Consultants, for whose inspection teams I designed the initial version of the Reading Profile. Deserving of a big vote of thanks are my inspector colleagues, particularly Marie Gibbon, and also Pamela Evans and Wendy Simmons, who acted as sounding boards for my ideas, helped with collecting examples of writing, visits to schools, and spent hours reading through drafts and giving me feedback. Others who helped with reading and the preparation of the book, to whom I am most grateful, are experienced teacher Celia Chester, and my efficient secretary Suzanne Philpott. I must also mention help from my computer expert, Rob Pepper.

Most of all, I must thank many schools, their headteachers, deputy heads and their English co-ordinators, who have helped by reading and discussing text, providing ideas and allowing me to use examples of pupils' work; I must, of course, include thanks to all those pupils themselves as well. These schools include the following primary schools:

All Saints Junior School, Hastings
Glebe Junior School, Rayleigh
Guardian Angels RCP School, Bethnal Green
Hernhill CP School, Hernhill, Faversham
Hollybrook Junior School, Southampton
John Scurr Primary School, Tower Hamlets
Lyon Park Junior School, Wembley
Meon Junior School, Portsmouth

Oliver Tomkins Infant School, Toothill, Swindon
Our Lady of Lourdes RCP School, Rottingdean
Rucstall CP School, Basingstoke
St Anne's RCP School, Basingstoke
St Helen's RCP School, Southend-on-Sea
St Paul's Cray CEP School, Bromley
St Peter Chanel RCP School, Bexley
St Saviour's CEP School, Westgate-on-Sea
Sandgate CP School, Folkestone
Sir Francis Drake Primary School, Lewisham
Summerlea CP School, Rustington
Swanmore CEP School, Swanmore, Southampton
Tenterden CP Infants' School, Tenterden

Secondary schools include:

Holsworthy Community College, Holsworthy
Kingsmead Community School, Wiveliscombe
and Greendown Community School, Swindon, where Assistant Headteacher
Tim Noble provided information about the Swindon Millennium Shakespeare
Festival for local schools, and related work and activities.

Finally I must record that I have tried to be accurate in factual matters and in
reflecting opinions, and have made every effort to trace sources appropriately:
any errors, omissions or ambiguities are entirely unintentional.

Dorothy Latham

Preface
About this Book – A Route Map

This book traces the processes involved in children learning to write, and uses some implications from these to show how certain strategies can enhance progress in writing. It is in line with the English National Curriculum for England and the National Literacy Strategy Framework for England and their related documents, and shows how the factors important for teaching and learning underlie such recommendations for practice. The target age range of the book is from 3 to 13, within the National Curriculum for England key stages of the Foundation stage, and Key Stages 1, 2 and 3. Issues such as the gender gap, teaching pupils for whom English is an additional language and left-handedness are discussed.

The book is intended as an information book about learning to write, from which further studies in particular areas of interest can be followed up by reading referenced publications. It is intended both for student teachers and serving teachers in schools wishing to study the context of writing in further depth. It provides activities for teachers and their colleagues, or whole staffs, to do and to discuss, and gives useful links for further reading. It can thus be used for school-based INSET.

The book is divided into two main parts: Chapters 1–5 deal with the underlying processes and skills needed in becoming a writer, and Chapters 6–10 show how children make progress in their self-generated writing, with a look at some of the major influences that can enhance their development as writers. Some ideas for sound but easy ongoing assessment of writing are included.

There is a short Introduction giving an overview of the derivation of the Western alphabet and how it contrasts with other world writing systems. The book ends by summarizing the most salient points for improving children's progress in writing, and a perspective on writing in the twenty-first century.

The following is a brief breakdown of the chapters and their main focuses:

Introduction – The alphabet

Chapter 1 – Brain development and structures

Chapter 2 – The acquisition of speech

Chapter 3 – Language and thinking

Chapter 4 – Working memory

Chapter 5 – Secretarial skills

Chapter 6 – Milestones in composition

Chapter 7 – Writing purposes and cross-curricular applications

Chapter 8 – Basic strategies for enhancing self-generated writing

Chapter 9 – Using reading to enhance writing

Chapter 10 – Using speech and drama to enhance writing

Epilogue – Pointers for improving writing and a perspective on writing in the twenty-first century

National Curriculum Terminology

In order not to repeat explanations of the ages of pupils attached to key terms used in the National Curriculum for England and related documents, the following notes are provided:

The National Curriculum – the National Curriculum for schools in England: it comprises ten subjects. Where reference is being made to the National Curriculum for England in the subject of English, the term 'The English National Curriculum' may be used, or if it is clear we are talking about English as a subject, merely 'The National Curriculum' may be used. **NC** also means 'The National Curriculum'.

Scotland, Wales and Northern Ireland have different curricula.

Key Stages – the key stages are as follows:

■ The Foundation Stage – ages 3 to the end of the Reception Year, the year in which children become 5

■ Key Stage 1 – ages 5–7

■ Key Stage 2 – ages 7–11

■ Key Stage 3 – ages 11–14

■ Key Stage 4 – from age 14.

Levels:

■ ELGs – Early Learning Goals – usually achieved by most 5 year-olds

■ Level 1 – usually achieved by most 6 year-olds

■ Level 2 – usually achieved by most 7 year-olds

■ Level 3 – usually achieved by most 9 year-olds

■ Level 4 – usually achieved by most 11 year-olds

■ Level 5 – usually achieved by most 14 year-olds.

P-Scales – stages for assessing children achieving below the ELGs and Level 1.

NLSF – National Literacy Strategy Framework for England.

NSFTE – National Strategy Framework for Teaching English (Key Stage 3) for England.

Introduction: Writing and the Alphabet

◼ ABC

Different writing systems – How did our alphabet arrive?

NB Words included in the glossary (page 177–186) are given in bold type on their first occurrence in the book.

Different Writing Systems

When we write or teach our children to write in English, we use the **alphabetic** system which developed from ancient times through the cultures of the Western world. The alphabetic system, though, is not the only writing system, and some pupils in our schools for whom English is an additional language may well come from cultures where the writing system is of a different nature.

Writing systems can be divided into two main types. First, there are those that represent things by **pictographic** symbols, a bit like the laundry symbols inside our clothes, or notices at airports and other public places. Then there are those that actually represent spoken words, either by symbols that stand for a whole word, or a **morpheme**, a meaningful part of a word; these are called **logographic** systems. Finally, there are those where symbols stand for sounds, called **phonographic** systems (Sampson, 1985). A morpheme may be a word, the root of a word, or a suffix or prefix, or even a syllable that has its own meaning, such as 'un', for instance. The separateness of such units is usually obvious to native speakers and children do not, as a rule, have to learn how to segment the stream of spoken meaning, or **semanticity**. However, there are times when young children have minor difficulties, as when a 5 year-old asked 'How do you spell *smorning? I've done the!'*, although this is rare.

In a logographic system the stream of sound has been split up into morphemes, but in a phonographic system there is a second splitting of the morphemes into individual sounds; this is a double analysis, called double articulation. As speech is symbolism itself, then in systems which represent spoken words the writing is a further level of symbolism built upon the first, sometimes referred to as second order symbolism. Thus in a phonographic writing system, such as we have in English, not only do we have a second order symbolic system, we also have a double layer of sound analysis represented in the splitting down from morphemes. Acquisition of such skills does not come naturally, and both analysis and synthesis, the splitting and spelling out, or the decoding and encoding generally need to be learned (Downing and Leong, 1982; Bradley and Bryant, 1983).

In both types of system, of course, the repertoire of symbols and the meanings or the sounds they represent have to be learned. However, in a logographic system the repertoire of meaningful units is very large, imposing an enormous learning load. In a phonographic system, once blending and splitting skills have been learned, the load is reduced. If the phonographic system is syllabic, the learning load is still very large, of course, and in ancient times this led to writing being learned only by a scribal class.

Today, whereas some writing systems are **phonological**, others are in logographic form. Where the case is the latter, being literate is usually an attribute of the learned, rather than of the ordinary person. In China the writing system is basically logographic, although there are some phonographic elements. Origins were iconic, that is, pictorial, but these are lost in the mists of time. There are a vast number of symbols to be learned. However, one advantage is that since most symbols are not linked to sounds, all the different Chinese languages, which are distinct and not merely dialects, can use the system with equal ease. In modern global business, though, such a system is a handicap for the use of word processors and computers. In Japan there are two systems, one is a logographic system long ago derived from the Chinese, called *kanji*, while the other is phonetic in nature, a phonological system known as *kana* (Robinson, 1995). Today, an educated Japanese person is supposed to know about 2,000 *kanji*, while a literary individual may have a repertoire of about 5,000. Careers, income and status depend on the mastery of *kanji*, and this often produces extreme stress. Primary school children are expected to learn about 960 *kanji*. On top of this, they must also learn their sounds for *kana*, of which there are two different sets, one formal and one less so. Today there is a third set, with intrusions from the West, called *romaji*, Roman letters. A breakfast cereal packet in Japan may have text written in *kanji*, *kana* and *romaji*. There are difficulties for computer use, of course, which at present is only really possible in *kana*.

How did our alphabet arrive?

Although our language is Indo-European in origin, our alphabetic writing system grew from the Semitic languages of the past in which early writing was developed. At first writing was done on clay tablets, and it is not surprising that it arose in the area of the Middle East known as 'the fertile crescent' where clay was plentiful in the area between the two great rivers of the Tigris and the Euphrates. Early writing grew from pictographic to **syllabic** forms, but later forms were phonographic, and by the middle of the second millennium BC an alphabetic system was being used, with 30 signs. The first appearance of a truly alphabetic system, using letter shapes, began in the second millennium in Sinai, employing a characteristic of Egyptian hieroglyphic writing. Here the symbols of items for the first sound of a spoken word were often used, as if we were to use S to indicate a snake, although their writing was in hieroglyphs. This feature became combined with initials from a Semitic vocabulary, and this was the starting point of the alphabet we use today.

Sinai is close to Lebanon, the ancient Phoenicia, and the Phoenicians were great sea-traders. Soon their alphabet of 22 letters was being used by the Greeks, across the other side of the Mediterranean, who called them 'Phoenician letters'. However, this alphabet only represented consonants. This made a dense form of script, not easy for the uninitiated to use. The big contribution made by the Greeks was that of the addition of symbols for vowels, using some of the Phoenician consonantal symbols they did not need in their language. By the third century BC, the Romans had a 21-letter alphabet, which had travelled to them via the Etruscans, their forerunners in Tuscany, where it had arrived from Greece. It is from the Etruscans, whose language is little known, though, that we get the origins of our words literature and **literacy**, from their *litterae*, meaning writing (Robinson, 1995). Since then, between the second century AD and mediaeval times, five more letters have been added to complete the alphabet as we know it.

The basic shapes of our capital letters are still like those used for the chiselled inscriptions of the Romans, made on stone monuments and buildings. The lower case letters have changed and developed, through usage in writing at speed by hand using pen and ink, at first on papyrus, then vellum or bark and, much later, on paper. With a highly segmented phonographic, alphabetic system the economical learning load thus provided has allowed reading and writing to become possible on a widespread basis, and not just the property of a scribal elite. Later, in the fifteenth century, the invention of the printing press began to make literacy even more widespread, but it was only gradually that universal literacy became the norm in Western societies.

1 | Early Brain Development, Laterality and Gender Differences

■ Brainpower and Boys and Girls

Early brain development – Critical periods and functional changes – Hemispherical characteristics – Laterality – Implications for dyslexia – Gender differences – Gender differences in the educational situation – Some implications for teaching and learning in English – Chapter summary – Teacher activity

Early Brain Development

Writing depends upon the use and understanding of speech. The use and understanding of speech depends upon the acquisition of language, and this in turn depends upon early brain development. Motor skills, used in writing, also depend upon brain development, involving the growth of **sensori-motor** structures and functions leading to hand and eye co-ordination.

Dr Mark Porter, writing in the *Radio Times*, states 'The human brain is a complex living computer that weighs just over 2 lbs/1 kg, contains more than 100 billion interconnected cells, and has the consistency of blancmange' (Porter, 2001). The brain advances more in its development and grows faster in the early years than at any other time in life. At birth it is 25 per cent of its adult weight, but by the age of 5 it is 90 per cent of it, and by 10 years old it is 95 per cent of the final weight (Brierley, 1976). Greenfield refers to this 'astonishing growth', and states that by the age of 16 it approximates its adult size (Greenfield, 2000b). All the nerve cells have been present since the middle of foetal life, and none are made beyond that period. Many of the supporting cells, though, grow after birth, and are generally present in large numbers by a year or so. The nerve cells, however, enlarge, develop longer processes and make new connections, which we may visualize through the metaphor of an electric wiring system.

The growth of these is extremely fast, reaching a peak at about eight months old, but still continuing rapidly as general growth takes place. Greenfield (2000a) explains that 'the advantage of this mind-boggling increase in connections is that it makes the human brain incredibly flexible, able to adapt to the unique life of the individual.' Furthermore, she adds that the human brain 'responds to use by making new connections and reforging old ones', and while depending on the individual persons and their attributes and situations, different parts of the brain may need to adapt more than others. This wiring, then, increases at a phenomenal rate in the early months and years. Regular use stimulates the brain to develop more connections, while neglect has the opposite effect. Experimental evidence shows that areas stimulated more by use show a greater richness of connections (Greenfield, 2000a).

During infancy and childhood, the density reaches even greater levels than in adults. A phase follows when the density begins to reduce, gradually reaching the adult levels. It is thought that perhaps the less useful connections become automatically 'pruned'; Greenfield refers to this process as one of atrophy (Greenfield, 2000b). Johnson likens this process to that of a newly planted tree, where roots growing into stony ground gradually wither, while those finding fertile soil strengthen and become firmly established (Johnson, 1997).

■ Critical Periods and Functional Changes

While some interactive development is general, other kinds of experience are quite specific in terms of responding to very critical sensitive periods during the growth sequence. If such critical periods are not 'hit', or sufficiently stimulated, by environmental experiences, and are missed, deficits can result (Greenfield, 2000a). On the other hand the brain, and particularly the cortex, owns a remarkable plasticity and adaptability, and where critical periods are not involved, development and adaptation can continue to take place.

As well as growth, there are functional changes in children as they develop. For instance, the quality of their movements changes as co-ordination becomes more efficient and refined, and as musculature develops to allow more strength and precision. Compare a 3 year-old kicking a ball with a 7 year-old kicking a ball, or observe a 4 year-old on a tricycle and compare his action with the skill and manoeuvrability shown by a 10 year-old cyclist. Generally, growth tends to proceed outwards towards the extremities, so that an infant reaches out and uses the arm and hand more as a unit rather than being able to adopt a complete range and flexibility of movement in the different parts of the limb. Progression takes place from gross motor skills, i.e. those using limbs and trunk, such as in climbing, kicking, jumping, cycling, to fine motor skills such as drawing, picking up and fitting together small items or using scissors. Movements tend to be overlarge for the fine motor skills to begin with, and lack precise co-ordination, but gradually become fine-tuned. It is also known that some fibre tracts of the brain are not fully functional till around the age of 4, and in particular those involved in the fine control of voluntary movement. This has implications for teachers dealing with young children trying to write, draw, and play with a variety of toys in the nursery and reception classes. Sheridan gives a useful sequence of development in terms of movement and behaviour in the early years (Sheridan *et al.*, 1997).

In order to transmit messages through the nervous system, the nerve fibres need to be covered by an insulating coat or sheath, to preserve the impulse and prevent it leaking away or discharging before it reaches its destination.

Our metaphor of electrical wiring gives a ready parallel. First the fibres have to grow. Then the covering, called **myelin**, develops around them, before they can transmit their messages. The effect of **myelinization** is sadly demonstrated by its breakdown in the disease known as multiple sclerosis, where patients gradually lose control over many functions. Myelinization is, however, a very prolonged process, and is possibly associated with continually developing sequences of social behaviour, speech, and later with thought processes. Between the ages of 2 and 4 considerable myelinization occurs, allowing the increased development of movement and motor intelligence, and this, in turn, may stimulate more. At puberty, the further surge in myelinization enables far greater control and development in many areas of function and behaviour.

Hemispherical Characteristics

Although the brain has the ability to make new connections through external stimulation, despite this plasticity there are certain usual patterns for the various pathways and circuits involved in particular functions within the brain, which are common to most people. Language has a number of related functions, including verbal reasoning, which are normally located in the left **hemisphere** of the brain, while spatial and non-verbal functions are usually located in the right hemisphere. The brain, with its **cerebral cortex** over-mantling the rest, somewhat resembles a large grey walnut kernel, with two convoluted hemispheres joined centrally by a harder core, rather like a sunken ridge. The latter is called the **corpus callosum**, and is an elongated bridge between the two hemispheres where pathways cross from one to the other, enabling intercommunication. This is a crucial crossover effect since the left hemisphere controls the right side of the body and the right hemisphere controls the left side. Most language areas tend to be set up in the left hemisphere, although there are also some specific verbal functions which usually belong on the other side. It is suspected that the right hemisphere may be responsible for **prosodic** aspects of language, such as intonation and cadence in speech.

The two hemispheres work together, due to the connections running through the corpus callosum. Paul Broca, a French doctor in the nineteenth century, was the first to realize that there was a specific location for some language functions, through his study of a brain-damaged patient. This area, in the left hemisphere, is now called Broca's Area (Pinker, 1994; Greenfield, 2000a). There are other areas, too, discovered through studies of brain-damage, such as that first identified and described by Carl Wernicke, a German physician, also of the nineteenth century, dealing with speech impairment. In Wernicke's **aphasia** people can articulate satisfactorily, but the content of their speech becomes garbled due to the loss of reasoning elements connected to the speech areas.

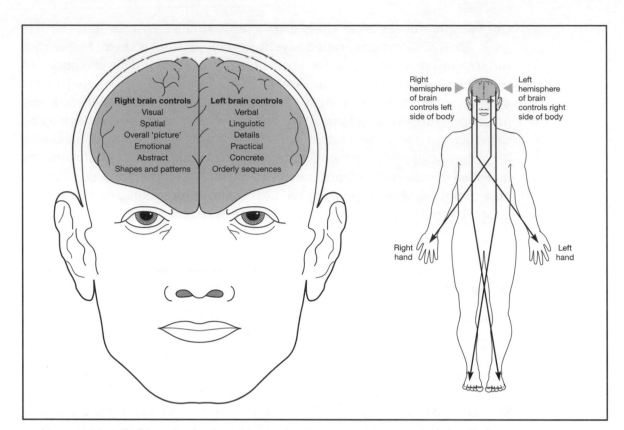

Figure 1.1 and 1.2 ■ These figures are reproduced by kind permission of Penguin Books Ltd, from pages 40 and 41 of **BRAINSEX: The Real Difference Between Men and Women** by Anne Moir and David Jessel, published in London in 1989 by Michael Joseph, copyright © Anne Moir and David Jessel, 1989.

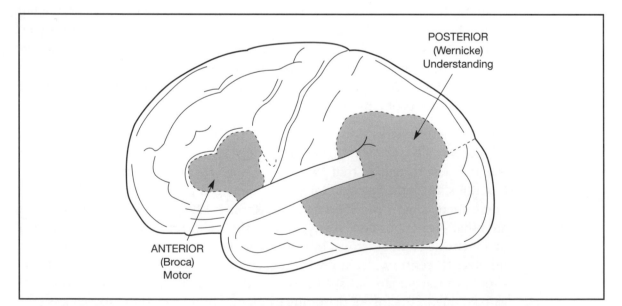

Figure 1.3 ■ The diagram is reproduced by kind permission of John Brierley from Figure 12 in his book **THE GROWING BRAIN**, published in Slough in 1976 for the National Foundation for Educational Research.

In a recent study in Japan, participants listened to passages from different literary genres, including a philosophy text, a newspaper report on global warming and some jokes. Brain imaging techniques showed that all genres activated language regions on the left side of the brain, although difficult sequences showed greater activity in the areas known to be involved in processing meaning. The humorous material aroused activation of Broca's Area augmented by activity in the frontal part of the cortex (Ozawa *et al.*, 2000). Both Broca's Area and Wernicke's Area are normally on the side of the left hemisphere, with Broca's rather further forward than Wernicke's. Grammatical processing appears to be centred to the front of this, including Broca's Area, while to the rear of it, including Wernicke's Area, the sounds of words, especially nouns and some aspects of their meaning are processed (Pinker, 1994). Carter discusses the two important language areas and their roles, suggesting that among the varying causes for **dyslexia** is a form of dissociation disorder caused by a lack of parallel functioning, i.e. working in concert together, between Broca's Area and Wernicke's Area (Carter, 1998). The picture is complex, but the study of brain-damaged patients and the modern use of brain scans are rapidly accelerating understanding of such interactive processes today.

Laterality

The dominant hand in right-handed persons is controlled by the left hemisphere, which also usually has the speech and language areas laid down within its connections. In left-handed people, the dominant hand is controlled by the right hemisphere, of course, with its greater specialization for spatial and visual aspects of processing, among others. Dominance of one hand or the other is usually well established between the ages of 2 and 3, although some children are much later in arriving at this stage (Sheridan *et al.*, 1997). Carter, in fact, gives evidence that hand preferences can even be discerned prenatally (Carter, 1998). There is, however, some variability in the establishment of handedness. Along with a strong preference for the use of one hand over the other, is the development of dominance of one eye over the other as a kind of 'lead ' eye, and connections formed between hand and eye are important for the efficiency of both fine and gross motor skills through hand-eye co-ordination. One leg or foot is also usually preferred for kicking, stepping off and initiating leg or foot movements. The establishment of the dominant hand, eye and foot are together called the establishment of **laterality**. In most people the three components of laterality are in line, being all right-sided or all left-sided, and thus controlled by the same hemisphere of the brain. For the majority of people, being right-handed, laterality is right-sided, involving the left hemisphere. The opposite is true for left-handers, despite language centres generally still being located in the left hemisphere for left-handers. However, in some individuals laterality is mixed; this means that either or both the dominant sides for the lead eye and foot are not the same as for the hand.

Pinker thinks that this is determined genetically. He says that '90 per cent of people in all societies and periods in history are right-handed, and most are thought to possess two copies of a dominant gene that imposes the right hand (left brain) bias' (Pinker, 1994). He goes on to add that those with two copies of the recessive version of the gene develop without a strong right-handed bias; in this category are right-handers with some ambivalence, those who are ambidextrous and the left-handers. He also tells us that left-handers are not mirror images of the right-handers. Carter agrees, and tells us that the left hemisphere controls language in virtually all right-handers (95 per cent of these), but the left hemisphere only controls language in about 70 per cent of left-handers, while in the other 30 per cent most have language areas in both hemispheres (Carter, 1998). Pinker suggests that about 19 per cent of left-handers have most language areas in the right hemisphere (Pinker, 1994). There is some evidence that left-handers, though better at mathematical, spatial and artistic activities, are more susceptible to language impairment, dyslexia and stuttering. Both Carter and Snowling agree with the genetic determination of handedness, but add that it may also be attributable to prenatal influences in some cases (Carter, 1998; Snowling, 2000).

■ Implications for Dyslexia

A wealth of evidence is summed up by Gredler in support of his opinion that an appreciable proportion of dyslexic children show poorly developed laterality or mixed laterality. However, he comments that though this might be interpreted as demonstrating that poorly developed laterality can be linked with incomplete cerebral dominance, it cannot be established as a comprehensive cause, since many children with poor or late establishment of dominance or mixed laterality do not show any difficulties in becoming literate (Gredler, 1977, in Reid and Donaldson; Hulme, 1987, in Beech and Colley). Certainly a sense of directionality is necessary in acquiring reading and writing skills, with a recognition that the letter order in a written word reflects the sound order of the spoken word, and laterality may be linked with this. Some other studies quoted by Gredler have indicated that mixed laterality only becomes a prominent factor below certain levels of general ability, and certainly below average levels of ability. Snowling quotes research showing that although it was expected that left-handers would be at risk of having speech difficulties, including dyslexia, results were not clear, and there was some evidence that children with very strong right-handedness as well as very strong left-handedness were more numerous among poor readers (Snowling, 2000). While the cognitive difficulties of dyslexia are more than likely to stem from inherited differences in the speech processing mechanisms located in the left hemisphere of the brain, further research is needed in this area.

Some children have not developed dominance fully by the time they come to school, or may have uncertain or mixed dominance. Teachers can check for this easily, by giving a kaleidoscope to the child, ensuring that presentation is made centrally towards the chest. The child will then use one or other hand to accept it and will usually place it to the eye on the same side as the chosen hand. If this is repeated on different occasions, and the same hand and eye are used each time, then the dominant hand and eye have been identified. Notice, too, which foot is used for dribbling or kicking a ball, in physical education lessons or playtimes. If a child uses either hand on numerous different occasions, try to notice if one is used more frequently than the other. There should never be any attempt to force a left-handed child to write or draw right-handedly as once used to be the case.

There is an important exception in the crossover control from the brain to the opposite sides of the human body, and that is a partial exception which involves the eyes. Interestingly, the eyes are actually brain outposts, since embryologically speaking the retinas are formed from brain tissue, later specialized and adapted. Each eye feeds information to both the hemispheres of the brain, with the fibre tracts of the **optic nerve** crossing at a point in the part of the brain known as the **optic chiasma** (meaning a crossover, from the Greek letter X, called chi). Thus fibres run from the left eye to both hemispheres and from the right eye to both hemispheres, one bundle remaining on the same side as the eye, the other bundle crossing at the chiasma and joining those from the other eye. So the visual area of each brain hemisphere builds up a half picture of the total visual field as a 'double exposure'. Through the complicated connections between the hemispheres, the two halves of the picture are welded together, emerging as what we consciously experience as a single stereoscopic view. The nerve impulses go through a special structure on each side, in the visual processing channels, before entering the two brain hemispheres.

According to Greenfield, scientists have recently discovered that the whole visual system consists of two systems working in parallel and is extremely complex. While one system deals with perceiving movements, the other deals through further sub-systems with colour and form. Greenfield endorses the view of the importance of early experience and states that for vision to develop normally in children, both eyes have to be used during a specific sensitive period, very early in life (Greenfield, 2000a).

Advantages for the visual input to the left hemisphere have been found with right-handed people in word-naming tests, with both vertical and horizontal arrangements of words (Young, 1987, in Beech and Colley). Further, the inclusion of studies conducted in the Hebrew language, which is read from right to left, show the same effect. Support for the explanation of this phenomenon in terms of cerebral asymmetry, i.e. the specialization of the left hemisphere for language processing, is provided by the fact that this superiority for word recognition is reduced or absent in left-handed people, and by their superiorities in non-verbal tasks. Both hemispheres are able to process letter recognition, although the left hemisphere is more sensitive to the **orthographic** properties of pronounceable non-words using high frequency spelling patterns. This might raise the question as to whether this is a factor in blending ability when learning to read and to spell, since synthesis and analysis of word components, in practice, seems not to vary particularly with general intelligence but to be an independent and specific phenomenon. Young also concludes that expressive language abilities belonging to the left hemisphere are superior to those on the right. These, of course, are involved in the productive skills of speaking and writing (Young, 1987, in Beech and Colley).

While left-handers may have a spatial superiority, right-handers are more likely to have a verbal superiority in cognitive functioning. However, this is only one of many factors operating within the context of cognitive functioning, and other individual differences too may mask or enhance such effects in different ways. Thus some left-handers will certainly perform in many speaking or writing tasks at levels superior to many right-handers, but nevertheless these differences are important to note, helping to raise our awareness of individual differences, including difficulties and aptitudes. We need to remember that mixed dominance often leads to directional confusion, and direction is important in both the literary skills of reading and writing, in decoding or encoding letters in the correct order in a word, or words in sentences.

■ Gender Differences

In general, boys tend to be slightly ahead of girls in development at the time of birth, but passing through the same sequences of changes, girls develop faster from birth onwards until puberty. Girls' development also shows greater stability than that of boys, and is less easily affected by adverse circumstances. These differences were given prominence three decades ago, in the national study which tracked the development of 11,000 seven year-olds (Davie *et al.*, 1972). Breaking new ground, Hutt explored gender differences in physiological and cognitive terms, backed up by a huge range of critically reviewed research (Hutt, 1972). She clearly puts the case for psychological sex differences, stating that the basic mammalian template is female, or as we might say today, the default design is female. Since male differentiation takes place through alterative mechanisms, the male of the species tends to have greater variability than the female, including variances in structures and functions. The male in general has greater vulnerability, and also generally shows slower development towards maturation than the female. However, warns Hutt, this cannot be merely regarded as simple retardation of the male compared with the female, since differences in genders mean that for some maturational sequences boys may be following slightly different paths of specialization.

When gender differences are reported, these are generalized differences belonging to the group of one or other gender as a whole, and within this context, as with laterality, individual differences operate. These can be both large and varied. So, if we say the male sex is better at something, it does not mean that all boys will be better than all girls, or vice versa: it is a general trend noticeable when large samples are involved. The slower general rate of male development, states Hutt, begins early in foetal life and continues to adulthood, although there are some areas where boys' development exceeds that of girls, such as having a greater vital capacity with stronger muscles, larger heart capacity in operation during stress or exertion, and increased capacity for persistence in muscle activity (Hutt, 1972).

Females have greater sensitivity to touch and pain, even from birth, and they also have better auditory discrimination. Even at a few weeks old, says Hutt, boys show more interest than girls in visual patterns, while girls attend more than boys to sound sequences, speech and changes of tone. Hutt reviews the evidence on differences in the bilateral functioning of the brain, with its two hemispheres, and outlines differences found in these between men and women, suggesting that the right hemisphere functions operate rather differently in the two sexes, and that the laying down of linguistic functions, in particular in the left hemisphere, is accelerated in the female. However, the position of bilateral control, she concludes, implies more efficient control, allowing for the well-known male superiority in spatial functions.

Moir and Jessel (1989) have extended these assertions by critical scrutiny of a vast array of subsequent experimental research into this area. It is now accepted that although there are specific language areas in the left hemisphere, in women these are rather less specifically centred, with many aspects of both language and spatial skills controlled by both sides of the brain, whereas in men the areas for the two types of skills are more specifically located in the two hemispheres, right for spatial skills and left for verbal ones. Thus men's brains are more specialized, and in women's the functional division is less clearly defined. Also, connections via the corpus callosum between the two hemispheres tend to be richer and more dense in women (Moir and Jessel, 1989; Carter, 1998). Further, brain functions related to the mechanisms of language, such as grammar, spelling and speech production, are organized in rather different ways in men's and women's brains, say Moir and Jessel. Men, with more specifically developed brain functions, once engaged in a task, may not be so easily distracted by superfluous information, they suggest. An example of this is given in a map-reading situation familiar to most of us as a bone of contention on family journeys in the car! Whereas for a man map-reading will be specifically a right-hemisphere activity, and talk a left-hemisphere activity, a woman is more likely to be confused in trying to listen to instructions or follow a conversation while studying the route, since both hemispheres are likely to be involved in both tasks.

The language skills relating to grammar, spelling and writing, however, are different. In women, these are all much more specifically located in the left hemisphere, while other language skills, such as comprehension, are very often in the right. In men, although all these functions are usually located in the left hemisphere, they are more spread out across the hemisphere from the front to the back areas of the cortex. Additionally, because of the greater facility for connections via the corpus callosum in women, allowing more information to be more easily exchanged between the two sides, alluded to as 'superior switchgear', women have the advantage where a task involves both sides for both sexes. So boys, say Moir and Jessel, will have to work harder than girls to achieve these skills (Moir and Jessel, 1989). They add that recent research shows that the more connections people have between the hemispheres, and of course again there is a huge range of individual differences crossing the gender divide, the more articulate and fluent they tend to be.

It has been suggested that this also relates to links between emotion and speech. In men emotions are centred in the right hemisphere, and speech clearly in the left. In women the brain has some emotional capacities on both sides, and connections anyway, as we have seen, are stronger. With weaker hemispherical connections, men may find it more difficult to express emotions, with information about feelings flowing less easily to the verbal areas on the left of the brain. Carter says that the stronger hemispherical connections in women may explain why they are usually more aware of their own and others' emotions than men (Carter, 1998). These are, however, minimal differences in many cases, and again, individual differences must be understood to be operating. This situation, though, may have implications for choices in literature, and for the ability to empathize through reading, or in imagination through writing in role. Boys certainly enjoy different kinds of books from girls, to some extent, and tend to go for those with high levels of adventure and even violence and aggression, nonfiction, or those with quirky humour in their reading.

In the pre-adolescent years, the mathematical and scientific aptitudes of boys are generally better than those of girls, a most noticeable cognitive difference and well documented. While girls may learn to count earlier than boys, the boys soon show superiority in mathematical reasoning, with their more specific tightly and exclusively organized visuo-spatial area in the right hemisphere of the brain. These sex differences become even more marked as boys get older, and Moir and Jessel state that male hormones enhance visuo-spatial skills, as they do with the drive for competition and aggression, and female hormones tend to depress them. As boys reach full maturity, albeit a couple of years later than girls usually, the differences in higher maths between the sexes generally become very marked indeed (Moir and Jessel, 1989). Eventually, boys will catch up with girls in their basic verbal skills, although they will never be quite as fluent as girls, but these skills will also combine successfully with the greater powers boys have for perceiving ideas and logical relationships. It is at puberty that the dramatic acceleration takes place in boys' development, catching up with girls on verbal scores in tests, and in writing abilities. While general intelligence levels, although within individual limits, soar between the ages of 14 and 16, those of girls, previously ahead, level off.

Summarising, Baron-Cohen, in Carter, states: 'After decades of research into whether and how the sexes differ psychologically, some differences are repeatedly found that, though not true of every individual, certainly emerge when groups are compared' (Baron-Cohen, 1998, in Carter). Among the listed attributes differing between men and women are: for women, a faster rate of language development, doing better than men on tests involving social judgment, empathy and co-operation, and doing better at matching items; for men, doing better than women on mathematical reasoning tasks, doing better in tests involving distinctions between figure and background, mental rotation of objects, and better accuracy in hitting targets (Carter, 1998).

Gender Differences in the Educational Situation

What implications does all this knowledge carry into the educational situation? There is currently great concern about the gender differences found in the end of Key Stage national assessments, particularly in English, involving reading, but most particularly writing. In a 1998 publication produced by the Qualifications and Curriculum Authority (QCA) in connection with the National Curriculum in English about raising boys' achievement in English, this statement is made: 'There are still major issues to be addressed relating to girls' achievements and aspirations, and these must not be forgotten. However, more recently public attention has shifted to boys and their relative under-achievement up to and including GCSE across wide areas of the curriculum. In some subjects, including English and English Literature, the difference in achievement is particularly pronounced. It is clear that the problem emerges early' (QCA, 1998/081).

■ At Key Stage 1, 21 per cent of girls achieved level 3 in the English tests compared with 14 per cent of boys.

■ At Key Stage 2, 69 per cent of girls achieved level 4 and above, compared with 57 per cent of boys.

■ At Key Stage 3, 66 per cent of girls achieved level 5 and above, compared with 47 per cent of boys.

'At age 16+, GCSE results in 1997 showed 67 per cent of girls achieving grade C or above, whereas the figure for boys was 43 per cent. Given the undoubted importance of literacy in achievement right across the curriculum, this evidence of an early gap is particularly disturbing' (QCA, 1998/081).

Detailed findings by Her Majesty's Inspectors (HMI), reported in the same document, include the facts that boys were more likely to have problems with basic literacy, where there was setting girls were more numerous in higher sets, girls in all years read more fiction, girls wrote at greater length, boys made less use of school libraries and participated less in extra-curricular activities associated with English, and insufficient time was spent on poetry, even though it was less popular with boys.

Again in 1998, an official publication by the Office for Standards in Education (OFSTED) gave a résumé of recent research on gender and educational performance, providing a statistical summary of the evidence for the gender gap, and showing both similarities and differences in male and female achievement. Even at GCSE level, the percentage differences in subject choices were clearly significant, with mathematics, physical sciences and technology being much more prominent for boys, and English and the creative arts much more prominent for girls. While it has been suggested that such differences may be enhanced or minimized by type of schooling, i.e. single-sex or co-education, the proportion of change indicated is small compared to the gender effect itself, and other factors connected with the research situations on this matter render it more or less inconclusive (Arnot *et al.*, 1998).

Even where later studies have shown subject performance advantages for separate sex sets, other disadvantages, including social drawbacks, are involved (Henry, 2001). Strangely, role model effects from teacher gender are rarely mentioned in studies of stereotyping, but family therapist Biddulph thinks these important and stresses that both sexes need to be represented within children's teaching experience (Biddulph, 1997). On the other hand, in some very recent and ongoing research into learning situations for boys, in Suffolk, the effects of teacher gender are refuted (Rundell, 2001). Evidence for this aspect of the situation remains equivocal.

National data show that at age 7, in Key Stage 1 national end of Key Stage assessments (SATs), girls, on average, always outperform boys by a considerable margin in writing, spelling, handwriting, and in speaking and listening. In Key Stage 2, by age 11, the differences still strongly persist and are still there in the Key Stage 3 assessments at 14. In mathematics and science at age 7, while girls have done marginally better than boys in these subjects, by the end of Key Stage 2 at 11 this difference has begun to disappear, being very similar but with a very slight advantage for the boys by the age of 14, at the end of Key Stage 3. However, during the 1970s and 1980s, the main gender issue was at that stage worry about girls' performance in mathematics and science, and considerable work went in to trying to redress this balance, and the QCA report that girls' performance in these subjects at O level and GCSE now matches that of boys (QCA, 1998/081). It does not, however, give details of the proportion of girls and boys selecting these subjects for their subject options. In value-added research, say Arnot *et al.*, girls were shown to make greater progress between the ages of 7 and 16 than boys, but levels of academic progress were reversed at A level (Arnot *et al.*, DfEE, 1998). While there has been improvement of results overall in national tests in the last decade or so, at the same time that the proportions of pupils doing better are on the increase, there are signs that the two-way gender gap is actually widening.

In view of the findings about brain differences, supported by a vast range of corroborative experimental evidence, it is surprising that the OFSTED survey centres so heavily on social stereotyping as the most salient factor. A body of evidence in terms of social influences, teaching and learning styles, and types of schooling is marshalled as a rationale for the existence of the gender differences, with hardly any reference at all to the cognitive differences produced by the **dimorphic** nature of brain function. Referring to a 1992 review by Halpern of the evidence for biological explanations for these psychological phenomena, the 1998 OFSTED survey reflects his views by reporting 'Despite a resurgence of interest in biological explanations for psychological phenomena in recent years, it is now generally acknowledged that such explanations are unlikely to provide an adequate account of gender differences in academic performance, and especially changes in the pattern of male and female achievement' (Arnot *et al.*, DfEE, 1998).

However, the OFSTED survey does acknowledge that differences between male and female performance on tests of verbal and spatial abilities have been recorded and that cerebral lateralization (handedness) has been demonstrated to combine with sex differences in a number of ways. Quoting Halpern, Arnot *et al.* agree that high ability left-handed boys do better on tests of verbal abilities and less well on spatial abilities than right-handed boys, with an opposite pattern for girls, while among boys with lower ability there is a high proportion of left-handers. They accede that language acquisition in the early years may be influenced by biological processes. Halpern reports that girls have been observed to acquire some language concepts, like understanding the difference between the active and the passive voice, earlier than boys, and he puts this down to 'a female advantage in maturation and not just family conversational patterns in favour of girls' (Arnot *et al.*, DfEE, 1998). Even if biology sets limits to human abilities, states the OFSTED survey, there is no certainty about what these limits may be, and this, of course, is an incontrovertible statement.

While certainly allowing for a situation in which social stereotyping and both teaching and learning styles may play a part, Moir and Jessel would place far more reliance on dimorphic brain function as a prime factor in the rationale for the two-way gap. Moir and Jessel say clearly, that while the prejudices of society may reinforce natural advantages and disadvantages, today there is too much biological evidence for the sociological argument to prevail as the main causal factor. This is supported by recent evidence provided by Carter as well (Moir and Jessel, 1989; Carter, 1998).

Both nature and nurture have an interdependent role to play, and neither factor may be ignored in our search for optimum ways of teaching and learning for both sexes. To summarize, in childhood the rate of maturation for girls is faster than boys. Girls do better during childhood, and to some extent in some aspects even after puberty and into adulthood, in language, and this includes reading, writing, spelling, grammar, and speaking and listening. Girls also show greater ability to retain random pieces of information. Boys generally do better than girls in mathematics and science, technology and reasoning by the secondary school stage, and certainly onwards. They are also good at speaking and listening in rather different ways from girls, enjoying the competitive nature of repartee and of speaking in class, although they do not tend to persevere well in small group and paired discussions, especially if working only with other boys (QCA, 1998/081). Boys are more interested in the technological aspects of life, in competition, and are more likely to display aggression, while girls are more interested in social aspects of life, in relationships and emotions.

In literacy, in aspects of reading and writing, boys are more likely than girls to have special educational needs, as indeed they are with behavioural problems, and they are more likely than girls to be among the dyslexic pupils. An information sheet from the British Dyslexia Association provides some figures about the incidence of dyslexia, although we are warned that these statistics are not precise: up to a tenth of the population, in the Western world, is thought to show some signs of dyslexia, with four per cent being seriously affected; it is thought that it is about four times as common in boys as in girls (BDA, 2001).

■ Some Implications for Teaching and Learning in English

Are there some lessons to be drawn from this information in terms of the ways teaching strategies in literacy need to be focused? The OFSTED research review of 1998 finds that girls are more attentive in class, more willing to learn, do better on sustained open-ended tasks requiring independence, and do better on course work, while boys show greater adaptability to more traditional approaches which require memorising facts, acquiring and applying rules, and in tests and exams than in course work. They are keen to answer speedily and less likely to spend time thinking deeply or giving sustained effort (Arnot *et al.*, DfEE, 1998). There are clear differences in choices of literature, with a tendency for boys to have a lack of interest in poetry, to select non-fiction, dramatic and often bloodthirsty adventure, and wacky humour. Literature favoured by girls often emphasises relationships and personal experience. Of course, there is a huge overlap and there are many fictional styles enjoyed by both sexes, notably the passion 9, 10 and 11 year-olds have for the Harry Potter books by J.K. Rowling at present, and also the Roald Dahl repertoire, but teachers in Key Stages 2 and 3 will recognize the differences.

Efforts are being made in primary schools now to change what was previously an over-rigid school literary culture (Beard, 2000). Beard reiterates the conclusions of work by Millard, stressing the value of a broad range of genres, lively and up to date book stocks, and careful choices for shared reading activities, including the use of some non-fiction forms of 'pop-culture' which may be topical (Beard, 2000). Schools today are much more aware of the need for a good range of fiction and non-fiction, and for selecting varied texts as focuses for text study in the literacy hours, and this change of attitude has been greatly helped by the implementation of the English National Literacy Strategy (NLS). While the balance in English cannot be totally redressed for boys, given the obvious and likely origin of the literacy gap, nevertheless it may be minimized by endeavouring to ensure a lack of social stereotyping in schools, a careful balance of teaching strategies, and a breadth of literary choices, rather than strengthening the differences.

It is, therefore, of crucial importance to continue to attend to these factors and to make every effort to develop understanding of how they work and interact. A balance is needed, introducing boys to those aspects more favourable to girls, together with using with impact those features of classroom practice which cater better for boys' learning preferences and interests, to the benefit of both sexes, within a harmonious breadth. Included in these must be a greater emphasis on structured teaching, in particular in phonic instruction and practice, and this is already coming about, again due to the implementation of the NLS in England. Mixed gender groups for discussion in small group work and varying the groupings is also beneficial, since this has been shown to aid boys' persistence in discussion at greater length; boys enjoy group work (Arnold, 1997). This effect may not be as salient in paired work, however.

The rapid early brain development reminds us of the vital importance of early learning, not only for cashing in on what may be critical periods for the learning of language, but also because early experience enriches the functional capacity of the brain. Learning is also incremental in nature, that is, at each step it is built upon previous prerequisites and foundations. Thus we can also see the importance of early intervention where special educational needs are at stake, and where there is early language deprivation. Laterality is important in the directional aspects of learning to read, write and spell, and left-handers may need specific attention in writing and spelling skills. While there are differences in cognitive functioning patterns and interests between the sexes, both genders have valuable attributes to bring to the learning situation, and teaching strategies need to exploit the strengths and minimize the weaknesses of both, through understanding and a balanced range of techniques.

■ Chapter Summary

1. The early years, when the brain connections grow fast, are crucial for establishing a good foundation for the development of later cognitive abilities.

2. Laterality usually develops early, and handedness or mixed laterality may be one factor involved in individual differences in spatial and verbal abilities. Left-handers may need special attention and care in learning to read, write and spell.

3. Gender differences in performance in different subjects, and in interests, are likely to stem from differences inherent in the brain and, in particular, in hemispherical differences, even though social influences may enhance or detract from these.

4. In English, boys on the whole usually do less well than girls, until the late puberty stage; this is the gender gap in English.

5. Left-handed boys, especially with lower general ability, may be at greater risk than others of developing difficulties in reading and writing, including dyslexia.

6. Early learning, early intervention for those with special educational needs, and a broad range of teaching techniques in specific areas of English, can help to minimize the gender gap effect and enhance learning for both sexes.

■ Teacher Activity

In the Foundation Stage, observe the use of the writing table and of the role-play area in free choice times by both boys and girls – are there any differences in numbers using them, or in length of time spent there, or in how it is used? In Key Stage 1, notice if girls tend to write more, i.e. at greater length, than boys in free writing tasks, and if there are any differences in 'show and tell' sessions. In Key Stages 2 and 3, try to see whether more girls or more boys usually answer questions in class discussion times, and/or do a class or group survey of kinds of books preferred, and analyse the results by **genres** and gender. Discuss your findings with your colleagues.

For following up further interests

Arnold, R. (1997) *Raising Levels of Boys' Achievement*. Slough: NFER.

Arnot, M. *et al.* (1998) *Recent Research on Gender and Educational Performance*. London: DfEE for OFSTED Reviews of Research.

Biddulph, S. (1997) *Raising Boys*. London: Thorsons.

Barrs, M., and Pidgeon, S. (1993) *Reading the Difference*. Centre for Language in Primary Education (London Borough of Southwark).

Carter, R. (1998) *Mapping the Mind*. London: Phoenix Paperbacks, Orion Books.

Greenfield, S. (2000a) *Brain Story*. London: BBC Worldwide.

Millard, E. (1997) *Differently Literate: Boys, Girls, and the Schooling of Literacy*. London: Routledge Falmer.

Moir, A., and Jessel, D. (1989) *Brainsex: The Real Difference Between Men and Women*. London: Michael Joseph.

QCA (1998/081) *Can Do Better – Raising Boys' Achievement in English*. London: Qualifications and Curriculum Authority.

Rudduck, J. (1994) *Developing a Gender Policy in Secondary Schools*. Buckingham: Open University Press.

Sheridan, M. D. (1997 edition, with revision by Frost, M., and Sharma, A.) *From Birth To Five Years – Children's Developmental Progress*. London: Routledge.

2 | Early Speech, Language Acquisition and Related Theories

■ Babble and Babel

> *Language acquisition and stages of early speech – Acquiring basic phonology – Looking at grammar – Linguistic universals and related theories – Young children's uses of language in the early stages – Chapter summary – Teacher activity*

Language Acquisition and Stages of Early Speech

The acquisition of speech and the learning of language is one of the areas where critical periods appear to operate quite strongly, centred in early childhood (Pinker, 1994; Greenfield, 2000a). Greenfield allows that we do not know how the brain makes language possible, but she emphasizes that it develops both naturally and spontaneously, while the stages of development are similar in every culture (Greenfield, 2000a). She sums up the sequence thus: at 6 months babies are babbling, by about a year they produce one-word utterances, around 2 years utterances composed of two words begin to appear, by 2¹/₂ they can put three words together, and by the age of 3 years, most children are speaking in sentences. By 4, the majority of children are able to use language with a capability close to that of an adult.

The babbling stage, though one of the most important as the foundation of language development, is one of the most mysterious of stages, since the sounds emitted include a range not necessarily needed for the child's native language, later to be reduced and limited to those belonging to the mother tongue. Babies enjoy making sounds, and do so even when alone, suggesting, says Bancroft, internal motivation to babble (Bancroft, 1995 in Lee and Das Gupta). He describes how vocal play gives way to what he calls reduplicated babbling, a series of repeated syllables made up of a vowel and a consonant, such as 'dadadadadada'. Such sequenced babbling is sometimes referred to as **echolalia**. Towards the end of the babbling stage, and when single words are about to, or beginning to, erupt, stress and intonation become noticeably imposed on the babbling. This intonational variety and sense of rhythm and cadence is part of the **prosody** of a language; it allows even a very limited range of words to express a number of feelings and attitudes. This differs from one language to another, and is a characteristic part of its structure. Once the initial babbling stage has initiated the process, the communicative context is crucial for the development of language. Pinker argues that what he calls 'Motherese', with its conversational give and take, and its repetitive simple grammar, is not the whole story and other mechanisms which he thinks are innate are operating, nevertheless tragic cases have shown that language development, though it starts, does not continue without the conversational context (Pinker, 1994). Carter also refers to the active nature of babies' contributions within the conversational situation, with what she calls 'motherspeak' as the corresponding component (Carter, 1998). Bancroft states that by about 18 months of age, children are likely to have a vocabulary of about 50 words, and that evidence suggests that they are able to understand a much larger vocabulary than that they can produce (Bancroft, 1995, in Lee and Das Gupta).

Carter refers to this emergence of words as the beginning of 'proper' language, and says this happens with the activation of the two major speech areas in the brain, Broca's Area and Wernicke's Area, the former dealing with articulation, the latter, as we have already seen, with aspects of comprehension (Carter, 1998). She states that language initially starts to develop in both hemispheres, but by the age of 5, in the majority of cases, 95 per cent, it has become mainly fixed in the left hemisphere. She suggests that the abandoned speech areas in the right hemisphere are then given over to other functions, and that these include gesture.

The single word utterance, with contextual meanings supplied by gesture and often by intonation, is a capsule sentence, often known as the **holophrase**. In the recently updated English **'P Scales'**, produced by the DfEE, for assessing performance below English National Curriculum Level 1, particularly for use with children with special needs, this stage corresponds to P4 (DfEE, 2001 rev.). If the child utters '*dada*', is he meaning 'look at dada', 'is that dada?' or 'pick up my toy, dada'? The word is being used as a one-element sentence (Crystal, 1982; Pinker, 1994). Most of these first words forming holophrases will be nouns, naming people or objects. As the repertoire grows, and two or three words begin to be strung together, the holophrase becomes elaborated by another descriptive or modifying word, or words. The meanings of phrases such as '*sweeties more*' or '*allgone milk*' are obvious, but does '*daddy socks*' mean 'daddy is putting on his socks', 'the dog's chewing daddy's socks', 'I'm giving daddy his socks', or 'mummy's putting daddy's socks in the washing machine'? In the communicative context, the adult or adults present are likely to be able to make a good informed guess, and can model for the child the expanded version of his comment, such as 'Yes, mummy's putting daddy's socks in the washing machine' or 'Yes, these are daddy's socks'. It will be some time before the child may be able to echo the fully modelled sentence or phrase, but gradually he will become aware of the other elements in such sentences and begin to extend his own.

When two or three words are put together in this way, it is sometimes called the stage of **pivot grammar**, with the noun as a pivot and the other word or words as a context around it, modifying the meaning (Gurney, 1973). This stage corresponds to P5 in the DfEE P Scales. Notice that these pivot grammar phrases are not parroted from adult models, and the 'Motherese' of reducing a sentence to a pivot grammar phrase such as in a peek-a-boo game, saying 'Bye-

bye teddy' instead of 'Look, I'm hiding teddy' is probably a natural response to the utterances of the child himself. When learning negative forms, children tack on the word *no* or the word *not* at the beginning or end of a pivot grammar phrase, whereas the adult is likely to have modelled negative statements using *doesn't* or *aren't*. The acquisition of language here is not a copycat procedure, but one where elements are learned and combined in ways that make sense to the speaker using his limited repertoire; it seems to be an **inductive process**, with structures and rule being formed and adapted as new elements are experienced and learned.

From the pivot grammar stage, children progress adding more words to their utterances, verbs, adjectives and pronouns appear, but the utterances may still not be full sentences, or may be very short brief sentence forms (P Scale P6). These are sometimes described as **telegraphic speech**, described fully by Roger Brown (Brown, 1976). Words in an old-fashioned telegram cost money to send, comments Brown, so there was pressure to express the message as economically as possible and reduce the number of words. For example, a full message like 'My car has broken down and I have lost my wallet; send money to me at the American Express in Paris' Brown suggests might be redrafted as 'Car broken down; wallet lost. Send money American Express Paris' (Brown, 1976). Today, there is a similar drive for economy in letters and words in text messaging on mobile phones! In telegraphic speech, the child's pivot grammar or simple phrase or sentence can be unpacked by the hearers, who are able to expand the meaning by understanding the child's needs and interests within the conversational context, as we saw above. While emergent forms disappear and standard forms become permanent, these differences remind us that languages other than our own may have different grammatical categories, with different focuses of meaning as a consequence (Clark, 2001, in Bowerman and Levinson).

As utterances expand, basic words and phrases extend, **inflections** of words such as plurals and tense endings for verbs begin to be apparent. Full grammar is beginning to be acquired, and the inductive and rule-formulating process is very obviously at work (this is around P Scale stages P7 and P8, and then progressing onwards through national Curriculum Level 1). We are all familiar with the over-generalized forms, sometimes known as **over-extensions**, when a child says something like *'he runned'*, *'he goed'*, *'a scissor'* (Bancroft, in Lee and Das Gupta, 1995). Learning from forms of verbs with a regular past tense ending of *-ed*, this morphemic element has been applied, quite reasonably, to another verb stem, and in the case of the scissors they are, after all, one object although we call them a pair. Gradually these glitches are ironed out as the child becomes aware of the irregular forms in his language. This is also the stage where children produce **neologisms**, new words, or new forms of words, of their own making. Pinker gives a lovely example of a child saying *'Don't giggle me!'*, making a **transitive** verb out of an **intransitive** one (Pinker, 1994). A similar instance is *'I'm torching!'*, pressing the torch on and off, making a verb out of a noun, and after all, why not? We say *'I'm bicycling!'*. These are other signs of the rule-making structure or the deductive process taking place, rather than mere copying from models. The acquisition of language is a dynamic and creative process.

Gradually the over-extensions and the emergent categories disappear, and sentences are fully formed. The ability to create different types of sentence from the kernel sentence's structure appears, and questions, commands and negatives are clearly present. The basic foundation is laid, although we go on learning more grammar and adding to our understanding of vocabulary throughout childhood, and even through our adult years. Crystal provides a clear description of the stages of speech acquisition. His stages of speech acquisition are divided into phonological and grammatical aspects of development, with rather more emphasis upon the grammar (Crystal, 1982).

Acquiring Basic Phonology

Crystal comments that at the babbling stage the basic phonology of the native language is being practised, refined and developed. Towards the end of this stage, the child begins to learn the use of sound in a contrastive way for **semantic** purposes, that is, to represent meaning. The learning of this sound system of the native language begins around 9 months of age, and the child begins to discriminate and to produce the vowel and consonant phonemes of his language, in the contexts in which they happen to occur. While we have seen that by 4 or approaching 5 most children are able to use language with a facility close to that of an adult, Crystal states that the process of acquiring a full and accurate knowledge and use of the phonology of the native language is not completed generally until around the age of 7 (Crystal, 1982).

His first stage is roundabout the age of a year or so, and as Crystal comments, is the stage when the prosodic framework has already been founded. It is also the holophrasic stage. Stage 2 corresponds to that of the pivot grammar, and Stages 3, 4 and 5 extend from the pivot grammar to the phrase or very short sentence, probably taking place between the ages of 2 and 3 plus. Crystal also gives a clear sequence of phonological acquisition in respect of consonant phonemes in English, with average age estimates for these:

- By 2 years – p b m n w
- By 2½ years – t d k g ng h
- By 3 years – f s l y (as in you)
- By 4 years – sh v z r ch (as in chew) j (as in juice)
- By 5 years – th (as in think) th (as in this)
- By 6 years – the soft j sound as in measure.

He adds that the difference between *f* and *th* often causes difficulty until 7 or beyond. More complex consonant clusters can also represent difficulties, such as in the word *twelfths*.

Are there some implications here for the introduction of phonemes in a Foundation Stage or Early Years phonics programme? In the English National Literacy Strategy Framework (NLSF) knowledge and use of all the letters of the alphabet plus the combinations *sh*, *ch* and *th* are expected by the end of the reception year, for the majority of children. This is therefore roughly appropriate in terms of Crystal's estimates, but there may be difficulties for the less able children if their sequence of phonological acquisition is slower, and this might be particularly the case in terms of the sounds represented by the common **digraphs**. Since the NLSF post-dates Crystal's description by more than a decade, we may ask whether the view of the acquisition of phonology has changed, or does the actual teaching and learning involved as a result of the NLSF being applied produce the necessary acceleration to enable the achievement of this goal? While the situation is not clear, the research conducted by Bradley and Bryant, and Goswami and Bryant, discussed by Oakhill, indicates that while young children have difficulty in differentiating between the phonemic components of words, which are meaningless units, they have no such difficulty with meaningful units such as words themselves, or syllables, and that **onset** and **rime** are naturally able to be distinguished (Oakhill, 1995, in Lee and Das Gupta). Further, she suggests that phonics instruction works well for beginning readers because it fosters an awareness of speech units, showing how these can be mapped onto written words aiding understanding of the analysis of words into smaller components. Thus it seems likely that early teaching, carefully applied step by step so as not to confuse, may aid the achievement of the goals set in the NLSF.

■ Looking at Grammar

At about age 2¹/₂, at Crystal's Stage 3, inflectional endings begin to emerge (eg *daddy kicking ball*, or *daddy kicked ball*), and first uses of auxiliary verbs and pronouns. By Stage 4, the majority of types of **simple sentence** (i.e. a sentence with only one clause, a main clause) are in use; these include statements, questions and commands. With this sentence structure comes the ability to put together words in the word-order characteristic in English, and which is part of the **syntax** of the language. Also emerging is the use of *and* as a **connective** within phrases, together with more elaboration such as noun phrases, describing the noun, such as Crystal's example of '*the man with the hat on*'. By Stage 5, the use of *and* is extended to join clauses, and **compound sentences** and **complex sentences** begin to be a common part of the speech pattern. A compound sentence is two main clauses joined by a connective such as *and*, while a complex sentence consists of a main clause with one or more subsidiary clauses. From Stage 6 onwards, Crystal indicates that various grammatical systems still being developed come to be more thoroughly acquired, such as the whole pronoun system, the auxiliary verb system, and the understanding of passives, which may not be understood until the age of 9 or 10 (Crystal, 1982). However, he says that full understanding of these actually takes several years longer (Crystal, 1982). This brings the culmination of this area of knowledge and understanding, for the average child, at least into Key Stage 2 or even into Key Stage 3.

Crystal goes on to explain that learning does not cease at 10 or 11, and there still remains much further learning to take place in the realm of understanding grammar. He sees this in two perspectives: new learning, and then learning to comprehend familiar structures more fully (Crystal, 1982). In the first category he puts sentence connectivity, the use of connectives to join clauses within a sentence. Although the latter does begin according to him by the age of about 4 or 5, this only happens with the use of relatively few and unsophisticated connectives, and these gradually extend to more sophisticated forms over several years. Certain types of dependent clause are relatively late in developing, and include those introduced with an adverbial connector such as *really*, *however*, *frankly* and so on. In addition, he says that the child has to learn 'that there are layers in the interpretation of a sentence that are not immediately apparent from perceiving the form of the sentence.' He goes on to say that sentences do not always mean what they seem to mean, and that it is only when this process starts that children begin to appreciate the possible effects that can be produced in the use of language, such as idiom, and jokes, riddles and puns. Comprehension, of course, often involves the use of inferences to gain the full meaning of a passage, in more mature levels of text, such as those used in the upper Key Stage 2 years and onwards. Crystal reports that at about that stage the nature of the language learning process alters radically, along with some evidence that the ability to learn foreign languages differs from pre-puberty to post-puberty, becoming more difficult to acquire. He speculates that while pre-puberty speech may be more homogenous, the use of speech post-puberty shows greater idiosyncrasy and inventiveness, although evidence for this is rather limited. Finally Crystal reminds us that the learning of vocabulary and style is never-ending and is a lifelong process (Crystal, 1982).

Bancroft suggests a further convention comprising just two stages, over and above that of the stages just outlined, and one which makes a watershed division between the stages of telegraphic speech and speech which employs grammatical markers and inflections (Bancroft, 1995, in Lee and Das Gupta).

■ Linguistic Universals and Related Theories

Altmann outlines two goals involved in the study of language acquisition, firstly, understanding the gaining of knowledge about individual words, and secondly, understanding the gaining of knowledge about how words combine to form meaningful sentences (Altmann, 1997). The latter must include not only grammar, but also the structure of meaning through the putting together of words, and there are several theories concerning this aspect of language acquisition. These have generally looked at patterns common to many or all languages, termed universals, which underlie the processes involved and the observations we are able to make of children's developing speech.

In the first part of the twentieth century, the ideas of Piaget began to play a prominent part in views of children's cognitive and language development. He stressed the important role that the child plays in his own development through his actions. The mechanism for learning in Piaget's theory was that of adaptation. We adapt our knowledge and understanding through accommodating new information, sometimes modifying it as we link it to previous learning if it does not quite fit, so that elements of conflict between new and old learning cause us to move forward in our understanding (Piaget, 1959; Das Gupta and Richardson, 1995, in Lee and Das Gupta; Bremner, 1999, in Messer and Millar).

At the same time the Russian psychologist, Vygotsky, was producing his own ideas about learning. Vygotsky maintained that although children might learn some concepts through their everyday experiences, they would not develop modes of thought or skills using symbolism, such as speaking, reading and writing, without adult modelling, help and instruction. From this, he developed his idea of the **zone of proximal development (ZPD)**, sometimes called the zone of potential development. This is what we today might call 'next steps learning', that which the child can go on to achieve next with adult help and guidance, but which he would not learn by himself at that stage (Vygotsky, 1962; Das Gupta and Richardson, 1995, in Lee and Das Gupta).

While Piaget stressed the active role of the child in his own learning, Vygotsky placed his reliance largely on the social context and its impingement upon the individual. Both their theories related to cognitive development in general, in which they saw language as a part. While the stage system Piaget produced still has some validity, it has been discovered that cultural contexts do have an effect upon the time periods, although not the sequence, of the stages (Das Gupta and Richardson, 1995, in Lee and Das Gupta). Many studies emulating Piaget's work have shown that context and the language used to children in the experiments also produce different effects in terms of the time periods for the sequenced effects (Donaldson, 1978; Drozd, 2001, in Bowerman and Levinson). Thus the notion of social context, the basis of Vygotsky's theory, has been seen to modify Piaget's hypothesis.

A most prominent theorist in the field is Noam Chomsky, who originally argued that babies are born with a specific language acquisition device, and who holds that they have very specialized inbuilt information processing mechanisms. Chomsky's view of the mind and its functioning developed from this, and incorporated three crucial features derived from the close observation of children's developing speech: creativity, complexity and universality. The human being's ability to speak and understand an infinite number of original sentences, i.e. those never heard before, demonstrates the complex, inexhaustive and innovative nature of language. Furthermore, he thought that the ease with which children learn their language before other cognitively simpler tasks, and in what must be seen as an inductive manner from only fragmented information, strongly suggested specific innate mechanisms. These he also thought from the same evidence must be of a restrictive or constraining nature, operating on the organization of language. If this were so, he argued, then such specific principles of organization would be shared by all languages (Lyons, 1970; Bancroft, 1995, in Lee and Das Gupta; Smith, 1999; Clark, 2001, in

Bowerman and Levinson). Chomsky's **principles and parameters theory (PPT)** reflects some of his later thinking. He has also, more lately, focused on some meaningful aspects of children's speech and has attended to the way they develop understanding of both word meanings and grammar (Smith, 1999).

Other views and theories have begun to make their appearance. A number of these are based on the assumption that cognitive processes are based on our genetic inheritance. Much of this latest work uses the notions of modules and domains to explain differences in learning abilities (Spelke and Tsivkin, 2001, in Bowerman and Levinson). Bancroft explains that 'Modules are different subsets of our neural networks which are genetically pre-structured for processing different kinds of input information: for example, language information, or musical or mathematical information.' He goes on: 'A domain is the set of representations on which a particular kind of knowledge and the cognitive processes that go with it are based.' (Bancroft, 1995, in Lee and Das Gupta.) Bancroft also discusses a new challenge in terms of language acquisition theories, with a perspective combining information from the fields of artificial intelligence (i.e. using information technology) and psycholinguistics. This is known as **connectionism**. As a model of language development it is based on the idea of the interconnected operation of the large number of neurons in the human brain, which together form very complicated functional networks (Bancroft, 1995, in Lee and Das Gupta). Messer concludes that none of the various important theories of language acquisition are completely satisfactory, but that the connectionist view provides an alternative to the parameter setting ideas of Chomsky (Messer, 1999, in Messer and Millar).

Although Messer holds that environmental influences are strong, he thinks the special social environment created by adults for children is not likely by itself to make the acquisition of language possible. Thus both the structures in the brain, whether more specific or more general, and whether more restrictive or more loosely constraining in their effects, and the environmental influences and experiences from the social context of language are features essential to learning to speak (Messer, 1999, in Messer and Millar). Both are essential, but neither one alone is sufficient. The argument thus restates itself as a matter of the relative emphases between these two major participants in the process. Messer suggests that in recent research more attention is being paid to the way adults actually speak to children, and that this is the way forward. He states 'For too long, research has been influenced by grand theories. Instead, we need to spend more time watching and listening to children.' (Messer, 2000.)

■ Young Children's Uses of Language in the Early Stages

One of the most striking of the phenomena of early language use is that of the **monologue**. Sometimes referred to as **egocentric speech**, it is a sort of sporadic running commentary uttered by the child, usually accompanying play or activity of some sort, and not emitted in the expectation of any particular response from those around him. Early noted by Piaget, who also began to realize the progressive differences in the quality of play, it often happens when the child is absorbed in doing something of interest, and may fulfil the function of maintaining self-directive thoughts to do with the ongoing activity (Piaget, 1959). An example of monologue is the following, playing with toy cars in the sandpit: *'I'm going to make it go up here...Brmm brmm brmm...Whee eeee ee! It's coming down now...Wheeeeee Now the red one's going...Brmmm brmmm brmmm...It's crashing, it's crashing!'* This function of language appears around 2 years old, and continues until around the ages of 4 to 6. At the same time children are developing their abilities to engage in **dialogue**, and this happens spontaneously, more frequently, as time goes on, so that as children develop socially they become more likely to interact with others verbally.

At the stage when the monologue is very prominent, the child is usually most absorbed in playing by himself, engaging in **egocentric play**. Later, he is more aware of those around him, and likes to play alongside his peers, throwing occasional remarks to them to tell them what he is doing: *'I'm making a monster – he's fierce – he's going to eat you up!'* This is the stage of **parallel play**. Gradually, social interaction develops and arguments and co-operative ventures become frequent during play, showing the beginning of true collaborative play and work; this is the stage of **co-operative play**, and with it comes the advent of the prominence of dialogue. At the stage of co-operative play, language becomes conversation, with a cut and thrust between the participants; sometimes it is general conversation, sometimes argument and justification, and sometimes one of the participants takes the lead and issues commands, but communication is taking place. An example, during construction play with bricks, would be something like: *'Look, put that big red one here, put yours here, we're going to make the highest tower...it's got to go here...oh, yeah, that's good...we've done it!'* There is considerable overlap as this gradual process takes place. Eventually, the monologue completely disappears, as far as language spoken aloud is concerned, at least, and from his dialogue with others the child gradually acquires the facility to communicate in a variety of ways, using his speech for a wide repertoire of functions.

Children learn and consolidate language by using it, and the uses children make of their language skills has been another aspect of language acquisition which has proved fertile ground for research, although the range, variety and detail produced in this field has been nowhere near as great as that concerned with the theories of acquisition themselves. Crystal, in discussing this area of interest, questions whether it is indeed possible to create detailed and determinate specification of language functions (Crystal, 1982). However, he goes on to mention the pioneering work done by Halliday, who produced a means of classifying the grammatical functions of early speech (Halliday, 1969). His categorisation of the many-sided nature of the child's linguistic experiences and uses by the time he starts school is composed of seven models, or types of use: Instrumental ('I want'), Regulatory (language as control), Interactional (maintaining relationships), Personal (awareness of self), Heuristic, (language to learn), Imaginative (pretence, fantasy), and Representational (communicating information). Additionally, there is the function of language which might be termed the ritual use, and which Halliday likens to table manners, used by adults to define a social group, and gradually imposed upon children, but playing no actual part in the child's own needs for using language.

Halliday also discussed what he called the notion of **transitivity**. How much is actually communicated between participants in a conversation or discussion? It is dependent on the common understanding of the concepts and ideas represented by the words. This is a salient point for teachers, and in particular for the teacher of pupils with English as an additional language. Meanwhile, on a very simplistic level, we may be reminded of this by the misinterpretations sometimes made by young children, such as the old favourite of 'Harold be Thy Name...', and more up to date, perhaps, 'I am the Lord of the Damp Settee'.

Corden suggests that some of Halliday's work on aspects of talk is especially important for teachers since it identifies the learning potential of what he calls **exploratory talk** (Corden, 2000). Exploratory talk, he explains, is concerned with working things out together, rather than speaking to an external audience, and is sometimes called process talk. He gives interesting and illuminating examples of this kind of interactive speech.

In a different way from Halliday, Tough devoted a great amount of time and effort into observing and noting the language forms and uses of young children (Tough, 1973; Tough 1977). She adopted a fourfold classification of functions, called the directive function, the interpretive function, the projective function and the relational function. Her study of children's communication skills was done at a basic level, and served very much to inform teachers working with children in the early years about how children communicate, and how to allow time and stimulus for enhancing such development. Her main sevenfold categorisation is as follows: Self-maintaining, Directing, Reporting, Reasoning, Predicting, Projecting, and Imagining. Despite criticism from those examining and replicating her work, her ideas were seminal and had impact in making teachers more aware of the importance of speech and conversation in the early years' classroom.

Wells maintains that language develops vitally through interaction, and he points out unequivocally that literacy depends upon the foundation of speech and understanding of language, in many aspects, through the development of meaning (Wells, 1981; Wells, 1977). Corden, in reviewing investigations into the translation of speech into literacy, supports this view and gives a range of information on the practical application of sound findings and theory (Corden, 2000). In the classroom, Corden states, children use language in a variety of ways (see summary at the end of this chapter). Corden shows how teachers can support and extend such uses to good effect in the classroom (Corden, 2000).

SEQUENCE OF DEVELOPMENT OF SPEECH		
Terminology	**Stage**	**Example**
	Babbling – playing with sounds – responding to adults	

Holophrase
 	
(P4)
	Single word utterances
	      – naming people or
	         objects
	
	      – representing variety of
	         meaning
		Dadda
		Bow-wow
		Din-din
		
		Daddy =
		Daddy help me (?)
		Daddy's here (?) etc.

Pivot grammar
 	
(P5)
	Two or three word utterances
	
	      – adding descriptive
	         or modifying word
		Peas more
		Mummy gone
		Daddy socks

Telegraphic speech
 	
(P6) (SS3)
	Words/phrases
	
	      – expanded by adult
	      – reduced by child
		
		Daddy socks
		Give daddy his socks
		Daddy socks

Grammar
 	
(P7 & P8)
(SS3, 4, 5)
 	
(Accidence)
 	
(Syntax)
	Imitative speech and production of own
	creative speech
	
	      – monologue
	      – dialogue: learning and
	         applying rules
	
	      – word order
		
		He fighted mouses
		Don't giggle me
		
		John kicked Jack
		Jack kicked John

Transformation (of a kernel sentence) (P8) (SS4, 5 & ELGs)	Different types of sentences	John has a hat Has John got a hat? John hasn't a hat
Diversification (NC Level 1+)	Range of use and functions	

Table 2.1 ■ 'P Scales' references taken from 'Supporting the Target Setting Process', rev.2001, DfEE, Stepping Stones and Early Learning Goals references from Curriculum Guidance for the Foundation Stage, DfEE, 2000. Table updated and adapted from 'Becoming a Writer', KCC, 1984

LANGUAGE FUNCTION AND USE – HALLIDAY AND TOUGH		
Example	**Halliday**	**Tough**
I want	Instrumental	Self-maintaining
Go away Do what I say	Regulatory (controls others)	Directing
You cut and I'll stick	Interactional (interacts with others)	Directing
Here I come	Personal (expresses feelings, interest etc.)	-----------
I've got something to tell you	Informative	Reporting
I'm getting a bike for Christmas	Informative	Predicting
The boy ran away from the witch	Imaginative	Imagining Projecting
How did this happen?	Heuristic (seeking information)	-----------
The desert is hot and I think you'll get sand blown over you	-----------	Predicting
Cars can't go in floods but boats can	-----------	Logical reasoning

Table 2.2 ■ Adapted from 'Becoming a Writer', KCC, 1984

According to Corden, children use language in the classroom to:

■ Relate new information to existing experiences and knowledge;

■ Investigate, hypothesize, question, negotiate;

■ Argue, reason, justify, consider, compare, evaluate, confirm, reassure, clarify, select, modify, plan;

■ Demonstrate and convey understanding, narrate, describe, explain;

■ Reflect upon and evaluate new perceptions and understandings.

■ Chapter Summary

1. Children's acquisition of speech and language follows a basically universal sequence; learning language takes place relatively quickly, and basic language structures are usually in place by the age of 4.

2. An amazing feature of young children's speech during the process of acquisition is its originality and creativity. This has led to much theorizing about the way speech is acquired.

3. There are different theories about the acquisition of speech, but it is now accepted that both innate biological development in the brain and social interaction with a language basis are necessary for it to happen. The difference between the theories is based on differences of emphasis and the mechanisms modelled.

4. The monologue is characteristic of young children's language development, and seems to disappear from spoken speech when the stage of dialogue becomes prominent, roundabout the same time as the development of co-operative play.

5. Children use a surprisingly wide range of speech strategies in support of the functions of meaning they draw upon in their communications with others. Some of these are to do with the development of the inner knowledge of self, others to do with relationships, with learning and with fantasy.

6. Some features of grammatical structure, especially some forms of logically related clauses, are not fully understood until late childhood or early adolescence.

7. Early intervention is indicated in cases of linguistic deprivation.

■ Teacher Activity

Briefly transcribe a few utterances of young children, or try one or two of different ages; note length of utterances in number of words. With older children listen and notice any use of dependent clauses in complex sentences, or note whether boys and girls use a different vocabulary, particularly in description or reporting on attitudes and feelings. Are 11–14 year-olds using any causal type dependent clauses, i.e. explaining causal links of a logical type, such as those involving the use of *if* followed by *then*, or using *because*?

For following up further interests

Lee, V. and Das Gupta, P. (eds.) (1995) *Children's Cognitive and Language Development*. Oxford: Blackwell.

Pinker, S. (1994) *The Language Instinct*. Harmsworth: Penguin Books.

3 Language and Thinking, and Cultural and Social Influences on Language Use

■ **Floating Cargoes Across Time and Space**

Language and thinking – The development of meaning and the idea of transitivity – Some social and cultural differences between languages – Implications for teaching pupils with English as an additional language – Social and cultural influences within English – The importance of oracy for literacy – Chapter summary – Teacher activity

Language and Thinking

There has been considerable debate about the relationship between language and thought, as psychologists try to develop the understanding of how ideas and reasoning develop in children. Bancroft suggests that categorizing experience, involving the use of concept formation, is an important way of simplifying the world as it impinges upon the individual, and that language is likely to be involved in this process. Concepts, as they develop gradually from experiences, are likely to differ from person to person, although as more experience of a common sort takes place, the closer these representations become. This allows some commonality of understanding within the communicative context to develop. Since they are individually constructed, though, Bancroft points out that boundaries between concepts may be varied and indistinct (Bancroft, 1995, in Lee and Das Gupta).

Following older classic studies, including Carroll and Casagrande in the fifties and Berger and Luckman in the sixties, Waxman has investigated the contribution of language to conceptualisation, and in particular, the effect of naming, or labelling upon the imaging and remembering of ideas (Carroll and Casagrande, 1958; Berger and Luckman, 1967; Waxman, 1990). Discussing this conceptual mechanism, Bancroft quotes Waxman: 'Providing a common label (e.g. '*animal*') for multiple referents is in itself an act of classification. Likewise, providing different labels (e.g. '*dog*', '*horse*') reveals conceptual distinctions among referents.' (Bancroft, 1995, in Lee and Das Gupta.) Berger and Luckman use the same simile as that of Piaget, in describing the construction of outside reality inside the mind as a process of sedimentation, as words gradually acquire meanings as labels for objects and experiences.

Thought can exist without language, for instance in spatial and pictorial forms, and in movement memories, and even toddlers show evidence of this when they seek the ball that has rolled underneath the sofa. However, the development of the thinking processes in general, and the eventual ability to reason in abstract terms, depend to a considerable extent upon language use. For young children, much of their thinking seems to be inextricably linked with speaking out loud.

Both Piaget and Vygotsky noticed the monologue as a characteristic feature of the speech of young children at play. According to the emphases of their different theories, they attached alternative explanations to its developmental role. Vygotsky believed that the egocentric speech of the monologue eventually became 'inner speech' rather than petering out altogether, and that such internalised language served to develop logical thinking (Vygotsky, 1962; Piaget, 1959). Vygotsky asserted that such egocentric speech provided an adaptive planning function. Both he and other notable authorities on the subject accept that language is a prime agent in cognitive development.

Vygotsky initially identified two roles for language: language as the means of communication, and then as the means of thought. He thought that these strands started as separate, but came together around the age of 2, in their interdependent and intertwined common nature. Bruner also emphasized the primacy of language for cognition and the ability to reason, through what he termed the symbolic mode of representation (Bruner, 1966; 1985).

There are, of course, different opinions about the relative contributions of language and experience to cognitive development, and a particular stance was adopted by a couple of theorists called Sapir and Whorf, whose work became prominent around the middle of the last century. The Sapir-Whorf hypothesis, also known as the **linguistic relativity hypothesis**, held that language determines thought, through the influences of the social world both concepts and understanding gradually grow, imbibing cultural constraints and modes (Whorf, 1956; Sapir, 1966). There is a so-called weaker form of the Sapir-Whorf model, in which language is taken to frame or influence thought, rather than to wholly determine it. Today this is perhaps the more acceptable version, and Bancroft puts forward the current thinking on this, saying that it is accepted that language does indeed have some influence on the way in which one thinks of the world (Bancroft, 1995, in Lee and Das Gupta).

In learning a first language, Bancroft claims, the child is learning the conceptual relations implied by that particular language. He holds that both language and the social context in which it is used seem to be implicated in the development of children's concepts and their ability to reason. He shows that although young children have been found to have more understanding of concepts like cause and time than was previously held, nevertheless evidence demonstrates that the process to full understanding is very gradual, and is not complete until the late childhood years, around 11 to 12.

Exploring further the notion that the language we hear all around us can actually influence the way in which we understand the world, Alison Gopnik suggests a neo-Whorfian relationship between language and thought (Gopnik,

2001, in Bowerman and Levinson). Her thesis is that the relation between language and thought may be seen as 'analogous to processes of theory formation and change in science', and this hypothesis she calls **the theory theory**, as children generate their own theories and make inferences. Although sharing broad emphases with the Piagetian stage theory, this approach owns a number of specific differences from it, allowing that young children have greater capacity for logical reasoning and are likely to own 'abstract representations of the world that are removed from direct perceptual experience or action schemas.' (Gopnik, 2001, in Bowerman and Levinson.) She recognizes the strong effect language has upon thought, and states 'Children do pay attention to the particularities of the adult language, and these particularities do affect the child's conception of the world.'

The Development of Meaning and the Idea of Transitivity

Children thus gradually acquire the facility to communicate, reason and think in a variety of different ways, using an extensive repertoire of functions. Thought is likely to be influenced, structured even, by social context, and growth in using language and in thinking may be facilitated and enhanced, or limited and deprived by linguistic experiences. This returns us to the question of transitivity, to use the term coined by Halliday, the actual nub of communication. Is the understanding common to both the speaker and the listener? Do they have the same ideas of what the words mean, and how they are arranged and even spoken? There are two important issues here: one is concerned with differences in interpretation of words and phraseology by speakers of the same language, and the other is to do with the way mind-sets are structured or influenced by a person's native language and how these may affect understanding in another language being learned, or already learned. Where we are dealing with literacy, and using reading and writing, different forms of the same language may have developed over years, decades and centuries, or with slightly different usages for some words in geographically differently placed communities.

Words come to us like boats, carrying their meanings like cargoes transported over space and time. Traces of the meanings others have invested in them travel to us, some from the immediate past and from our near communities, others from older eras or far-away places. Some traces become overlaid and obliterated, as the basic meanings gradually change, and new usages take their places (Carroll and Casagrande, 1958). Where young children are concerned, and first hand experiences are valuably exploited in their learning, this reminds us of the importance of accompanying talk and commentary, providing the appropriate words to encapsulate an aspect of experience, to graft on new words, and to provide the labels for storage and retrieval of the experience in memory as part of the process of concept formation.

Tomasello emphasises two particular aspects: the pattern of cultural interactions in the social world into which the child is born, and the child's own capacity for tuning in to that world (Tomasello, 2001, in Bowerman and Levinson).

Children come to internalise the thought-forms prevalent in their culture, through the relationship with parents, family and through a gradually expanding social life within their own community. Reviewing substantial evidence from cross-cultural linguistic studies, Smith concludes that children learning different languages do develop different attentional biases which seem to be specific to different languages (Smith, 2001, in Bowerman and Levinson). Different language uses encountered during the journey through life can thus influence thought, while language itself changes in terms of the meanings it represents as people use it. The role of language in cognitive development is thus a complex one, difficult to unravel or to assess, yet it is plain that it has a crucial and essential part to play in thought processes and their development throughout life.

■ Some Social and Cultural Differences Between Languages

Returning to the idea of transitivity, we need to take account of the way thought forms may be framed or influenced by language uses. There are implications here for children in our schools whose first language is not English. English as we know it today is a language which has been produced from the impact between several different languages, buffeting each other across the centuries from the intrusions of invaders and conquerors; it is like a rolling stone, from which not only the moss has been rubbed away, but which has been polished smooth from all rough parts and protuberances by the tumbling and knocking it has received (Crystal, 1997).

When people pick up a language with which they are not familiar, they tend to latch on to the roots of words more ably than they do to the suffixes and prefixes, the agreements, tenses and cases. Thus morphology is reduced. This has happened to English, which has few instances of case changes; although these existed long ago, overt forms of case only remain now in the personal pronouns (Pinker, 1994). German has four cases, while Latin had five, but Finnish uses 15. In English nouns do not have gender, as they do in French, Italian and German, for instance. On the other hand, while it may be easy from the point of view of using agreeing endings, or changing articles, the English language has a vast repertoire of words, a huge vocabulary, making learning all the nuances able to be expressed in the language quite a daunting task for the non-native speaker. In addition, its spelling system is not fully regular, having many alternative rules for the same sounds. These characteristics are also the inheritances of the swirling mixture of linguistic intrusions that so long ago forged the English language. Bill Bryson writes that 'English retains probably the richest vocabulary and the most diverse shading of meanings, of any language' (Bryson, 1990). The availability of alternatives makes English a tool for expression which has great scope for both clarity and creativity.

A language of Indo-European origin, our language has evolved from the ancient Germanic language of the Angles, with intrusions from Celtic, Saxon, Jutish, Viking, Norman French, while influences came from Latin through legal and religious commerce. This is the mixture that formed our mongrel language, gave it its flexibility, its precision, its extensive vocabulary, and its strange mixture of regular and irregular spelling.

Our language, of course, is still living and developing, and the adoption of words and phrases did not cease with the Norman conquest. Referring to the wide range of words adopted from languages around the world, Bryson tells us that even as far back as the sixteenth century English had already adopted words from 50 different languages. He explains that Greek influences entered through Latin forms or from Latin and then French forms of usage (Stevenson, 1999). Intrusion continued into English from many other sources and peoples. From as early as the sixteenth century, Romany people had settled in England, and we use some of their terms in our everyday language, for instance, pal, cove and cosh; Romany, or Rom, is a language of Indo-Aryan origins, from north-western India (Stevenson, 1999). We need to remember that meanings are capable of shifting, and that as a language is used this happens, often imperceptibly, over time and over distance. Bryson gives us the example of differences for meanings of the words vest and pants, developed between England, where they are underwear, and America where these words mean waistcoat and trousers (Bryson, 1990).

We are all able to think of words which have changed their meanings, or acquired additional meanings, in our own lifetimes, such as the changes in the use of words like chip, grass, joint and hardware. This demonstrates how words are mere labels for constructs of meanings. If these constructs have a different make-up for one person to another, the transitivity of communication between them is not going to be complete or accurate. For those who are learning English as an additional language, apprehension of English forms and structures, and their meanings may pose difficulties, or even may be tinged with aspects of meaning from the characteristics owned by the native tongue. Gradually, with full fluency and the commerce of using the language, commonality of understanding will be generally achieved. However, it is important for those teaching children at early stages of the acquisition of English in our schools to attend to building the understanding of meanings behind the labels of the words and phrases being taught.

Apart from differences in calligraphic form and direction, contrasts between languages fall into two categories, those of **lexical**, and those of **syntactic** or grammatical differences, the latter including word order patterns. Lexical differences have been described by Slobin as being mostly in the categories of missing as opposed to present terms and different divisions of semantic domains, all hinging on the way concepts are coded by words (Slobin, 1971). For example, in Chinese there is a word meaning 'fruit and nuts', whereas this has no parallel in ordinary everyday English. The use by Aztecs of a single word to indicate snow, ice and cold is another example. Some languages, albeit rather rare, have no words for left or right, others for up or down. Another interesting area which has been studied is the naming of colours, useful since the rainbow of colour is actually a continuum, broken up in different ways;

thus blue and green may be seen as different shades of one colour by some peoples. We have already seen how certain grammatical structures, such as case and case agreement, differ from one language to another, in the contrast between English, and German and Finnish. While Slobin thinks it is possible to express virtually any idea or concept in any language, he qualifies this by pointing out that certain ideas may be easy to express with precision, with perhaps one word even in some languages, but difficult and needing substantial circumlocutions in others (Slobin, 1971).

Turning to syntactical differences, Pinker gives a very useful and clear list of six ways in which other languages may differ from English (Pinker, 1994). First, he says, English is an 'isolating ' language, by which he means that sentences are built by the rearrangement of word units, without the alteration of noun or verb word units by using case endings or affixes, for instance. It is a 'fixed word-order' language, and of course this use of word order to indicate meaning renders the case changes redundant (Pinker, 1994). The way questions are asked is also often different in other languages from the structure used in English. In English, question words are conventionally placed at the beginnings of sentences, whereas in languages that use the order 'subject-object-verb', the question words will usually come at the end of sentences (Pinker, 1994).

Finally Pinker explains that in English a noun remains the same in any sentence construction, apart from the change when plural is indicated. In some other languages nouns may be in gender classes, or may be classified as animate or inanimate, whether part of a cluster or a particular category of use, and other classifying features, and these need to be indicated by endings or other affixes, or by accompanying words (Pinker, 1994). Contrast the learning needed in English for noun forms with that required in Finnish, where there are 15 case changes; this is equivalent to learning 15 different spellings for words such as cat, dog, house and so on (Bryson, 1990). Again, in some other languages, adjectives have to accord with the gender of the nouns, as in French and also in Russian. English, says Bryson, is mercifully uninflected, an aspect of the linguistic structure which, despite other difficulties, makes it easier for additional language learners.

Chinese, of which the main language is Mandarin, is thought to be one of the oldest living languages in the world, and uses no prefixes or suffixes. Yen Mah tells us that it is a non-inflectional language with very few grammatical rules: it has no cases, endings, different forms of words, gender agreements, and not even any tenses. She writes that there is an almost complete reliance on word order and the use of auxiliary words to convey meaning (Yen Mah, 2000). Words tend to be root words, and gain their grammatical category by their position in a sentence; this carries the corollary that a word cannot be fully understood except in relation to its textual context. Yen Mah adds that Chinese sentences do not need to have a verb: 'Big house', she says, is a sentence, but it can also be the subject of a larger sentence. She informs us also that there is no verb 'to be' in Chinese, and that a precise translation of 'To be or not to be...' is therefore impossible; she has seen it translated as 'Let me live or let me die...' (Yen Mah, 2000). Summing up from her position as a fully fluent speaker of acquired English, she claims that the characteristics of Chinese make it, as a writing medium, an imprecise and often ambiguous tool. Abstract sequences of logical reasoning are particularly difficult to translate accurately from English to Chinese, she states. 'Western reality is based on substance and causality, whereas Chinese reality is centred on relative contrasts and relational thinking.' (Yen Mah, 2000.) China has, however, one great advantage, in that among all the different Chinese languages spoken there is only one writing system, and because it is pictographic, it can be used equally well in all the Chinese languages.

In some languages, homonyms are differentiated by the use of different voice tones, something which does not happen in English at all. Yen Mah gives the example of a Chinese word *ma*, which can mean mother, numb, ant, horse or scold, according to the tone or cadence of the voice when it is spoken. Although we do not have tone representing meaning in English, we do have characteristic stress patterns in our speech, which form natural rhythms in cadences of speech and particularly in poetry. Stressed and unstressed syllables enable specific intentional rhythms in poetry, by means of the selection of words to form different types of **metrical feet**. Rhythms and cadences of speech form characteristic attributes of languages, and are part of their prosody; these can differ widely. Consider the speaking of French, as a contrast to English, where all syllables generally receive equal stress, so that while syllables may be counted, the stressed and unstressed patterns providing different rhythmic effects in poetry in English cannot be mirrored in quite the same way in French.

It must be stated that no value judgements about languages are being made here, and there is no intention to rate any language as better than any other. Contrasts have merely been outlined as examples of some of the ways in which languages may differ, and particularly in the ways they may differ in framing or influencing thinking, through linguistic cultural heritages. All languages own features which make both for ease and for difficulties for the non-native learner, and for communications between languages.

Implications for Teaching Pupils with English as an Additional Language

In teaching pupils with English as an additional language it is important that the children's own cultural heritages are valued and celebrated, and that they continue to have experiences of literacy in their own native tongue, as well as in English. Evans has a good chapter on this, showing the value of reading and writing in the native tongue alongside the additional language (Evans, 2001). Close attention needs to be paid to pupils' understanding in spoken communication, and their comprehension in reading, as well as the way they use words and grammar in their writing. Words and phrases may be acquired and used, seemingly correctly, but often the conceptualisation behind the word usage remains limited for some time, until use and experiences have enlarged the original ideas. Tenses are often difficult to acquire correctly, especially with irregular forms which are difficult in English, together with the fact that we have two different ways of expressing the present tense. Whereas learning vocabulary is difficult enough, it is the way that words are used in sentences, the morphology, and syntax which are hardest to acquire (Bryson, 1990). Colloquialisms are a particular hurdle, sometimes, because they demand an understanding of inference and further symbolism. Bryson's example of a computer translating 'out of sight, out of mind' into another language and then translating it back as 'blind insanity' illustrates this well. Care with explanations, showing the way rather than pointing out mistakes, will help.

However, for the teacher to have some ideas about the native languages of pupils in the process of acquiring English, even in the most general way, is likely to pay dividends in understanding how children's knowledge and understanding is being mapped by them onto the English words and phrases. While acquisition of an additional language follows much the same sequence as learning a native language, there are some points of difference which may occur: there is often a 'silent period' when children are listening to the new language at the beginning, and before they start to speak, and this can sometimes last for weeks or months. Other differences are word order problems, difficulties with verb agreements and/or tenses, a lack of full understanding of concepts behind the apparently competent use of words for which they form labels, and lack of full understanding of idiomatic phrases.

Useful sources for support with teaching pupils with English as an additional language include the Key Stage 3 Strategy for English, among other official documents, as well as the guidance on teaching, learning and assessment given in both Gravelle and Gregory (Gregory, 1996; Gravelle, 2000; DfEE, 2001/0019).

Most local education authorities have some information about the range of mother tongues spoken in their areas, usually available from their Ethnic Minority Assistance Services (EMAS), and some provide useful information or book lists of dual language books and books in the various languages needed, so that schools can widen their library repertoire by providing these for pupils. An example of this is an annotated list of books, produced by Southwark Education Department, reflecting the cultural and linguistic diversity of children in the borough's schools (CLPE/Southwark, 1999). In addition, many local education authorities have produced schedules showing the sequence of acquisition of English as an additional language, and identifying milestone points in the process as specific stages. This is very helpful, and class teachers, as well as English co-ordinators and specialist teachers for English as an additional language, should be aware of any such schedule recommended by their local education authority. An example of one such schedule, produced by the education department of the London Borough of Lewisham, is given in the Appendix. The progress of such pupils learning English also needs to be evaluated by reference to the English National Curriculum levels, and for young children, where relevant, by the English nationally recommended Early Learning Goals and the steps by which these are reached (DfEE, 1999a; DfEE, 2000). Whereas it is sometimes recommended that only the National Curriculum levels should be used for assessment in the acquisition of English as an additional language, since it is the only national set of benchmarks, the periods between the attainment of the levels (one or two years) are too long to be of any specific use, and there is a need to supplement these by use of the more specific acquisition schedules. An OFSTED report *Raising the Attainment of Minority Ethnic Pupils* stresses that evaluation and assessment of progress is important for progress (OFSTED, 1999). Remembering the notion of critical periods in the context of learning a second or third language, Smith suggests the window of opportunity lies within the first decade of life, and that perfect mastery of additional languages is possible if children's exposure to them comes sufficiently early (Smith, 1999). Carter supports this, reporting that once the phase for learning a native language is over, additional languages being learned are processed in a different part of the language area of the brain (Carter, 1998).

Social and Cultural Differences Within English

In the sixties there was considerable concern about differences in language use between social classes, and there was a number of prominent studies investigating such issues. The main focus of the argument was that education is promoted mainly through a middle-class type of language use, highly differentiated and more flexible, and less dependent on the here and now for its referents, whereas many children come to school limited to only one type of language use. The latter is assumed in some cases to be of an immediate situational type, peer-orientated rather than individualized, yet personal rather than abstract. Bernstein, famous for his work in this field, drew attention to the way different types of language use within the same English tongue may reflect and perpetuate certain attitudes and values characteristic of the culture to which they belong (Bernstein, 1960; 1971). He thinks that some children are limited to a kind of language use of an immediate and undifferentiated type. This places pupils at a disadvantage in school where the medium of learning is a more flexible, individuated and well-differentiated mode of speech (Bernstein, 1960; 1971). That education needs to be conducted in the latter is accepted for reasons of precision, abstraction, reasoning and flexibility. Such a disjunction, in effect at the extreme a gulf, between the different uses, Bernstein thought, might lead to alienation from school and antagonism towards authority.

The rigidity with which he labelled the contrasting linguistic experiences as **restricted code** and **elaborated code** have been questioned. Wells did not find such characteristic differences as he had been led to expect by Tough's work, in line with Bernstein's ideas, when he surveyed language used in the home across a wide section of society in Bristol (Wells, 1981). Wells suggested that social background could no longer be seen as the strong determinant it had previously been thought to be in terms of either rate or style of language development (Wells, 1981). Wells also began to think that schooling itself develops the child's use of language, rendering it more individually differentiated in terms of meaning, and detaching it more from the immediate context, aiding abstraction. Crystal maintains that appropriateness is what is important in language teaching contexts. He thinks it is widely recognized that 'there is no single or universally correct or most logical use of language, and that acceptability depends primarily on seeing any language use in relation to its purpose' (Crystal, 1982).

Today, this perspective has held sway. Barnes reminds us, though, that unless there is a meeting of minds through the medium of language the work of the classroom may become an empty formality for some pupils (Barnes *et al.*, 1969; Barnes, 1976). Altmann must have the last word here: 'In the end, there is just one view from Babel. Language, quite simply, is a window through which we can reach out and touch each other's minds. Anyone can reach through it – regardless of race, regardless of belief. It is the most intimate act we can ever perform. We must be sure, always, to keep that window open.' (Altmann, 1997.)

■ The Importance of Oracy for Literacy

Thus spoken language forms a constraint, a ceiling not only on the ability to comprehend, but also on the ability to write, beyond which literacy cannot progress. Not only does speech form a basic foundation for starting to write, or writing in the early stages of schooling, but it is an ongoing process which supports and propels writing abilities forwards. Rather like riding an escalator, the ability to develop in writing rises as it is carried to new heights by further development in speaking and listening.

Maclure writes about the gathering momentum of the oracy movement, and the centrality of talk in education (Maclure, in Maclure *et al.*, 1988). She concludes that the path of developing spoken language extends across many situations, and many years, with the interaction with others as a facilitating factor (Maclure, in Maclure *et al.*, 1988). It is assumed today, therefore, and appropriately so, that schools are able to contribute towards the development of children's oral abilities. In the past, traditional classroom techniques and structures were often characterized by much direct teacher talk, placing pupils in an overly passive role. Nowadays, although obviously some elements of direct teaching are essential, there is a more positive and productive emphasis on active and interactive modes of communication in the classroom. Corden has shown very effectively how learning through talk supports the process of becoming literate, and in particular, the teacher strategies and types of language intervention that can enhance such learning (Corden, 2000).

Corden also discusses the position of speaking and listening in relation to the other two major strands of English, reading and writing, in the English National Curriculum, and in the English National Literacy Strategy Framework (NLSF). Corden suggests that the framework is 'in danger of imposing an instrumental, ethnocentric and static model of literacy in our schools'

(Corden, 2000). He comments that the Literacy Hour (LH), a structure of the English NLSF, has received some criticism for appearing to be too rigid and not allowing ideas or themes to be extended. However, he also reports that Stannard, involved in the production of the NLSF, has pointed out that teachers may use the LH with a degree of flexibility, particularly as they gain confidence (Stannard, 1998, in Corden, 2000). There is some evidence to be seen in schools that this is beginning to happen, very positively, in response to the needs of pupils in pursuing and approaching specific literacy goals.

While the inception and development of the NLSF in schools has had great impact and has brought about a great deal of improvement in teaching and learning, teachers need to recognize that the LH forms only part of the teaching of English. The NLSF itself states that 'The Literacy Hour is intended to be a time for the explicit teaching of reading and writing. Teachers will need to provide opportunities for practising and applying new skills in independent work at other times.' (DfEE, 1998.) Areas not specifically focused on in the NLSF, although they are frequently included in some form or other as aids to the achievement of the literacy goals, are handwriting, extended writing, drama, and speaking and listening.

Speaking and listening is a distinct attainment target in the English National Curriculum, and is part of the English 'Orders' which schools are obliged to deliver. The fact that it does not own a central role in the NSLF does not mean that it is a less valuable part of English. While it cannot be seen as separate from reading and writing it deserves prime status, and needs its own developmental and sequential framework. Incorporating both formal and informal activities, such a framework also needs an evaluative structure for guiding assessment, to ensure progress is taking place in this key aspect of English. Although the NLSF acknowledges the interrelationship between the three major strands of English, and encourages schools to pay due attention to the development of speaking and listening, too many schools have not realized the essential nature of this interaction.

As they accepted and took on board the NLSF, many assumed that the framework would take the place of their own former English schemes of work, and ditched these documents in favour of the new framework. In these cases, despite the actual wording in the NLSF, the differences between the demands of the English National Curriculum and the content of the NLSF were not fully realised. Early awareness of this soon followed in relation to handwriting, extended writing and drama, but frequently speaking and listening, the third major strand of the National Curriculum in English, has been left to lie fallow. Generally without any framework, developmental scheme, evaluation and assessment guidelines, and not incorporating any particular and specific objectives or goals for speaking and listening, a number of schools seem to have assumed that speaking and listening just grows.

Good opportunities are generally provided in the reporting back activities in the plenary part of the LH, and opportunities for paired or small group discussions are also available. More is needed, aimed at specific speaking and listening objectives, and these need to be planned for on a regular basis. Some schools do make a feature of incorporating small, focused activities in speaking and listening very regularly, even including these sometimes in the LH. This is good practice and it is surprising how well integrated speaking and listening can become within aspects of literacy as teachers become more confident and used to thinking about including it. Grugeon *et al.* give a good range of teacher strategies for promoting speaking and listening at both key stages in the primary school, together with ideas for assessment of this strand of English (Grugeon *et al.*, 1998). Corden also provides a huge range of ideas for the promotion of talk and shows how it may become integrated with literacy learning. He says 'Whatever our conception of literacy may be, spoken language should be seen as an integral and important ingredient.' (Corden, 2000.)

■ Chapter Summary

1. The development of the thinking processes in general, and the eventual ability to reason in abstract terms, depend to a considerable extent on language and language use.

2. Different aspects of language use are thought to canalise, frame or influence ways of thinking and understanding.

3. Transitivity, which is the nub of communication, depends on the commonality of understanding between speakers and listeners, or writers and readers.

4. There are a number of differences between English and other languages, and it is important for teachers with pupils who are acquiring English as an additional language to be aware of this, and how it may affect the work of such pupils.

5. There are also differences within English itself, in a range of different usages appropriate to different contexts.

6. While schooling provides opportunities for the development of the kinds of language use which facilitate reasoning and abstraction, teachers need to be alert to possible differences in understanding which pupils may have, due to different language uses, and to ensure that effective communication is taking place.

7. Schools need to pay attention to structuring the programme for speaking and listening as a crucial part of the English curriculum.

■ Teacher Activity

Listen to some children's conversation while they are working or playing – how much do they use intrinsic comment or gesture, in place of specific description or extrinsic comment? Given an object to describe in speech, can your pupils describe it without recourse to touching or demonstrating its function or use? Discuss your impressions with your colleagues.

For following up further interests

Altmann, G. T. M. (1997) *The Ascent of Babel*. Oxford: OUP.

Bryson, B. (1990) *Mother Tongue – The English Language*. Harmondsworth: Penguin Books.

Corden, R. (2000) *Literacy and Learning through Talk – Strategies for the Primary Classroom*. Buckingham: Open University Press.

Evans, J. (ed.) (2001) *The Writing Classroom*. London: David Fulton.

Gravelle, M. (2000) *Planning for Bilingual Learners – An Inclusive Curriculum*. Stoke on Trent: Trentham Books.

Gregory, E. (1996) *Making Sense of a New World – Learning to Read in a Second Language*. London: Paul Chapman.

Maclure, M., Phillips, T., and Wilkinson, A. (1988) *Oracy Matters*. Buckingham: Open University Press.

OFSTED (1999) *Raising the Attainment of Minority Ethnic Pupils – School and LEA Responses*. London: OFSTED Publications.

Stevenson, V. (1999) *The World of Words*. New York: Sterling Publishing.

4 | Some Cognitive Functions in Literacy – How Working Memory Affects Reading and Writing

■ Brain and Bottlenecks

Differences between oracy and literacy – Working memory and its constraints – Memory spans in adults and children – Developing effective skills in writing and reading – Using assessment in setting challenges for progress – Dyslexia and dysgraphia – Chapter summary – Teacher activity

☐ Differences Between Oracy and Literacy

Wilkinson has classified the language arts as follows:

	Production	Reception
Oracy	Speaking	Listening
Literacy	Writing	Reading

(Wilkinson, 1971)

Since production of language involves creating, and creating something understandable, whereas reception involves understanding of the message, the cognitive load is greater for production than for reception. Writing therefore requires more effort than reading, despite reading including the mental effort of bringing meaning to the symbols. Writing also involves a physical component, that of recording the message, another complication, whether through handwriting or typing. While in reading it is possible to recognize or understand a word from minimal cues, such as word configuration and some of the letters of letter clusters, in writing the encoding of words into letters has to be precise and specific (Snowling, 2000). Thus in writing we have the creation of thoughts, the encoding into written form, and the physical manipulation of writing tool or keyboard.

A text needs to use a precision and complexity of linguistic structure which is not demanded of speech. A reader can take his time over reading a text, if he wishes, and give it his whole attention, or he can scan the text quickly for an overall impression. Either way, the reader can vary his speed to match his understanding of the text. He is able to go back and re-read, to glance forward to cross-reference, to pause and reflect about a meaning or an idea. On the other hand, the listener has to receive his message immediately, catching it on the wing. Because of its immediacy, speech is often **elliptic**, with pauses, corrections, repetitions and so on. These are not generally appropriate in written text, unless, of course, speech is being represented as part of the text. Spoken language is responsive to changing demands in the immediate situation, such as the non-comprehension of the listener leading to further explanation, or the interest of the listener encouraging further detail. Written language, however, cannot respond in this way to situational changes, and therefore must, in its relative permanence, have more resistance to misunderstanding. Written language enables thoughts and ideas to be stored and retrieved, and to be transmitted across space and time, transcending the immediate moment. Thus textual language differs from spoken language in a number of ways:

■ Text does not record a number of features present in speech, such as speed, volume, intonation, and hesitation, while the subtleties of facial expression are also lost.

■ Written text can overcome the limits placed on language by the immediacy of speech, and transcend both space and time, whereas speech is suited to face to face situations, particularly those demanding co-operation in a mutual task where speed of exchange is essential.

■ Written text can be a more precise and exact form of language than speech, because it is relatively more permanent and time can be taken in composing it to produce a more specific and finished article.

■ Text often uses language in forms particularly suited to the specific nature of writing, rather than the immanent nature of speech, in terms of vocabulary chosen, the completeness of syntactic forms with no ellipsis, breaks and repeats, and in terms of conventional phrases suited to the purpose of the writing, such as 'book language' in story form.

■ Text uses some conventions not present in speech, such as word separation, punctuation and paragraphing; these help when nuances of speech are lost.

■ Text has to be encoded and decoded into a writing system, in English, an alphabetic one: spelling rules and irregularities therefore have to be learned, and handwriting and/or keyboarding skills have to be developed in the case of writing.

For both reading and writing, then, specific learning and acquisition of skills is needed, and these do not come naturally, given a literate environment, as speech does in a spoken language environment (Downing and Leong, 1982; Bradley and Bryant, 1983). For a while, it was fashionable to assume that the reverse was the case, and that given an environment where they were bathed in literacy, children would naturally acquire the relevant skills. Frank Smith, despite many valuable insights into the processes of both reading and writing, tended to adopt this view when dealing with the initial stages (Smith, 1973; 1978; 1988). Oakhill debunks his ideas on this quite firmly, and brings supporting evidence from experiments with learning readers, showing that children generally use context cues less to help their word recognition as they become more skilled readers (Oakhill, 1995, in Lee and Das Gupta). This is after the initial stages, of course, when they are able to recognize or decode some words for a start.

Splitting words into their component syllables and phonemes is a complex system for children to learn. Both reading and writing, explains Carter, call on much more in terms of brain function than just the activation of the language areas (Carter, 1998). She shows that in reading, while the visual cortex is feeding in impressions of shapes from the page, in writing the motor cortex is needed to activate the muscles used in the fine motor skills for recording those shapes (Carter, 1998). She adds that if there are disruptions or blockages between brain areas involved in the flow of information during the reading and/or writing processes, then forms of dyslexia may be the result (Carter, 1998).

How can children come to acquire the difficult skills of analysis and synthesis, the splitting up and spelling out, or the blending and fusing of the alphabetic symbols to make the words which represent sounds, and to put words side by side to makes phrases and sentences, in their writing? Oakhill suggests that today it is generally accepted that children move from using a visual code to using a phonological code to gain meanings from words, although the strategies they use may vary (Oakhill, 1995, in Lee and Das Gupta).

This multi-aspect fitting into place may be likened to the process of fitting pieces into a jigsaw puzzle. It is not just a question of being told or of being shown once or twice how to blend and decode, but of gradually practising and speeding up this complex skill until it becomes almost automatic. Two decades ago Arnold noted a pattern in the use of different types of cue during the process of acquisition of reading skills which fits nicely with Oakhill's modern view. Initially, children use visual cues only, such as word configuration, together with context cues to form guesses about word meanings and syntax. Then as phonic skills are taught and learned there is a phase in which there is great dependence on these, almost to the exclusion of other types of cue. Finally, as the rate of reading speeds up and semi-automation is achieved, there is a balanced use of all three types of cue being used collaboratively (Arnold, 1982). This fits in with Frith's stage theory of reading, described by Oakhill, and which uses logographic, alphabetic and orthographic stages. It is also fairly consonant with the causal model of Goswami and Bryant: pre-school phonological skills including logographic aspects give way to alphabetic skills as independent skills, and finally become merged with orthographic components (Oakhill, 1995, in Lee and Das Gupta; Goswami and Bryant, 1990). Oakhill points out that phonological coding remains very important even after words have been recognized, as it actually facilitates retention in the memory of parts of the text, aiding comprehension.

■ Working Memory and its Constraints

In putting together the graphemes of written language, representing the phonemes of the spoken words, to write (or in recognizing and decoding the symbols in reading), we use cognitive functions which are represented in a theoretical model known as **working memory**. There are other theories of memory as well, including those involving semantic networks and also connectionist models (Coulson, in Lee and Das Gupta, 1995). However, the system which generated the idea of working memory is perhaps the most developed to date. There are a number of different types of memory which have been inferred from observations of memory functions in both adults and children, and also sometimes in brain-damaged patients. Bristow gives a good survey of these, including some details of memory in the different sensory modalities, and the contrast between **long-term memory** and working memory (Bristow *et al.*, 1999). The idea of working memory needs some explanation. The characteristics of working memory have been ascertained from experimental evidence on a wide scale, and are well established in a huge range of relevant literature. Working memory is what we generally use for ongoing thinking and for what we might call 'working things out'.

Carter gives a clear and up to date picture of this model, of which the main proponent and developer is Baddeley (Carter, 1998; Baddeley and Hitch, 1974; Baddeley, 1976, 1986). Working memory has three basic components. First, a **central executive** which has an organisational role, and is able to switch and direct attention to enable focusing on relevant information; it is able to combine information coming from the other two components. These are a **visuo-spatial scratch pad**, which can hold images, and a **phonological loop** which deals with acoustic and speech based information, and through which rehearsal of such information may be practised. Together, these parts of the model represent the function of working memory (Baddeley, 1997). Looking at recent brain imaging studies, Carter reports that three parts of the brain shown to become activated in relevant tasks correspond very precisely to the three parts of the working memory model (Carter, 1998). As we might expect, the phonological loop appears to activate areas in the left hemisphere, a part near to Wernicke's Area dealing with inner speech, while Broca's Area is also involved. When the visuo-spatial scratch-pad is thought to be in use, this is indicated in the right hemisphere. The central executive is at the front of the brain and is shown as belonging to both hemispheres (Carter, 1998).

So how does it work in terms of everyday phenomena? We are surrounded by floods of sensory impressions which pass almost instantly unless we focus selectively upon them. Even when we do so, there are limits to our intake of new information or of information that we want to operate on mentally or work with. These limits are caused by a phenomenon much observed and established firmly through a great deal of experimentation, which is best described as a bottleneck for the flow of information into our memory store. While the main long-term memory store has no known limits, information is stored there in terms of meaning, and this is much facilitated by links with previously stored meaningful material. Think of it as a system of hooks upon which new items may be caught and suspended. Before items of new information can arrive in the store they must become significantly meaningful, or else, when not very meaningful, repeated often, to penetrate in to the storage system.

■ Memory Spans in Adults and Children

Working memory does not code information in terms of meaning, but in the images of the sensory mode through which it has entered, thus where literacy is involved, visually or auditorily. Working memory was developed from a previous short-term memory model, which reflected the ability only to accommodate seven plus or minus two items, that is a usual range of five to nine items, in the normal adult (Miller, 1956; Baddeley, 1976). In young children it may be less, and some experimental indications show limits of three or four (plus or minus two) by the end of Key Stage 1 (Latham, 1983). Limits of between four and six (plus or minus two) have been found in the Key Stage 2 years (Fontana and Evans, 1980). Furthermore, the memory traces fade very quickly, and were thought to do so in around ten to 12 seconds for adults (Miller, 1956). Figures have, though, been given which range from ten to 30 or more seconds for adults, but such variations may be influenced by contextual factors (Craik and Lockhart, 1972; Baddeley, 1976). However, Baddeley has commented that the memory store of the phonological loop in working memory fades very fast indeed, and he gives a figure of only one to two seconds for this; it may be slightly enlarged by rehearsal, but the rehearsal procedure itself tends to impair further storage (Carter, 1998). This means that without rehearsal or incoming influences from long-term memory, we would only be able to repeat words or numbers we have heard for very few seconds (Bristow *et al.*, 1999).

The capacity of working memory, when tested to see how many items are more or less immediately recalled in this way, is referred to as **memory span**, or working memory span. While this is the basic paradigm for much research into the verbal functions of working memory, Baddeley warns that working memory and memory span are not actually synonymous. This is because of the different ways in which working memory may be functioning, for instance, using rehearsal, and more lately discovered, the influences upon it and merging with it of some aspects of activity from the long-term store (Baddeley, 1976; Baddeley, 1986; Engle *et al.*, 1999, in Miyake and Shah). He says 'Working memory allows us to use our memory systems flexibly. It enables us to hold on to information by rehearsing it in our minds, to relate that information to older knowledge and to plan our future actions.' (Baddeley, 1998, in Carter.)

To illustrate these functions, look at the following two imaginary situations:

1. If you looked up a telephone number strange to you, including the code, say 11 digits in all, and then crossed the room to the telephone, you would be unlikely to remember it all unless you either wrote it down, or else rehearsed it to yourself all the way across the room. If you were looking up a

local number, and knew both the code and the first two digits representing the district anyway, you would be likely to be able to remember the rest of it, since the patterns of the code and local prefix would be meaningful to you and in the long-term memory store already. You remember all your own phone number, and some of those belonging to friends and family, because through repetition the sequences have become thoroughly learned and are stored in the long-term memory as meaningful sequences.

2. If you are driving along on the motorway, and see a car doing something dangerous or causing an accident, assuming you can see its registration number and want to report it to the police, would you find it easy to remember all of it by the time you can telephone? Generally seven items, a registration number would be possible to recall theoretically, but with other things to attend to, such as driving the car and anticipating events, it might be difficult without being able to rehearse or write it down. However, if you can straight away impose some meaning on the letters and numbers, immediately you have a better chance of retaining and recalling them. Suppose a registration number such as this: F 527 LGO. If you said to yourself 'Fool! 52 weeks in a year, 7 days in a week and let's go!' you might get it! Or try this: N 230 RRM – how about 'Newmarket, 2.30, Red Rum'?

To summarize, working memory characteristics are as follows:

■ Capacity limit of seven plus or minus two for adults (three to six for primary school age children).

■ Fast fade, generally in very few seconds.

■ Codes specifically in the sensory mode of the stimulus, usually visual or auditory for verbal activity.

How do we get over the bottleneck and learn to read and write at all? Since the bottleneck restricts information, we have become adept at 'chunking', that is, bundling together or linking together pieces of information. As adults we are really skilled at this, and in reading we take in phrases in single visual gulps, between intervals known as **saccades**, and transfer them to our long-term memories speedily in terms of translated meanings called up by the symbols we see on the page. According to Nicolson, the eye jumps about five times a second in reading, and fixates on the visual gulp between the jumps or saccades (Nicolson, 1999, in Messer and Millar). He also suggests that the perceptual span cannot be increased beyond the usual three words or so for looking ahead and the intake. We have also learned to operate extremely fast to beat the fade, and unless with very unfamiliar material, we constantly rehearse until storing becomes possible. While we do know that we become more skilled with age, how much of this is due to learning and how much to general maturational processes is not clear.

Thirty years ago Conrad put forward the idea that the ability to recode phonologically from visual inputs is essential to the task of reading, and he claimed that children first begin to remember pictured objects in terms of their names at the same time that they start to learn to read (Conrad, 1972). Before 5 years old, indications of phonological coding were not present, but appeared in a significant degree by 6 years old, according to his experimental findings. Whether this was actually due to the teaching they received or to a maturational milestone is not clear and does not seem to have been fully investigated as yet; however, children in school today are being taught the basic elements of phonics far earlier, and certainly usually before 5, with the majority being successful in the early stages of simple blending and analysis. Byrne gives sound evidence showing that young children do indeed benefit in ability to decode and encode from specific early instruction (Byrne, 1998). This facility, at whatever age it becomes acquired, Baddeley suggests is connected with the utilization of the phonological loop which is probably articulatory in nature (Baddeley, 1976).

Gathercole and Adams suggest that while the ability to rehearse is available by the age of 3, its deliberate use as a strategy does not seem to develop till about 7 years old (Gathercole and Adams, 1993). Coulson suggests that age related differences are more likely to be due to the gradual acquisition of strategies only developed as we get older, rather than to actual capacity (Coulson, in Lee and Das Gupta, 1995). On the other hand, age related differences in working memory have been investigated by Miyake and Shah, who think that processing speed is likely to be a more important factor in differences between age groups than it might be in accounting for individual differences in working memory function (Miyake and Shah, 1999).

Links between reading performance and **visual memory span** in pupils in the Key Stage 2 age range were experimentally established by Fontana and Evans (Fontana and Evans, 1980). Latham also found links between visual memory span and reading performance in children of 7 (Latham, 1983). Strong evidence for close links between working memory capacities and the achievements of 7 year-old children in vocabulary, language comprehension, reading and mathematics have recently been reported by Gathercole and Pickering using the English National Key Stage Standard Assessment Tests and Tasks (Key Stage 1 SATs) as measures (Gathercole and Pickering, 2000). Children who had low levels of attainment in curriculum assessments showed marked impairments on the measures of central executive function, and in particular of visuo-spatial memory. However, Gathercole and Pickering think that it is the central executive which is the crucial factor, while the roles of the phonological loop and the visuo-spatial scratch pad are still not clear and may be less important than previously thought (Gathercole and Pickering, 2000). They conclude: 'Complex working memory skills are closely linked with children's academic progress within the early years at school.' (Gathercole and Pickering, 2000.) They add that the assessment of working memory skills may prove to be a useful method of screening children who seem likely to be at risk of poor progress at school.

■ Developing Effective Skills in Writing and Reading

In writing and spelling, letter sequences have to be called up, and this process to begin with is very laborious. With long or difficult words, the memory fade may blot out the end of the word before reaching it, because concentrating on the actual writing of it may have taken concentration away from the intended graphemic components. While the same system for word meanings forms the basis for both understanding what is written and producing written forms of language, there are differences in the processing of the actual writing: Ellis tells us that the letter strings (graphemes) and sounds (phonemes) come from two separate word production systems, and these, of course, have to be related (Ellis, 1984). When writing becomes automated, the letter sequences we want to use are stored as **kinaesthetic** memories, that is memories of the movements involved, as well as being combined with the images of the letters and the word shape. Thus in learning handwriting and spelling, practising over and over again is beneficial in that it encourages the building up of the visual and kinaesthetic imagery. This enables the speeding up of the processes, which eventually bring about the **automation** which can release thinking space in working memory for setting down ideas.

If pupils are reading texts which are too hard for them, slowly and laboriously, and meeting unfamiliar words, even with quite short sentences they will have forgotten the beginning of the sentence before getting to the end of it. They will not be able to concentrate on meaning: when children read an easy text they can report what they have read, but with hard passages often cannot recall what they have read. In the teaching situation the text must be easy enough to reduce errors to five per cent or below in order to sustain a good decoding speed (Betts, 1957). Betts' error levels are surprisingly low, but provide a model for good practice.

In writing, because there is no input as in the receptive mode of reading, children generally limit their textual levels to those that they can achieve, but teachers need to be aware of what is at stake here in order to support and extend writing skills without urging the impossible upon their pupils. Challenge is certainly good, and without it nobody would achieve their potential, but ongoing evaluation of that capability is necessary. Remember that in making a long sentence, children in the early stages of writing may forget what they have said at the beginning, and start going off on another tack, so that the sentence becomes distorted, or they forget the word they were going to write, or the phrase. For older writers, the problem is more to do with remembering the structure designed for the piece of writing, while getting on with the writing, or to do with trying to deal with presentation or even the use of descriptive language while getting the ideas down on paper. At these stages we can see the value of planning for the piece of writing, and of draft, proof-reading and redrafting. Presentation can be polished at the end. The opportunity to reflect and attend to different aspects of the writing process at different times relieves the cognitive pressure, and allows both better achievement and through it, progress.

At approach and lower levels of reading, English National Curriculum Levels 1 and 2, pupils of average ability or below will still be attending heavily to decoding and recognition skills. They look at each word in turn and as they decode it or recognize it, give it equally voiced emphasis with those which come before and after in the sentences. This is 'word by word' reading, sometimes described as Dalek-like. Pupils may or may not be able to report something about their reading at this stage, depending on the level of difficulty of the text for them, but the ability to attend to some meaning and remember it starts to grow. For most pupils, by the time they are in Year 3 and entering the work of Level 3, they are beginning to show semi-automation of decoding skills on appropriately matched texts. Speed is developing and they are able to look ahead to see what is coming, becoming more aware of meaning and phraseology. Expression creeps in, and fluency develops. Those who are more able will reach this stage while in Year 2.

The big watershed comes between these two stages, word by word reading and fluent expressive reading. After fluency is achieved on texts of appropriately matched levels, text study and comprehension activities are productive for pupils in developing reading skills further. **Cloze procedures**, **comprehension** questions, **prediction** and group prediction, **sequencing** and group sequencing, appreciation of dialogue, **characterization** and style, fact and fiction, and dealing with **persuasion** and **bias** all become possible. However, the roots of some of these activities can still take place with children who have not yet achieved fluent reading by using oral modes of presentation, such as oral cloze, prediction, or asking children to comment on characters and events in stories or pieces of text they have listened to or seen read to them, as in shared reading.

There is also a big watershed in writing which happens round about the same time, perhaps a little later, following reading development closely. Typical Level 2 writing is writing in a sequence which has attributes of a chain, one statement giving rise to the next, rather than a preconceived plan or plot, and in which the pattern of sequencing events is to join them with *and* and *then*, or even *and then*, often repeated. Gradually this changes to writing which shows some evidence of being thought of as a whole, a whole story or a whole report, for instance. With this change comes the use of more complex sentences, and a wider range of connectives introducing the subordinate clauses. This is typical Level 3 writing. It is as if the mechanics of setting down ideas limit the viewpoint of the writer to the immediate sentence he is writing so that, afterwards, the sentence he has just written is the limit of his perspective for generating the next, even though he may know the story he is writing or the event he is reporting. Automation of writing skills and speed of writing allow a broader overview.

Using Assessment in Setting Challenges for Progress

Pupils will not be able to use complex sentences with subordinate clauses if they are not using them in their own speech. Such use needs to be nurtured and encouraged in their speaking and listening, in appropriate and natural ways, by using question and answer activities and by modelling from adults. Ongoing evaluation and monitoring of children's speaking and listening skills is therefore important in this respect, and is part of matching their challenges to appropriate levels. It is an important part of supporting less able pupils and accelerating the learning of the more able pupils.

Setting levels of challenge which can be presented to pupils to extend their learning depends on the notion of evaluating just where they have reached in their prior learning, thus assessment is crucial to planning, and needs to form a recurring and cyclic pattern. For writing, assessments need to be made not only of children's actual writing performance, in terms of getting ideas down on paper, but in the initial stages of their fine motor skills which underpin the ability to scribe, and of their phonic skills for spelling; most of all, attention needs to be paid to the ongoing development of their ability to speak and to listen, and to notice developments in their speech. In the later stages, such as upper Key Stage 2 and Key Stage 3, teachers need to notice how far pupils use reasoning and thinking skills, and how far they are able to place themselves inside the mind of the reader of their work.

■ Dyslexia and Dysgraphia

Separate from brain damage, which can obviously be a cause of dyslexia, developmental dyslexia is defined as reading ability which is unexpectedly low when compared to an individual's general ability, and which has no obvious connection with inadequate learning opportunities or other noticeable causes. Dyslexia caused by brain damage, called acquired dyslexia, has been one source of information, however, and Sasanuma found interesting differences between Japanese patients, in their ability to read using *kanji* and *kana* writing systems according to the areas which were damaged; processing of pictographic figures appears to be centred in a different location from that of the phonetic processing. He views this as support for dual coding system routes for visual and phonological inputs (Sasanuma, in Coltheart *et al.*, 1980).

Dysgraphia is the correct term for specific difficulties with writing or inability to write, caused by brain lesions or malfunction, but so often difficulties in writing and spelling go along with reading problems that it is usually subsumed under the general heading of dyslexia. While reversals are common at the start of learning to write, persistence of frequent reversals by 7, and certainly during lower Key Stage 2, accompanied by difficulties and slowness in reading and writing against apparent average or better general ability, might indicate cause for concern and possible dyslexia. Dyslexia takes many forms, and has a variety of possible causes; some have single origins, while other forms may be caused by more than one factor.

Snowling believes that studies to date have been unable to assign all dyslexic children to particular categories, but she goes on to propound that it is very unusual to find a dyslexic child without some kind of phonological problem

(Snowling, 2000). She carries out a comprehensive and up to date survey of information about dyslexia, including possible causes of varying natures. She discusses phonological processing disorders, brain correlates, and the evidence that some forms of dyslexia may have genetic origins in detail. Some of the factors include atypical patterns of neuronal activity and hemispherical differences.

Thus, while some forms of dyslexia are acquired, due to brain damage, other types may be due to functional deficits which are inherent, and termed developmental dyslexia. There is, however, a distinction between what is called surface dyslexia and deep dyslexia. In surface dyslexia, difficulties seem to be caused by spelling to sound recoding problems; in deep dyslexia, difficulties seem to involve semantic and syntactic processing (Marcel, 1980, in Coltheart *et al.*). Marcel states that with deep dyslexia, non-words can hardly be read, while their errors often show some degree of understanding of the written word, whereas the understanding of people with surface dyslexia seems to be linked to their oral responses in decoding the word. He suggests that the situation is more fluid than that and may reside in the different depth at which items are processed.

As Carter has informed us, some forms of dyslexia may be due to missing or inactive connections between two particular brain modules normally involved in the task. Brain scans have shown, in particular, a lack of working together in co-ordination between Wernicke's Area and Broca's Area to be indicated in some forms of dyslexia, producing the phenomenon that words cannot be understood and spoken at the same time (Carter, 1998). Developmental dyslexics frequently report that letters tend to become blurred or move about when they are trying to read. Stein and Walsh take the view that such visual confusions stem from abnormalities in a specific pathway in the visual processing system, which has the role of processing incoming visual information at fast speed. This is a different approach in looking for causes of dyslexia from those which focus on phonological, visual or motor systems (Stein and Walsh, 1997; Demb *et al.*, 1998). However, Skottun, in reviewing the experimental evidence for this hypothesis comes to the conclusion that it remains equivocal and unresolved (Skottun, 2000). On a completely different tack, Nicolson and Fawcett investigated some commonly noticed concomitants of dyslexia, and their experiments focused on the idea of an automation deficit, including poor balance and co-ordination, and difficulties with motor skills, sometimes referred to as **dyspraxia**. Results have seemed to indicate that a part of the brain which co-ordinates movement is involved (Nicolson and Fawcett, 1990; Fawcett and Nicolson, 1996; Fawcett *et al.*, 1996).

Another recent and interesting development in providing help for dyslexics takes an entirely different approach to any hitherto discussed, and is based on the inhibition of certain primitive reflexes usually only operating at the foetal stage, but which remain active in certain individuals beyond birth and have been found to have links with dyslexia (Smyth, 2001; McPhillips *et al.*, 2000). McPhillips claims success for this treatment which he believes turns off the unwanted reflexes by first using them in exercise routines. Children's ability to focus on the page and also to handle pen and paper improved, according to the experimental report in *The Lancet* (McPhillips *et al.*, 2000). It is clear that while important discoveries have been made about the causes of dyslexia, through vast amounts of careful work, there are still uncertainties, and unknown links still to be discovered within this field of research.

Focusing on ways to help dyslexics overcome their problems, Snowling includes phonological training as an important aspect of such help. Specific phonological awareness training is cited, but there is some evidence to suggest that younger children benefit more than older ones from this, supporting the benefits of early intervention (Snowling, 2000). Recent experimental work on a longitudinal basis agrees with this view of the value of phonological training (QCA, 1998/165).

Following the paradigm of Bryant and Bradley, using their onset and rime method, a controlled experiment contrasting reading recovery methods and phonological training showed greater beneficial effects for the latter, in the long term (QCA, 1998/165). For teachers, however, if dyslexia is suspected, expert diagnosis, assessment and advice to help compensate need to be sought, since the field is so complex, abstruse and specialized. A useful screen, produced by Nicolson and Fawcett and in use in a number of schools and local education authorities, as an early alert to seek specialist help, is the 'Dyslexia Early Screening Test', known as DEST (Nicolson and Fawcett, 1996). Hampshire County Council has produced an early screening for dyslexia, partly based on DEST measures and on some other cognitive research from Hull University, and this is linked with some resources for follow up training, including phonological training (HCC, 1997). In addition the BBC, in collaboration with the BDA, has produced a useful pack, including a video, for teachers on 'Dyslexia in the Primary School' (BBC, 1997).

■ Chapter Summary

1. There are specific differences between oracy and literacy, and between reading and writing as forms of literacy. Writing carries a heavier cognitive load.

2. There is a bottleneck in working memory which places considerable constraints upon children learning to read and write until they have learned to use particular processing strategies, including speed in semi-automating the skill, and 'chunking' information.

3. There is a watershed in learning to read and write which occurs usually round about the ages of 7 to 8, when semi-automation begins to be established.

4. Effective assessment is an important element in applying 'the match' and utilising the 'ZPD' to optimum advantage, in the learning and teaching of literacy skills.

5. Dyslexia exhibits a variety of symptoms in its presentation, and may have several different causes. Ongoing research is still trying to part the mists which shroud its mystery.

6. Dyslexia is complex and its study is abstruse; teachers need to get expert help and advice for children whom they suspect may be dyslexic.

■ Teacher Activity

Try a simple letter, word or digit span exercise with one child – say out loud, at intervals of about one per second, a short list of items, and see how many they can repeat back to you as soon as you stop; this is an auditory span. Do the same thing by showing a set of simple words on flash cards, one per second, and the recall will be in terms of visual span. Or ask your class to repeat some phrases after you, such as in learning a new song, poem or hymn by rote; at different times, vary the length of the phrase – note when ability to repeat effectively is impaired – how long is a manageable phrase? Discuss your findings with your colleagues who teach the same and different ages – are there any differences or similarities?

For following up further interests

Bristow, J., Cowley, P., and Daines, B. (1999) *Memory and Learning – A Practical Guide for Teachers*. London: David Fulton.

Fawcett, A.J. and Nicolson, R.I., (eds.) (1994) *Dyslexia in Children: Multidisciplinary Perspectives*. Brighton: Harvester Press.

Snowling, M.J. (2000) *Dyslexia*. Oxford: Blackwell.

5 | The Development of Secretarial Skills – Spelling, Handwriting and Presentation

■ Spelling, Scribble, Scrawl and Style

Components of the writing process – Encoding skills and automation – Blending – Orthography, roots and context – Facilitating strategies for spelling – Handwriting development, and more facilitating strategies – Chapter summary – Teacher activity

Components of the Writing Process

Wells proposes three distinct components of the writing process: assembling and organizing meanings relevant to the purpose of the writing, shaping the text to the assumed understanding of the audience, and encoding the message into words and grammatical structures. These do, of course, interact (Wells, 1981). Beard has suggested a slightly different perspective, made up of three sub-processes which need to be integrated in the production of a piece of writing: composing, writing and re-reading (Beard, 1984, 2000). Composing, he says, is sometimes referred to as planning or drafting, while writing is often referred to as secretarial skills or transcription. Reviewing is an alternative label for re-reading and editing. He also divides his reviewing sub-component into twin activities of editing, which he defines as correcting spelling and punctuation, and changing word order, while re-drafting is substantially to change the content or the structure in some manner, even if only partially (Beard, 1984, 2000). At first glance the triple distinctions of these two views may seem a little different, but the awareness of the audience could be viewed as a compositional factor, and is an area Beard does address, while reviewing the sub-process might be seen as part of an organizing component.

How does the English National Literacy Strategy Framework (NLSF) view the inherent structure of texts? Here, the focus is divided into three components again, but with more emphasis on the actual text itself rather than the processes by which it comes to be created: word level, sentence level and text level are the three major emphases on which the NLSF approach to text study is based (DfEE, 1998). Wells' encoding and Beard's writing could be said to underlie both word levels and sentence levels in text, while the finished text will have needed the processes of planning and organizing, or composing, of a sense of audience, and of reviewing. Sentence levels are, because of their syntactical nature, very much part of the composing for an audience, and of fitting the style of the text to its purpose, so here again there is the underlying process of planning, or of composing.

Four categories of skill in the acquisition of reading proposed by Ehri are described by Oakhill: prerequisites, facilitators, consequences and incidentally related factors. Within the latter are such variables as motivation, ability levels, and the use of literacy in the home (Oakhill, in Lee and Das Gupta, 1995). These can well be applied to the writing process as well. Certainly understanding the alphabetic principle is a prerequisite for writing in our language, including the fact that 26 letters (graphemes) are used to represent an unlimited number of spoken words by means of their sounds.

Encoding Skills and Automation

Firstly, children need to realize the system of **grapheme/phoneme correspondence (GPC)**, that is, understanding which symbols represent which sound units. Due to the multiple roots of the language, while spelling in English has a substantial proportion of regular rules, there is also a huge number of irregularities, and alternative rules for spelling the same sounds. Additionally, some groups of letters are used to represent a variety of different sound units (we are all familiar with the problems of *ow* and of *ough*, for instance). Again, there is not a simple one-to-one correspondence between graphemes and phonemes across the board, since some sounds are represented by letter combinations such as digraphs, **blends**, and **high frequency letter clusters**. In the aspect of spelling, English is much harder to learn than many other languages where spelling systems are more regular, or even virtually totally regular.

Secondly, children have to come to the realization that the spatial sequence in which the letters are placed in a word represents the time order in which the sounds occur in speech. This particular aspect of learning phonics and how to spell is not easy for young children. Left to right flow, as in our particular convention, has to be learned both in reading and writing, and, of course, applies not only to graphemes in a word, but also to words in a sentence.

In the initial stages of reading, realizing that marks on paper can represent speech, young children are at what is known as the logographic stage of acquiring the skill, the first of the three stages described by Frith (Frith, 1985, detailed in Oakhill, 1995, in Lee and Das Gupta). In this logographic stage, children notice the visual patterns and salient features of words, as well as guessing from context, and while they may come to learn some letters and the sounds they represent, they do not directly map speech on to letters and vice versa for some time (Oakhill, in Lee and Das Gupta, 1995). The strategies of the logographic or whole word approach are inadequate for all but a small range of words, and children then need to learn to crack the code by using letter to sound mappings. When they have achieved this mapping, children are then able to read unfamiliar words and even non-words, and to make correct or justifiable spellings of words they want to write. They frequently want to write words from their speech repertoire which are not in their reading or spelling repertoires, and this acquisition of the relevant knowledge enables them to do it.

From this alphabetic stage, also called the analytic stage, the second of Frith's stages, children extend their learning to cover the knowledge and understanding of larger units and spelling patterns than the single letters, digraphs and blends they have been using, and deal with larger orthographic units. In grasping the conventions of English orthography, they attain the stage labelled by Frith as the orthographic stage. These three stages, states Oakhill, have been evidenced by actual research (Oakhill, 1995, in Lee and Das Gupta). While these stages have been widely applied to reading, they are also apposite for the development of writing skills, too, except that though you can recognize words by whole word configuration and salient features, you cannot actually write a word without knowing at least some of the letters in it, if not all, and their appropriate sequence. There are not, therefore, strict parallels between reading and writing at the logographic stage, although there are in terms of the alphabetic and orthographic stages. The writing stage which parallels the logographic stage of reading perhaps includes what we might call early emergent writing, where some letter shapes are beginning to appear amid scribbly pseudo-writing, and gradually become more prevalent as letters and corresponding sounds are learned. The understanding that messages can be transcribed is understood, but GPC knowledge is lacking or too primitive and sketchy for successful encoding. Children playing in the role-play corner or at the writing table, in the Foundation Stage, like to 'write' messages and invitations. '*This says, "Come to my birthday party", you know*' announces a 4 year-old, waving a piece of paper with a pencilled scribble on it at the teacher. We might well term this stage in writing as the idiosyncratic stage, rather than the logographic stage, but alphabetic and orthographic stages make perfect sense when applied to writing.

There are some useful distinctions, first highlighted by Frith, in looking at differences in the sequences of development in reading and writing, however, at the latter two stages (Oakhill, 1995, in Lee and Das Gupta; Beard, 2000; O'Sullivan and Thomas, 2000). Progress in the two strands of literacy does not go totally hand in hand. The alphabetic skills are largely impelled forwards in use by writing, since letters are needed to write, while children are still at the logographic stage of reading. Later, when phonic skills are becoming overlearned and beginning to arrive at a semi-automated stage, this knowledge of spelling principles feeds back into their reading. In the orthographic stage of reading, on the other hand, spelling remains alphabetically focused still for some time, although moving into orthographic awareness may trigger, Frith believes, changes towards more sophisticated spelling strategies.

The beginning stages of cracking the code and learning GPC start with single letter phonemes, using the most common values of our alphabetic letters. However, letters have names as well as sounds, so there is a dual learning task involved. While Oakhill does not think that knowing letter names in themselves will help children to decode, she refers to research by Adams which suggests that knowledge of letter names may help children discover the link between letters and sounds, since the names of the majority of our letters when spoken do contain the phoneme to which the letter refers (Oakhill, 1995, in Lee and Das Gupta). On the other hand, Beard cites some research by

Blatchford, with a very large sample of children, which indicated that knowledge of letter names associated more highly with later reading attainment than letter-sounding, despite much evidence on this matter being inconclusive (Beard, 2000). Beard thinks that letter-naming may provide a firm foundation on which to build GPC knowledge.

Blending

Experimental evidence shows that 4 and 5 year-olds find segmenting words into their component parts, the phonemes, very difficult indeed, even though they are able to hear that similar words may have some sounds which are different. At 5 or 6 they may still have difficulty realizing whether two words begin or end with the same phoneme, but, Oakhill reports, they find it easier to segment a longer word into syllables (Oakhill, 1995, in Lee and Das Gupta). This reflects young children's awareness of morphemes as distinct units, rather than words or letters (Byrne, 1998). When pronouncing a phoneme by itself, it is often difficult to isolate accurately the sound as it is made within a word. Oakhill calls this the problem of **coarticulation**, and it is a problem later for **blending**. Modelling the isolation and identification of phonemes together with their actual articulated component within the whole word, so that the word context provides modifying auditory information, is the best that can be done to illustrate this to children.

Grapheme/phoneme correspondences are usually introduced as initial sounds in familiar words. Most, if not all, schemes of work for phonics give appropriate emphasis to the correspondences between single letters and the most common sound values they represent, at the beginnings of words, linking these initial letters with relevant visual images and providing a variety of games and exercises to display this correspondence with some impact. Focusing on final sounds in simple words, such as three-letter **consonant-vowel-consonant** words **(cvcs)**, comes next in the sequence. Much later, when they have had considerable practice in dealing with the final letter in a cvc word, children will be able to identify the medial letter or sound of a cvc word. The cvc word is the basic building block of phonics and decoding, and of spelling and encoding. In order to perform these processes, children need to develop the ability to blend, to fuse the sounds of the individual phonemes together in a synthesis, in the decoding process, and to split them up or analyse the word into its component phonemes, in encoding the spoken word. In doing this, children will at first vocalize aloud, and then sub-vocalize, before reaching the stage where they can do it silently, with auditory imaging. If their blending or splitting up skills are slow, they may rehearse extensively during the process, utilizing the phonological loop. This is necessary until the process has speeded up, because of the severe limits on the actual central executive of working memory.

Blending is dogged by the coarticulation problem, so that again it must be emphasized that saying component phonemes needs to be followed quite quickly by the whole word. Blending to decode is hard enough, but writing is productive, rather than receptive, so to spell a word from memory, by mentally or out loud rehearsing its sound, is harder still. Byrne cites evidence that specific instruction in blending helps children in their application of the alphabetic principle to move on as successful decoders and encoders (Byrne, 1998). The ability to blend is a curious aspect of learning to read and spell, and it does not appear to reflect general levels of ability. Regardless of varying levels of perceived intelligence, children vary enormously in their abilities to come to an easy competence in blending. It does not seem to parallel, either, progress in acquiring letter knowledge. There is only one way to help children with difficulty in blending to overcome it: this is sufficient practice, with adult and child together doing the saying. In pointing and moving the finger, the left to right direction is being practised, and with simultaneous vocalization, the parallel between time order and spatial order is being reinforced.

A considerable body of research has shown that young children's ability to discern and enjoy rhymes and alliteration is related to later success in reading, through providing a basis for later phonological processing, and in particular, awareness of onset and rime (Bradley and Bryant, 1983; Goswami and Bryant, 1990; Bryant, 1993). The ability to discern onset and rime links perhaps some little way with the idea of morphemic analysis, and may form a bridge across which children can progress in their journey towards the ability to fully perform the splitting of words into phonemes. This process is also, of course, involved in spelling. In early stages, using onset and rime, children may make analogies between words based on these units to help them, but as they develop their phonological skills more expertly, they become ready to use their strategies for analogy on their GPC knowledge (Snowling, 2000). Phonological training, following the Bryant and Bradley paradigm, formed the basis of some positive intervention in an experiment reported by the Qualifications and Curriculum Authority, and was found to have a more long lasting beneficial effect than reading recovery methods (QCA, 1998/165).

Orthography, Roots and Context

The use of common letter patterns, also known as highly predictable letter sequences, or **high frequency clusters (HFCs)**, and of **syllabification**, need to be taught directly and can, with older children, often be linked to word derivation to aid the division into relevant and sometimes meaningful syllables. For instance, taking the word *signalling*, we might divide it thus: *sig-nall-ing*. However, the word *sign* shows evidence of a common root here so perhaps a division like *sign-all-ing* might be more appropriate. Since the pronunciation of the root part of both words is different, though, it may be a debatable point, but one well worth discussing with pupils to extend understanding of word structure. This makes for more interest in spelling, and a wider understanding of word meaning links. With pupils towards the end of Key Stage 2 and in Key Stage 3 Latin and Greek roots can sometimes be profitably explored. In *Latin Roots and their English Spellings*, Laurita focuses on similarities between words in their spellings which developed from the same beginnings, while Morwood and Warman have produced *Our Greek and Latin Roots* (Laurita, 2000; Morwood and Warman, 1990). In a recent article, Jessie Randall analyses some of the vocabulary used in J.K. Rowling's Harry Potter books, and displays some of their literary, Latin and other lexical roots (Randall, 2001). High frequency clusters, such as est, ing, ence, ment, ough, need direct teaching to attract pupils' attention to them, and to confirm, perhaps, their analogy making strategies, and they need practice to aid the automation which needs to come to release more of working memory for the compositional aspects of writing.

The context in which words are placed is also a valuable aid to spelling at higher levels, since grammatical attributes often signal certain spelling patterns. Messer draws attention to the identification of grammatical classes of words, such as nouns, verbs and so on, from usage in speech (Messer, 1999, in Messer and Millar). Good examples of how grammatical aspects of word structure can aid spelling as well as word structure and derivation are given by Beard (Beard, 2000). Thus meaningful aspects of words, both semantic and syntactic, resurface to take spelling skills further, within the orthographical phase.

Oakhill gives the ages of 7 or 8 for arriving at the capability of using GPC rules competently, with accuracy in regularly spelled words (Oakhill, 1995, in Lee and Das Gupta). This corresponds roughly with the attainment of the English National Curriculum Level 2 in spelling, and moving on from there into Level 3 work. At this age children find irregular words, understandably, more difficult, but by about 9 or 10, she states, they are becoming equally accurate at spelling regular and irregular words. This reflects a decrease in dependence on GPC rules, and a greater dependence on orthographical cues and analogy. Analogy is suggested as a useful strategy for children, but their ability to use it must depend on their knowledge of words in general, in both spoken and written forms. This has implications for teachers, underlining the importance of provision of sufficient examples and of exposition to explain and focus attention. As pupils move through the upper Key Stage 2 and Key Stage 3 phases, they need to have a wide range of different strategies and rules which they can use flexibly, in acquiring higher spelling skills.

An overview of the stages through which children pass in learning to spell is, however, provided by Gentry, based on extensive work and research, and widely discussed and quoted in the relevant literature (Gentry, 1982). These are as follows:

1. Pre-communicative – children know symbols carry meanings, but invent their own.

2. Semi-phonetic – children begin to understand something of GPC, and use some letters appropriately but often in part words.

3. Phonetic – children focus well on GPC rules, often to the exclusion of other cues.

4. Transitional – children begin to use multiple strategies, including GPC, HFCs, and analogy, and to focus well on visual aspects of words.

5. Conventional (sometimes given as 'Correct') – children are able to use a whole repertoire of spelling strategies.

The first stage is before children have learned the conventions of GPC, and will be likely to be within the Foundation Stage, while the second stage will span the achievement of the Early Learning Goals in the Foundation Stage and the achievements expected at Level 1 of the English National Curriculum. Stage three is characteristic of Year 2 work, with some children in Year 2 moving into stage four. The transitional stage, stage four, would still be expected to be characteristic in the lower to middle stages of Key Stage 2, while conventional spelling would be likely to be achieved by most children by the end of Key Stage 2 and the beginning of Key Stage 3. Most pupils would be expected to be able to use a large automatic spelling vocabulary by these later years.

Facilitating Strategies for Spelling

We have focused almost exclusively on the prerequisites for spelling development, in terms of the categories proposed by Ehri, and have not yet addressed facilitating factors, consequences of engaging in the learning of the skill (Ehri, 1979). Looking at the facilitating factors, we may include teaching strategies which interest children, aid their visual and imaging abilities to develop, modelling, using meaningful contexts including for older children, derivations, and the teaching of higher level spelling skills together with the encouragement of analogy. The motivation of pupils is a crucial part of this, and Peters has pointed out the importance of maintaining a positive self-image in pupils (Peters, 1967). This is easily destroyed by focusing exclusively on what they have done wrong in spelling, rather than congratulating them on what they have done right. In the early stages marking needs to be selective, gradually coming towards a more conventional approach. A good strategy is for children to attempt the word they want themselves, before approaching the teacher or classroom assistant, even if it is only the initial letter; they can be praised for starting it right or for getting some letters correct, while accepting the help needed to complete the word. Other aids to independence in spelling such as lists, word banks and notices about rules, are helpful and support self-esteem in the development of competence.

The visual aspect of spelling is one of the most important factors in learning to spell, and Peters in her classic and seminal study of spelling pointed out not only the value of a multi-sensory approach, but the importance of training in imagery to improve spelling performance, leading to the strategy of 'Look, Cover, Write, Check', widely adopted now and generally known as '**LCWC**'

recognizable and have the same names, whichever way round they are and whichever way up they are. It doesn't matter whether a handle is sticking out on one side or another. However, in writing, the orientation of features is a crucial part of identifying and making identifiable for others the graphemes which represent the phonemes, the letters of the alphabet. Think about the differences, for instance, between b, d, q and p. To make such a jump in the comprehension of the way things are represented is a big hurdle for young children. Again, like so much else at beginning stages, it needs to be modelled, and commented on, rather than explained, and a lot of experience needs to be provided before the idea becomes second nature.

Children gradually progress through scribble to produce letter-like forms, and aspects of this process are described in useful detail by Beard. The formation and other specific features of these conventional concepts need to be specifically and directly taught for both accuracy and progress in writing, and errors in formation need early correction (Beard, 2000).

Many researchers and producers of schemes of work for handwriting have given prescriptions, not only for letter formation, but also for the use of letter families in reinforcing letter formation, and for joining letters in a cursive style. There is also a great deal of very sound advice in the NLSF book, *Developing Early Writing*, issued to schools in England (DfEE, 2001/0055). These are valuable aids for the teacher, but it is up to the school to select the style which is to be the basic element of school handwriting policy. However, there are one or two points to be made here, concerning when the introduction to joined writing is to take place, and this will inevitably affect the selection of a particular style, since some are more suited to easy joining than others. Observation of the timing of joining in many schools indicates that when joining takes place, it temporarily slows up the progress towards easy, fluent writing, and if that takes place early on, say in Year 1 or Year 2, writing may not be as neat at the end of Year 2 as it might be if joining had not been taught. But, if joining is not taught until Year 3, which was the expected stage for joined writing, according to the National Curriculum for England, then the slowing up of progress happens then instead, and relearning or additional concentration on movements becomes necessary for some time. By the time the end of Key Stage 2 is reached, the differences of the timing of this 'slow-up' have disappeared. Earlier joining would seem to have the advantage in that early learning is most advantageous, and to be slowed at the Year 3 stage, when writing is just becoming semi-automated and children are beginning to concentrate more on content, seems to make things more complicated. The NLSF *Developing Early Writing* recommends joining as soon as children have acquired a firm grasp of the letter shapes and their formation (DfEE, 2001/0055).

The aim with handwriting is to push progress forward to the stage where it becomes automated, so that the writer can forget about attending to making letters or joining them, and without realizing it set down the words which carry the ideas of composition from the mind onto paper. This involves the linking of the auditory memories of word sounds to the kinaesthetic memories of the movements involved in writing the necessary shapes, so that visual, auditory and kinaesthetic memories all have to be linked and overlearned, to produce very fast responses indeed. Nicolson has stressed the importance of skill automation in facilitating writing and spelling, and, of course, when writing words or practising handwriting with HFCs, spelling is being learned simultaneously (Nicolson, 1999, in Messer and Millar). Children need to understand what they are to do, and they need to practise it sufficiently to reach the stage where it becomes automatic. Nicolson states that to reach such a stage is at the heart of the ability to develop expertise in writing.

The crucial factor, once direct and careful teaching has been given, is sufficient practice. There has been recent emphasis nationally on giving more time to frequent weekly practice in handwriting, and this must be beneficial. Both frequency and amount are important, but frequency is paramount. Too often, a few slowly written lines two or three times a week have not produced the desired effect. In both Key Stages 1 and 2 a quick daily burst of handwriting practice is helpful, and if children are used to it as part of a daily routine, they will settle to it well. A good time is as soon as they come into the classroom from play, or with older children, early in the morning. If writing books are ready, they can sit down and start, while lesson resources are being arranged. In Key Stage 2, patterned sequences made up of spellings or of HFCs can be used to good effect, and at Key Stage 1, patterns of letters in word families, or the spellings of simpler words can be the basis. Patterning is a key strategy, since it gives the repetition of movements which need to be automated. Sometimes a stimulus for making up a pattern can be given, and sometimes children can make up their own. Varying the tools also helps, for instance the use of coloured pencils which can be chosen, or different pens for older pupils.

Other valuable strategies include modelling, for all stages of learning to write, and shared writing, the latter particularly with younger children in the Foundation Stage and Key Stage 1. Here it is important for teachers to do this with their backs to their classes, so that children are copying the movements with the same hand and in the same direction. Classroom assistants or other helpers can check on children from behind to ensure correct movements. The value of this sort of exercise lies in the fact that young children only refine their movements gradually, and can make more accurate movements on a large scale at first, only later making well-controlled movements on a smaller scale. Drawing letter shapes in the air can be fun, and following the same kind of strategy on a wider scale are the new ideas of dance-writing, where letter shapes are explored in larger sequences of movement in a wide space, and sometimes with the use of music.

For children who are left-handed, the paper needs to be angled differently from that of right-handers, to avoid both smudging and obliteration of just written words; the paper needs to be tilted, enabling better vision of what has just been written. Sometimes a slight raising of one corner of the paper helps, and an angled writing board is not difficult to construct. In addition, left-handers need space next to them for free arm-movements, without banging into a right-hander next door. Children with real writing difficulties, who are not responding to the usual teaching and support, including extra help and attention, whether mild or severe dysgraphia, will be likely to need expert help, and early intervention is crucial.

Pencil grip is something which affects writing, too, and with all writers, whether left-handed or right, the way the writing tool is gripped needs checking, preferably in the earliest stages so that wrong habits do not become entrenched. Where children have difficulty in holding the pencil, or find control of a thin tool like a pencil difficult, pencil grips are readily available and easily fixed. A word about erasers is apposite when considering writing: far too much time is wasted using rubbers, and rubbing out makes work look grubby and untidy. It is easy to ban rubbers and train children at all stages merely to indicate a mistake by putting a small x at the end of the wrong word, following it with the correct one. When used to the system they make far fewer errors, work still looks neat, and time is saved. When preparing final draft work for presentation, some errors may need to be erased, but the teacher can keep a few rubbers in a drawer for such occasions, to be used with permission, and older writers in pen may wish to borrow the white stickers or plastic paper dispenser.

Because writing is intended as communication, legibility is important, particularly so for presentation of work, and there is a difference in the attention needed to writing and arrangement of work on the page for a final draft piece of work and the planning and editing stages. In the latter, the writer writes in a preparatory mode, and getting down the ideas is more important than the appearance of the work. Good standards of presentation in final pieces of work need to include consideration of the layout, and of the suitability or otherwise of any patterns, decorations, borders and illustrations. These can make a difference to the impact of writing that is part of a display, or is to be included in a home-made book. Bookmaking is part of the presentational art, and can include attractive and intricate designs in paper engineering, such as envelopes to be opened, tabs to be pulled, and other ingenious surprises designed by the authors (Yates, 1993a; Washtell, 1998, in Graham and Kelly). They love to make it look real, too, and include things like a blurb and a bar-code on the back cover, as well as eye-catching designs for the front.

■ Chapter Summary

1. Writing involves composing, setting down, and reviewing in order to edit and polish.

2. Secretarial skills include writing and spelling, which depend on GPC knowledge as a pre-requisite, and on the understanding that the spatial order of phonemes, as represented in a word by the graphemes, is the same as the time order of those sounds when blended and spoken in the word.

3. Secretarial skills need to become automatic, in order to release capacity in working memory to attend to the compositional aspects of writing.

4. The main mechanisms to use to propel progress in these skills towards automatization are those of frequency and amount of practice.

5. High frequency letter clusters and syllabification also need to be taught, and examples provided for analogy. Word derivation study is interesting and may aid these aspects of learning to spell.

6. Employment of the metalanguage is important in reaching the stability of concepts in children's understanding of their language, enabling them to think and talk about their own and others' uses of their language.

(And, cut down on rubbing out!)

■ Teacher Activity

Collect three pieces of written work from your class, either handwriting, or a piece of self-generated work that includes both spelling and handwriting, one each from higher ability, average, and lower ability groups. Take them to an informal meeting with some of your colleagues, and looking at writing produced from different age groups, place in a developmental order. Are there any overlaps here? How are the English National Curriculum levels mapped across the year groups?

For following up further interests

Beard, R. (2000) *Developing Writing 3–13*. London: Hodder and Stoughton.

Bristow, J., Cowley, P. and Daines, B. (1999) *Memory and Learning – A Practical Guide for Teachers*. London: David Fulton.

O'Sullivan, O., and Thomas, A. (2000) *Understanding Spelling*. Centre for Language in Primary Education (London Borough of Southwark).

Sassoon, R. (1995) *The Practical Guide to Children's Handwriting*. London: Hodder and Stoughton.

Westwood, P. (1999) *Spelling – Approaches to teaching and assessment*. Camberwell, Victoria: ACER Press (The Australian Council for Educational Research).

6 | Stages of Writing Development and their Evaluation

■ Milestones

Composition – Structural development and stages – Early writing and support strategies – Organization of independent writing and developmental indicators – Prioritizing criteria for simple and effective ongoing assessment – The Writing Profile and The Reading Profile – Chapter summary – Teacher activity

■ Composition

While the secretarial aspects are merely the means to the end, composition aims to communicate, and here the ability to reflect is central (Bereiter and Scardamalia, 1987). Describing how this operates in both the compositional and the reviewing stage of writing, Corden includes in his list anticipation, critical evaluation, the ability to re-formulate, to elaborate, and to consider the intended audience (Corden, 2000). However, Corden comments that Bereiter and Scardamalia think that using reflection in this way is not characteristic of children in the primary school years, and he suggests that children need help in developing their abilities to reflect, and to be more aware of their own reflection. In particular, teachers need to model the process of thinking for composing through talk, and especially through interactive dialogue, thus supporting or 'scaffolding' learning. The scaffolding idea was initially developed by Bruner, inspired by the idea of Vygotsky's ZPD, and without this, children may not transfer ideas successfully from their literary studies (Bruner, 1985; Corden, 2000).

Essential to the processes of reflection, Bereiter and Scardamalia believe, is children's ability to think consciously about, and talk about, their own writing processes, as well as those of others, using metalinguistic skills (Bereiter and Scardamalia, 1987). Continuing the use of metalanguage through the various components and stages of writing development is thus a priority for teachers. Metalinguistic skills are thoroughly incorporated into the programmes of work designed for the different year groups in primary schools, within the NLSF, and also in the new Key Stage 3 strategy for secondary schools, as well as being encouraged by such documents as *Improving Writing in Key Stages 3 and 4*, produced by QCA, demonstrating how this can be integrated with literacy studies of poetry and Shakespeare plays (QCA, 1999/392; DfEE, 2001/0019).

Bereiter has formulated some different stages of the writing process, although there are some reservations about the use of the term stage, since the later stages are not always mutually exclusive but depend on the purpose of the writing.

However, in general they aid evaluation in composition (Bereiter, 1980). The first stage is the Associative Stage, characterized by the writing down of what comes to mind, the flow of ideas being combined with, or even constrained by, the need still to attend to secretarial functions. Next is the Performative Stage, where some stylistic conventions begin to emerge. In the Communicative Stage, the writer attempts to have a particular affect upon the reader, and in the Unified Stage, the writer is able to use reasoning and judgement to create and mould the writing. The final stage he calls the Epistemic Stage, where the writer shows evidence of a personal search for meaning through his reflections (Bereiter, 1980; Beard, 2000).

The maturity of the writer is, of course, revealed in the compositional elements. While the content may be the essence of what is to be communicated, the structure itself contributes to this meaning, enabling, aiding and enhancing the message. Where structural skills are limited or immature, the messages possible are inhibited or attenuated; as these skills develop, the content is also able to develop and expand in breadth, depth, amount, in detail and elaboration. The structure is, of course, firstly syntactic in nature, and secondly organizational. Together these aspects form a developmental framework which underlies children's progress in writing, and which will now be examined, looking at the structural skills themselves and the empowerment they allow in the production and communication of content.

■ Structural Development and Stages

Changes in these characteristics are gradual, and take some time before they become habitual. It is also an incremental process, so that subsequent learning and development increasingly build upon prior attainments. When describing features of structure and linking them to particular ages, stages or National Curriculum levels, the features will be used as descriptors of the stage where they become most prominent and characteristic of writing at that stage, rather than starting to be established or even well incorporated and used easily or automatically. Thus the milestones of writing development may be identified by certain characteristics at the period when they are becoming securely established and used as part of the writer's habitual repertoire. The value of such a simplification, with its lack of repetitive detail, means that an overview of progress can be more easily grasped for use in evaluation.

Taking the example of paragraphing, an organizational aspect of structure, we note that the first appearance of paragraphing comes in the NLSF for Year 3, when it is listed as something children can begin to use in their writing of letters, and it is also mentioned in the NLSF in work to be covered in Year 4, where organizing work into paragraphs is detailed. It reappears in the NLSF programme for Year 5, where the mapping out of links between sections and paragraphs is to be taught. In a 1999 report on the use in 1998 of the optional NC tests for Years 3, 4, and 5, it is mentioned, however, that although children performing at Levels 4 and 5 used features of textual organization well, and had a greater awareness of purpose and audience, only 56 per cent of children used paragraphs in their stories in the test, and of these only about half appeared to use them appropriately (QCA, 1999/282). The final functions of paragraphing appeared to be insecurely grasped by many pupils at that stage. Paragraphing is also given a profile in the Year 6 programme of the NLSF, though, where pupils are expected by the end of the year to be able to divide texts into paragraphs, paying attention to their sequencing, and the links between them.

Looking at the National Curriculum Level Descriptors for writing, however, paragraphing is not mentioned in the descriptor for Level 3 (usual year groups for this stage are Years 3 and 4), or in that for Level 4 (usual year groups for this stage are Years 5 and 6) but it is mentioned in the Level Descriptor for Level 5, which is normally reached in the secondary school years, and sometimes by the higher attaining pupils by the end of Year 6. While the NLSF gives very detailed programmes for teaching and learning, the Level Descriptors are extremely brief summary statements which cannot cover everything pupils are expected to know and understand.

The Key Stage 3 NSFTE details looking at paragraphing in Year 7 as part of cohesion and coherence, in particular homing in on the first sentence to make explicit to the reader the shift in the direction or emphasis of meaning as a new paragraph starts. QCA documents give helpful details (QCA, 1999/392; QCA 1999/418). Thus it is expected that pupils will generally paragraph their work by the time they achieve Level 4, evidenced again by references to the need for teaching this aspect of organization to those who reach Year 7 without gaining Level 4, as one of the 'catch-up ' goals, in the NSFTE and related documents.

The indication is that paragraphs will first be drawn to the children's attention in Level 3 work, with some exercises involving practice in organizing text in this way, and by Level 5 they will be using paragraphs habitually and with precision, understanding that a paragraph encapsulates a basic idea, and that the sequence of paragraphs links these ideas together. Paragraphing, therefore, may be viewed as a characteristic feature of work gaining prominence at Level 4, although it may appear sometimes at level 3, and will be used more precisely and with full understanding of the sequencing of paragraphs, as part of the coherence of a text, at Level 5.

Effective work on paragraphs was interestingly contained in a series of lessons in a Year 4 class, using a World War II scenario. Pupils were writing letters in role as prospective evacuees, either to the authorities to say why they didn't want to be evacuated, or as evacuees, writing home to their parents. First draft sentences were cut up into single sentences in strips, to be rearranged in different sequences. The aim was to arrange related sentences together to form paragraphs, and then, with monitoring from the teacher, the strips were pasted on to a fresh sheet of paper. Later, the letters were copied out with final amendments, in presentation form. This teaching combined a number of aspects of learning to write in a cross-curricular mode, utilizing history and English together in an effective integration. Paragraphing was introduced in a concrete way, aiding understanding and retention, and the drafting process was meaningful to pupils.

There seems to be a paucity of information about how the contents of the NC levels were originally assigned to different year groups, in terms of expectations about average performance. Evidence from the content of the programmes of study indicates that this is based on a wide range of sound and relatively up to date research, but the proportions of pupils achieving the various levels vary considerably, tending to decline with progress through school. These proportions do not seem to represent accurately the average expected for a certain end of year stage, but perhaps they are not supposed to do so. There is, however, great emphasis on pushing up these proportions, increasing standards. This is wholly desirable, but does it indicate that benchmarks have a floating nature, or are the specified targets for each age intended as a basic floor which the majority need to attain? It is probably the latter, although this is still not entirely clear. Information on the results of the writing tests in 1998 in Years 2 and 6 (SATs), and the optional ones in Year 4, showed that while 81 per cent achieved at least Level 2 in Year 2, 61 per cent achieved Level 3 in Year 4, and 52 in Year 6 achieved Level 4 (QCA, 1999/282).

These national tests are **criterion-referenced**, and not **standardized** in any way. This means that the level of difficulty of the tests is set without previous specific experimental referencing of test components, using a wide sample, and without the general proportions reflected by such a standard for those above and below the average. This is usually illustrated by what is termed the **normal curve**, a distributional pattern with a central tendency found in investigations of incidence in the sciences generally. Criterion-referenced tests are, therefore, tests that have been chosen as a selected benchmark, albeit with some evidence of age-related attainment in mind, but with the outcome of pass-fail proportions to be discovered and not necessarily related in any way to proportions of the normal curve. The idea of using criterion-referenced tests may have been chosen in order to escape the limiting of pupil progress to what may become out of date standards of the average, and to exploit the potential of pupils. A clearer basis for expectations may eventually emerge, however, as the data bank of statistics builds with each testing year.

Assessment of writing as it develops is a complex procedure, matching what Beard has called the very complex area of the study of writing development (Beard, 2000). He has pointed out that while a child may be advanced in one aspect of writing, other aspects may not keep pace. Further, Beard highlights the problem in that writing has no fixed point by which to judge outcomes, as in reading where teachers can anchor responses to the textual intentions, and this leads to the question of validity of evaluation, and the subjectivity of different markers. The NC, NLSF and NSFTE acknowledge this, as do the instructions for marking the end of stage and the optional tests linked to the NC, and though copious guidance is given to markers for the tests, advice is to allocate levels on the basis of the 'best fit' assumption. Agreement trialling of level allocations within school staffs helps to reduce subjectivity and to make guidance more salient for teachers.

Assessing and scoring is often a lengthy process, and after looking at some characteristic features of the different stages of development in writing, and progress made at different levels, together with some support strategies, some key pointers will be identified to provide some simple methods of evaluating writing on an ongoing basis. These may be useful to teachers when marking work, although they are not intended to form complete and definitive assessment, which must remain with the official tests and levelling criteria. Help with marking of writing is provided on a QCA website, and teachers are encouraged to decide which aspects of writing are relevant for their specific purposes in using such guidelines (QCA, 2001, website list, see page 201).

■ Early Writing and Support Strategies

When children become aware of people around them making marks on paper and then reading these, they begin to understand that writing carries meaning. To begin with they produce random marks and scribble, and pretend that the marks carry a message. This is **play writing**. As they learn to recognize and form a few letters, they begin to include these, randomly at first, then more systematically; they want to know how to write the words they need for their messages and captions, and seek help from adults for this. This is **emergent writing**, where there is some use of recognizable letter shapes, written with some idea of the symbol to sound correspondences. This grows gradually into written text where some words are correctly spelt, while others are attempted in a plausible way. At this stage, writing may be uneven, no particular format or layout can be expected, and the structure of the language is likely to be at first single words or short phrases or captions, developing into simple short sentences, without the use of **sentence markers** (capitals and full stops). Later writing at the end of this stage will have some awareness of full stops, and of putting a few sentences together, although these may not be in any sequential order. The content is very often about 'me'.

At the emergent stage, it is important to try to preserve children's desires to write and to communicate; if not inhibited by the restrictions of their minimal secretarial abilities, the ideas they want to express have a freshness and vitality about them. This differs from the stilted and attenuated writing of those who have been overlong trying to write with inadequate support for the setting down of ideas. The important thing is to provide support to prevent the swamping of the compositional aspects of writing by attention to encoding; the aim is to relieve pressure on working memory, allowing enough capacity to think about the content of the writing itself. A variety of strategies may be employed to provide such support, while an adequacy of GPC knowledge is being acquired. Some of these are:

■ **Teacher-scribe** (teacher or any adult helper or parent) – Adult writes text at child's dictation, eg as caption for child's picture. They read it together. The child may or may not trace over or copy under this, if sequence is short.

- **Shared writing** – Teacher/helper writes for group/class and uses children's contributions, reads it back.

- **Initial-letter shorthand** – Children draw a picture and construct a sentence to go underneath it, using only the initial letters of each word, thus '*I went to my nan's on Saturday*' would be recorded as '*I w t m n o s*'. The picture acts as a stimulus, both for making the sentence and for helping to remember it. Teacher and adult helpers move around the class or group as they finish, asking children to 'read' their sentence. Adults then become teacher-scribes and write the sentence in full beneath, pointing out the use of the child's initial letters at the beginning of each word. This works very well at the stage when children have acquired an understanding of the common sound values of most letters, and can isolate the initial sound, but are not yet ready to identify final or medial sounds or to blend.

- **Magic line** – Children can spell cvcs, and are beginning to attempt larger words, but sometimes get stymied. To avoid stopping the flow of ideas being set down on paper, when they cannot complete a word, they can merely put in a dash where the rest of it should be, usually the later part of the word, or the middle. As adults move round to help children or check their work, the missing letters in the word can be written in, above the line, and children congratulated for getting part of the word done.

- **Interactive journal** – This is where the child writes a phrase or sentence or two, but to write more is too laborious and the impetus becomes lost; the teacher or adult helper can 'share' the writing and take a turn to write more of what the child wishes to say. Usually 'journal' because it's usually about 'me', but not necessarily.

- **Word banks** – There are various forms of these, sometimes permanent and sometimes temporary to do with current topics.

- **Streamers** – A type of word bank, using A4 sheets mounted onto lengths of stiffer paper, 2 or 3 feet long, which can be hung from a hook by a bulldog clip, and thus easily added to, children's contributions can be recorded, or they can be invited to add them themselves, using a fat felt pen. They may be themed words for a topic, a list of colour words to do with art, say, or the story of Robin Hood, eg pea green, grass green, bottle green, apple green, olive green, sea green. Or useful alternatives for went and said.

- **Icon answers** – Promote **ideational fluency** by posing a question to make children think, and asking them to record as many answers as they can, using their own little pictures for answers; if they are able to do so, labelling with an initial letter is a half-way stage, or when spelling starts, they can attempt the words as well. Questions may be things like What goes up? What comes down? What is red? What is made of metal? Who might you meet in the woods? Reward originality, like the child who said 'My Nan says prices go up!'

- **Inventive spelling** – If not sure of a word, children attempt it on a piece of paper or in a spelling notebook, and ask for it to be checked or completed; praise is given for all attempts, like 'Well done, you've got nearly all the letters we need in this word!'

■ Organization of Independent Writing and Developmental Indicators

Independent writing develops usually during Year 2, as secretarial skills become easier in their growth towards automation. Handwriting becomes more regular, with letters generally appropriately formed, spelling of cvcs is correct, and so is spelling of more familiar words of other types, while harder words are plausibly attempted. Some common polysyllabic words using digraphs become familiar. There is the occasional use of an adjective, and alternative verbs to replace *went* and *said*. An idea of shaping text is beginning to emerge in the notion of story sequence needing a beginning, middle and end, while in writing a letter the form is different. Very early forms of planning and drafting can be accomplished, although these tend to draw out the writing process too long, often, and cannot be used all the time. Imaginative ideas and flights of fancy appear frequently. The writer is able to write half a page of description or a letter, and some stories become lengthy if writing is fluent, and may go on for two or three pages or more.

The prominent characteristic of this stage is in the sentence structure, which consists predominantly of simple and compound sentences. These are linked using the **early connectives**, *and*, *then*, and occasionally, *but*. Sentence markers (use of capital letters and full stops to demarcate the sentence boundaries) are sometimes used, often only occasionally. This structure is like a chain: one sentence, whether boundary marked or not, follows another, linked by the simple connectives. Reading such texts, it often seems as if the writer, to generate the next sentence, uses the content of the last one as a jumping off point. Ideas are associated from one sentence to another all the way through, and there is no feeling of a sense of the piece being conceived as a whole. Teaching about beginning, middle and end in story structure can gradually aid the beginnings of this perspective, however.

In the next stage of structural development sentences become modified, with the use of related ideas incorporated, introducing the habitual use of complex sentences. These are composed of **main clauses** with **subordinated clauses**, sometimes known as **dependent clauses**, attached. Sentence structure now consists of a mixture of simple, compound and complex sentences, as in all subsequent stages, although the quality, ordering and understanding of clauses will still continue to develop. These subordinate clauses enrich, elaborate, and sometimes explain, the main drift of the writing as represented by the main clauses, and are linked to them by a wider range of **basic connectives** than those generally used before. The range of connectives will further develop at subsequent stages and become more sophisticated, especially in relation to types of logical relations between the pieces of information. The range of connectives includes conjunctions, like *while, so, so that, because, when, where, while,* and also relative words, such as relative pronouns like *that, which,* and *who.* There is some apparent overlap of categories into which some of these words fall, depending upon their functions in sentences. Beard gives helpful and clear analyses of types of sentence and clause (Beard, 2000). These distinctions are also made clear in National Curriculum documents, in dictionaries and in other sources of English grammatical usage (QCA, 1998/052; DfEE, 1998a; DfEE, 2001/0107). The word *connectives* is used in the NC documents, forming a helpful umbrella term for all words connecting clauses within sentences.

Writing is usually joined up, in cursive style, and spelling is correct for many **bi-syllabic** and **polysyllabic** words, with justifiable spelling for lesser-known words, and sentence markers are used reliably. There may be the beginning of use of question and exclamation marks, and sometimes, speech marks. The organization of writing is more clear, with the order of any events or parts of a process in sequence, the beginnings of style in adaptation to purpose sometimes seen. The range of purposes increases, and there is some effort to create planned effects, with a greater increase in vocabulary to support it; there is more use of adjectives, and occasionally adverbs, in imaginative writing.

This stage generally corresponds with the usual characteristics of writing at NC Level 3, for work culminating at the end of Year 4 after Years 3 and 4. However, higher attaining pupils frequently reach this level while still in Year 2. In the Year 2 end of Key Stage National Tests (SATs), the achievement of Level 3 demands some of the features just described, including reliable use of sentence markers and correct spelling for most familiar words. The most revealing characteristic, however, is the sentence structure used: the inclusion of a substantial number of complex sentences. Sometimes a few are present in the higher grade of Level 2, 2a, but if the complex sentences number three or four to a page or more, it is likely that Level 3 will be achieved. The use of complex sentences goes on to be a habitual part of the writer's structural organization from this point. There is the watershed difference here, between the '**chaining**' of simple sentences using *and* and *then*, which is prominent at Level 2, and the complex structure being introduced and then used by Level 3. The clauses are indicated by the connectives employed, although sometimes the connective itself is actually missing and is only implied; if using the presence of connectives to assess use of subordination, care must be taken to note this. An example of a sentence with a subordinate clause introduced by a 'hidden' connective would be 'This is the house (that) Jack built.' Sometimes a clause is collapsed into a phrase, losing its connective and its verb, such as 'The flame (*that came*) from the candle shone into the darkness of the great hall…'. This, at a stroke, renders the text more economical yet more elaborate and vivid. When a clause is collapsed into a phrase in this way it is known as an **embedded clause**.

As children move into this stage of being able to use complex sentence structure in their writing, a range of connectives appear, indicative of subordinate clauses and modifying phrases. Children will not use such structure in their writing, though, unless they are already using it naturally and habitually in their speech. It cannot be implanted as part of teaching about writing, although once there, it can later be made more explicit using metalanguage, so that awareness may facilitate clause use for effect. It cannot be taught directly as part of speaking either, but it can be fostered by opportunities for speaking and listening, particularly by interactive conversation, and question and answer techniques. These include the sustaining of longer utterances through teacher modelling and

open-ended questioning, including personally targeted questioning, and the encouragement of elaboration. Open-ended questions are often those which begin with words such as *who, what, why, where, when* and *how*; the link is obvious. Thus the quality of teachers' skill in using open-ended questioning in Year R, 1, and 2, is a contributory factor to achievement in writing at Levels 2a and 3, and all that follows. The skill of teachers in using open-ended questions in the Key Stage 2 and Key Stage 3 years is also valuable, continuing as it does the promotion of reasoning and imagination.

Take the following complex sentence: *She met a little dwarf who was dressed in red*. The addition of *from top to toe* would be a further elaboration, using an additional phrase (implied connective and subsidiary verb). Note the implied connectives and verbs in the following example: *She met a dwarf (who was) dressed in red (which went) from top to toe (who was), dancing in circles and (who was) leaping in the air*. While implied connectives need watching, they are less likely at the emerging stage, but they are crucial for the distinction between Level 2a and Level 3. Other more sophisticated constructions are to be seen in the work of more able pupils, especially towards the top of the primary school, such as beginning a sentence with a dependent clause, connective and subsidiary verb implied, for both impact and economy of expression. An example of this would be something like: *Galloping through the woods, he came upon the castle, its towers gleaming in the sun, high above the treetops*. The underlying structure here is: *He came upon the castle* (main clause) *(as he was) galloping through the woods* (dependent clause). The rest of the sentence is made up of subordinate clauses describing the castle *(whose) towers were gleaming in the sun (or, the towers of which were gleaming in the sun)*, and *(which were) high above the treetops*. Notice that commas are needed where words have been implied, whereas with the words present, in some cases, they might be optional. Some of the influences on grammar here are different from those derived from speech. We don't talk like the last two examples: they are book language, generated from reading and from listening to stories. It is a more succinct and richer language form than normal speech, and demonstrates for us the importance of story reading and telling from the early years, as well as group story-making and story drama (Grainger, 1997; Corden, 2000).

Greater precision in the use of subordinate clauses is part of the programme for Level 4, and at this stage direct teaching can make explicit these formations. In a skilled lesson combining history and literacy a Year 6 teacher used the context of the blurbs pupils were composing for books on Greek mythology which they were making. The need to be sharp and succinct for this purpose appealed to them. One pupil wrote:

A long time ago in Ancient Greece, a child (who was) born to an unwilling grandfather was tossed into the sea (in order) to fulfil his destiny. To find out his destiny, read on...

The hidden, implied relative words, not part of the actual text, are given in brackets. Note the use of the adjective *unwilling*; this could be a conflated clause reduced to one word.

Work in Years 5 and 6 leads, for a majority of pupils, to the achievement of Level 4. The most prominent feature of writing at this level is the organization of the work. There is a much more obvious grasp of an overall conception before a piece of work is tackled, and planning and drafting become very important in helping to facilitate this. With a plan, the writer does not need to keep thinking about the development of the plot, scene or characterization all at once, but can tackle portions of the work at a time, referring back to the plan when the next section is needed. In this way, good concentration is preserved for attending to the actual writing, its immediate structure and its expression in the words selected. Coherence and cohesion are supported by a clear thread running through the organization of the piece of writing, including the paragraphing of the text showing shifts or elaborations of the meaning. There is evidence of some adaptation to purpose and audience, conveyed by style and vocabulary, and sometimes by form; words are chosen adventurously and for effect.

The differences between Level 4 writing and Level 5 writing lie in the range and variety of purposes and audiences for which pupils can write, effectively and with good adaptation, including a nice sense of appropriate style. They also lie in the degree of organization, part of that adaptation, so that the intended structure is obvious. Clause structure is used in a more sophisticated way, with a wider range of types of clause, and the use of clauses in different positions in the sentence, as for instance when a sentence begins with an embedded clause for impact, as in '*Slinking softly round the corner, he saw the creature outlined against the moonlight.*' Finally, differences lie also in the use of words with precision, not just for effect but for precise effect. The writer is strongly aware of the aim to communicate with the audience. Headings for the criteria used to evaluate writing in the Level 5 band include, apart from the secretarial aspects, clause structure, word usage, paragraphing and other features of textual organization such as coherence/cohesion, openings and endings and reader writer relationship (QCA, 1999/392).

Prioritizing Criteria for Simple and Effective Ongoing Assessment

To sum up, the most prominent features characterising the structure of writing at the different levels of independent writing are as follows:

■ Level 2 – a chained sequence of associations formed in simple and compound sentences

■ Level 3 – sentence structure which includes complex sentences, with related subordinate clauses, indicating a richer structure of a relational type

■ Level 4 – organized writing, the piece conceived as a whole, with use of paragraphing, and words chosen for effect

■ Level 5 – writing aimed at good communication, showing good adaptation to purpose and audience, some sense of style, paragraphing secure, and words chosen with precision.

Review is the third component Beard gives us in his model of writing, and this, although always a part of the process, comes much more into prominence where planning and drafting play a more vital role (Beard, 2000). Redrafting or editing is part of the review process, and so is proof-reading. Schools these days make good use of collaborative modes of working to facilitate these aspects of writing, sometimes with regular or different response partners, and sometimes in small groups. These are ideal ways of promoting the review process, which need stimulating by modelling by the teacher as well, because in the interactive process, talk and discussion is used, clarifying points, aiding reasoning and demonstrating the effect on a reader. Review is crucial for movement from Level 4 to Level 5, in making more explicit the focus on the audience.

Strategies for developing writing, then, need to include the encouragement of fluent writing at Year 2 stage, even if it is 'chained', and an emphasis on speaking and listening and story. In Years 3 and 4, elaboration is to be encouraged, including the widening of vocabulary, starting to plan simple drafts. In Years 5 and 6, a more workmanlike approach to planning and drafting is needed: it is difficult for some children to understand the role of the plan, and too often they write too much, actually starting the draft instead of a very brief plan. This needs teaching attention and modelling. Also direct teaching of paragraphing and the way to lay out and punctuate dialogue becomes important here. The range of purposes for writing needs widening, contrasting imaginative writing, whether poetry or prose, with informative writing where the need is for succinct and accurate reporting, and introduction of the feelings element with persuasive writing. The strategies for Level 5 work, or Key Stage 3 years, need to build on previous learning, sharpening it, making it more explicit and having greater awareness of the functions of the structures used in writing, through discussion, through models in literature, and through the use of the metalanguage. At this stage the contributions of speaking and listening, reading and writing become very intermingled and integrated, supporting the flow of learning as a whole approach to the use of the English language and the study of its literature.

Looking at ages and stages, a number of models have been proposed. Beard describes a model of early stages of writing put forward by Nicholls, which includes attention to the change from simple sentence structure to complex sentence structure in his final stage, which he calls 'Beyond Associative Writing' (Beard, 2000). Milestones have also been suggested by Kinmont, but without ages or stages linked to them (Kinmont, 1990). 'The Primary Language Record Scales' provide detailed models, one for ages 6 to 8, the other for 9 to 12. The age ranges are helpful, but there is little attention given to structure, in particular, clause structure and how this changes (Barrs *et al.*, 1988; CLPE, 2000). All of these models, different in their way, own many points of concordance, but the flow of development is divided rather differently in each; it is not entirely clear where the parallels lie in expectancies for ages and stages. Furthermore, lists of details, when long, tend not to be prioritised in terms of prominence of certain characteristics for the different stages.

For full NC assessment the official criteria need to be used, as they are in the marking of the SATs. However, there are certain aspects of writing at different stages which are key aspects, and can be used in simple ways to make ongoing assessment quick and easy. When marking children's work, keeping a finger on the pulse of pupil progress can be simple, effective and qualitative. Use underlining, circling or highlighting to pick out the following salient features quickly, until usage of this method habitually becomes second nature:

■ In Year 2, watch for the *ands* and *thens*; note the number of basic rather than early connectives used, as an indicator of subordinate clauses and complex sentences. If there are plenty, work will be likely to be at Level 3; if two or three, the writing will still be at Level 2, but moving in the right direction.

■ In Years 3 and 4, still look for these, but also note number of adjectives used, and see if there are any adverbs. Note verb variety. Look for signs reflecting awareness of purpose and audience.

■ In Years 5 and 6, check if paragraphing is used consistently, if vocabulary use shows evidence of selection for effect. Note the ability to use planning, drafting and editing. Look at verb variety, use of adjectives and adverbs. Any stylistic adaptation to purpose?

■ For the more able in Year 6 and for those in Key Stage 3, check if paragraphing is consistent and used with awareness of shifts in meaning and ways to join these shifts; look for precision in word use, double adjectives, imagery, metaphor and simile in expressive work. Above all, look for coherence and for adaptation to the communicative nature of the writing.

Examples of using connectives to assess a text follow below.

Fiona's writing – Year 1

> <u>When</u> you go camping you camp under a tree. Do you camp in a grassy spot <u>or</u> a plain spot? you have to light a fire <u>when</u> you go camping. I've never been camping <u>but</u> I want to. you must bring a light <u>when</u> you go camping. you need to bring you'r back pack. The end

Comments: Fiona has three clear subordinate clauses here, each introduced by the word *when*. In the first sentence, she has started the sentence with the subordinate clause, and the main clause follows. She has two compound sentences, one joined with *but*, the other with *or*. The last sentence is a simple sentence. Flora's writing shows characteristics of Level 3, or at the least, Level 2a; although we don't know what her work is like when she writes a longer piece. She has a good grasp of the use of sentence markers, although two capitals are missing.

Clare's writing – Year 2

> One day a sheep called Cedric whent for a walk and on the way he got lost he shouted HELP! Said Cedric I'm lost then he saw something it came closer to him and it was a sheep she was beautiful and they met and cared on gowing. Then they came to a lake...

Comments: Clare is definitely in the classic *and* and *then* phase characteristic of the 'chaining' so often seen in Year 2 writing structure.

Jenny's ghost story – Year 2

> Once upon a time there was a ghost (<u>and</u>) he was a bad ghost he was a very bad ghost. One day he went out for a walk <u>(and) on the way</u> he saw a very pretty princess he said to himself I want that princess <u>so</u> he creped behind the princess <u>and</u> calt her <u>and</u> put her in a very high tower <u>with</u> no door <u>but</u> there was just a window <u>coming out</u> of it was a very strange rope. <u>That night</u> the ghost went out and the princess got away. <u>On the way home</u> she saw a prince and the prince killed the ghost and...

Comments: Jenny has used mainly the 'chaining' structure typical of this level. She has a lot of simple and/or compound sentences joined by *and, so,* and *but,* using mainly *and.* Sometimes the *and* is implied, or else a full stop or a colon could have replaced it – but Jenny is not yet fully aware of punctuation. She has used some sentence markers but not consistently. However, there are a few constructions here, which though they look like phrases, are what we might call clausally derived, the embedded clause type. '*On the way*' means '*When he/she was going home*'. '*That night*' indicates '*The ghost went out <u>when</u> it was that night*'. '*A very high tower with no door*' is an interesting construction: '*with no door*' means '*which had no door*'. Also interesting is '*coming out of it was a very strong rope*', meaning '*and a very strong rope was coming out of that window*', but it links more economically and more elegantly. Even in this short excerpt, Jenny has shown evidence of some complex sentence structure, but overall, together with her unreliable sentence markers, she would not be at Level 3 yet, and hardly at Level 2a, though she is moving in the right direction in terms of her sentence structure.

Florence's letter – Year 2

Here are parts of Florence's letter in role as a little bird, to a fellow fledgling.

> Dear Plop,
> I have got a tingle in my toes and the butterflys have taken my tummy away, <u>because</u> guess <u>what</u> I realy did I flew!! I flew over the twisting silver river <u>that</u> runs round the city. I flew over the road, over tree-tops, I flew over house-tops and green fields. It was fabulous <u>when</u> I was flying... I was filled with joy <u>because</u> well it was the first time (<u>that</u>) I flew in my short little life.

Comment: Florence is using quite a number of subordinate clauses indicating complex sentence structure, in her writing. The word '*that*' is implied, not explicit. '*Guess what*' is an unusual construction and adds to the vivacity of the piece, even if she is not using punctuation appropriately here. Notice that she has twice used double adjectives, even in quite a short space, enriching her imagery. This work is certainly moving towards, or even within the range of, a Level 3, for a Year 2 pupil.

From sifting all the evidence concerning prominent characteristics of developmental phases in writing, as well as from substantial observation and experience of children writing at different stages, the model that follows (see pages 88 and 89) is suggested as a developmental profile. It is accompanied by a partner profile for reading, since there are points where the two processes go hand in hand or, in turn, lead each other forward.

■ Chapter Summary

1. Composition involves thinking, including considerable reflectivity. Some purposes also involve the ability to empathize.

2. Part of composition is structural, and this shows a clear developmental sequence, particularly in sentence structure between Years 1 and 4.

3. Support is needed in the early stages of writing, to enable sufficient working memory capacity to attend to composition, rather than being engulfed by the demands of encoding.

4. In upper Key Stage 2, and in Key Stage 3, use of paragraphing moves to a more precise use of it as an organizational feature, with the understanding of unifying ideas, and meaning shifts as part of a planned whole.

5. Also at these stages, words are first chosen for effect, and then become more precisely selected for very specific effects, as part of adaptation to purpose. Use of verbs in variety, adjectives and adverbs appositely used increase.

6. Developmental profiles are provided for both writing and reading.

■ Teacher Activity

Look at a piece of writing from your class or from the age group you usually work with, and assess it using some of the indicators given at the end of the chapter. If it is Year 1, 2 or 3, look at connectives, count them and divide into early and basic categories. How many in the basic category, indicating complex sentences? If it is in Years 4,5 or 6, look to see if you think the work is conceived as a whole, and what organization can be discerned: is it paragraphed or not yet, how much punctuation is there, is it coherent and sequenced? If it is from a more able child or in Years 7, 8 or 9, look particularly at the beginning and ending sentences of paragraphs to see if there are indications of a) links between the unifying ideas of the single paragraphs, and b) shifts of direction, emphasis or elaboration. Count adjectives and adverbs used; note any use of double adjectives. Look for similes, metaphors, and idiomatic phrases which aid adaptation to purpose and a sense of audience.

For following up further interests

Barrs, M. and Cork, V. (2001) *The Reader in the Writer – the links between the study of literature and writing development at Key Stage 2*. Centre for Language in Primary Education (London Borough of Southwark).

Beard, R. (2000) *Developing Writing 3–13*. London: Hodder and Stoughton.

Kinmont, A. (1990) *The Dimensions of Writing*. London: David Fulton.

Rees, F. (1996) *The Writing Repertoire – Developing Writing at Key Stage 2*. Slough: NFER.

QCA (2001) *Marking Guidelines for Writing*. Website: www.standards.dfes.gov.uk

A DEVELOPMENTAL WRITING PROFILE	
Context of the observation: **ASSESSING INDIVIDUAL WRITER** PUPIL: AA / A /BA	Estimated **NC LEVEL** ☐

Is pupil writing with support?
Is pupil writing independently?
Is pupil writing fluently?

Is handwriting legible?   Is pencil grip appropriate?

Are secretarial skills in line with the ability to generate ideas about content and support compositional progress?
Or do they lag behind and inhibit expression?

Is range of purposes presented for tasks appropriate for age/ stage?   Is length of written pieces appropriate for age/stage?

- -

Does pupil enjoy writing?
Or is reluctant to write?
Does spontaneous written work at home sometimes?   Completes written homework at home?

- -

APPROACH SKILLS – EMERGENT WRITING

Towards ELGs / at ELGs / Level W	Understands writing communicates messages Uses idiosyncratic writing in play Learns to write own name and to form some letters
Level 1	**Learning transcription skills** – acquiring knowledge of sound/symbol correspondence (GPC) Can spell some cvcs and use in simple captions, phrases and a few simple sentences

- -

LOWER WRITING SKILLS – ASSOCIATIVE STRUCTURE

Level 1/2	Spells cvcs well, and some 4/5 letter words Uses simple digraphs, vowel digraphs, consonant blends Writes 3–5 simple sentences
Level 2	Uses phonically justifiable attempts at harder words Uses common digraphs and blends securely – knows about "magic e" Writes in simple and compound sentences, uses *and, then,* and *but* as connectives **Structure is a chained sequence of associations** Uses some sentence markers Able to write more than 4/5 lines, often 1, 2 or 3 pages

- -

INTERMEDIATE WRITING SKILLS – RELATIONAL STRUCTURE

Level 3 (lower)	Good spelling patterns established for basic regular words, and for familiar irregular ones Handwriting becoming joined **Sentence structure includes complex sentences, with related subordinate clauses**
Level 3 (upper)	Use of sentence markers secure; understands sentence boundaries Uses wider range of connectives, like *if, so, while, though, since, when, who,* etc. Verb use wider, a few adjectives and adverbs used Fluent writing, understands basic story structure well
Level 3 / 4	Shows some awareness of reader and purpose in using different forms

- -

HIGHER WRITING SKILLS – ORGANIZED STRUCTURE

Level 4 (lower)	Fluent, expressive writing; accurate and automated use of secretarial skills **Conceives piece of writing for task as a global whole**
Level 4 (upper)	Able to use planning, drafting and editing skills competently Able to proof-read and review work, alone or collaboratively Uses paragraphing Uses correctly laid out dialogue Selects vocabulary for effect, verbs, adjectives and adverbs Awareness of adaptation to purpose for audience grows; wide range of forms tackled Note-making for study skills Précis & summarizing techniques used

HIGHER WRITING SKILLS – COMMUNICATIVE WRITING

Level 5	**Good adaptation to purpose and audience** Sense of style Structure and coherence in flow of content Paragraphing secure Precise use of vocabulary and of varied structure to evoke reader response
Level 6 and 6+	**Focus fully on communicating meaning**, autonomous writing as author, personal views and impersonal writing as well are both easily adopted Critical thinking developed through review, analysis, hypothesis, recollection and summary Extensive range of forms used

Table 6.1 (This may be photocopied for use within the purchasing organisation)

A DEVELOPMENTAL READING PROFILE

Context of the observation: **HEARING INDIVIDUAL READER**   Book used: READING SCHEME or LIBRARY BOOK?

PUPIL: AA / A /BA   Estimated **NC LEVEL** ☐

Is text matched to allow appropriate level of accuracy?
i.e. Independent level is 99% accurate (one error per 100 words)
i.e. Instructional level is 95% (five errors per 100 words)
i.e. Frustration level is 90% accurate or less (unsatisfactory)

Are type and range of texts appropriate? _____   How often heard? _____

Is there any evidence of cue use? (Levels 1, 2, 3) or textual understanding (Levels 4, 5)

- -

Does pupil enjoy reading?   Take it home?   Any favourite books?   Uses library?

- -

APPROACH SKILLS – EMERGENT READING

Towards ELGs / at ELGs / Level W	Has book handling skills
	Can discuss pictures
	Can recognize odd words / letters
	Learning decoding skills
Level 1	Recognize a number of familiar word and has some
	minimal idea of sound, symbol correspondence

LOWER READING SKILLS – INDEPENDENT READING

Level 1/2	Recognizes most words
	Usually accurate reading
Level 2	**Word by word reading – uses cues:**
	initial letter; cvc words decoded; other simple words.
	Able to use semantic and syntactic cues
	Knows alphabet sequence, understands content

INTERMEDIATE READING SKILLS – EXPRESSIVE READING

Level 3 (lower)	**Reading with expression**
	Able to use intermediate phonics
	Understands content and word meanings
Level 3 (upper)	Fluent, expressive and well paced reading
	Able to use all cueing systems
	Able to use all cues collaboratively
Level 3 / 4	Moving to advanced phonics

HIGHER READING SKILLS – INFORMATIVE READING

Level 4 (lower)	**Fluent, expressive, accurate; comprehension skills developing**
Level 4 (upper)	Study skills – skim and scan? Notemaking skills?
	Accessing skills – index, library? Knows about fiction and non-fiction?
	Can give reading preferences, authors, titles

HIGHER LEVEL READING SKILLS – INTERPRETIVE READING

Level 5	**Reads "between the lines" – understands inference, idiom, simile and metaphor well**
	Discusses genre, style, text; can refer to examples from text
	Sifts opinion and bias from fact

HIGHER LEVEL READING SKILLS – APPRECIATIVE READING

Level 6	**Awareness of author's intentions, and devices used to pursue these**

COMPREHENSION	Able to recount story or extract information –	Level 3+
	Prediction –	Level 3 / 4 / 4+
	Able to interpret using inference. Able to discuss and explain or expand –	Level 4 / 5 / 6

Table 6.2 (This may be photocopied for use within the purchasing institution)

7 | A Taxonomy of Writing Purposes and their Pertinence for Cross-Curricular Application

■ Purposes and Perspectives

Thinking and feeling – Content, style and form – Range of purposes for writing: a taxonomy of writing categories – Exploring some text-types – Cross-curricular uses of some text-types – Chapter summary – Teacher activity

Thinking and Feeling

We have seen that studying and discussing literature is the key to developing children's critical skills and enabling them to introduce some of the features they see into their own writing. This aspect is supported by the text study part of the English Literacy Hour (NLSF) in primary school work, and in the National Strategy for Key Stage 3 and its Framework for Teaching English (NSFTE), in the first phase of the secondary school. It is certainly a valuable element of teaching, the format for which is now becoming generally very well established in most primary schools in England, and now being introduced into the first key stage of secondary schooling (DfEE, 1998; DfEE, 2001/0019).

Apart from these thinking abilities and their effects on the development of writing, there are other personal aspects which wield an influence upon writing. Kinmont draws attention to the affective side of personality development and its effects upon the ability to write (Kinmont, 1990). Young children only slowly begin to emerge from egocentric stages. Awareness of others gradually develops, through play and interaction with those around them. Later, as older children and adults, if the process of socialization has proved adequate, they will be able to place themselves in the shoes of others, showing sympathy and empathy, or, alternatively, to be more objective in their views. This is an ability developing from growing outwards and away from the very egocentric viewpoint of the young child, and recognizing that others have feelings, and also that there are occasions when facts and not feelings or opinions are important. The process is a double-edged pathway forward, at once enabling more personal views in relation to others and at the same time, more impersonal ones. This process is sometimes referred to as the growing ability to **decentre**. Kinmont refers to the process of decentring as bringing about the ability of a writer to recognize the needs of the reader, in terms of the communication intended (Kinmont, 1990). She thinks that at first, when recognized, this tends to dominate the writer's style, but as greater control over text is achieved, the writer becomes more able to concentrate on the content, and to write more effectively in impersonal modes. She discusses writing as a process of self-discovery, and sees the major influences of decentring on different forms of writing as falling between 10 and 13 years old.

Children in the Foundation Stage or in Key Stage 1 are little able to think themselves into someone else's position or point of view, relatively speaking, but by the end of Key Stage 2 and in Key Stage 3, they should be able to do this effectively to a recognizable degree. The ability to see another's point of view or understand their feelings is a crucial part, not only of understanding literature and appreciating it, but also of bearing in mind the intended audience when writing. Will the reader need factual data, a clear argument, exciting action, detailed description of characters, and so on? Kinmont suggests that writing needs to be judged by this personal and affective dimension and how it reveals the writer's view of reality, as well as by looking at the organization and content of a piece. It is particularly crucial in writing in role, raising the reader's imagination and interest to a high level in stories, and imagining the reactions of the recipient in persuasive writing.

Using Moffett's hypothesis as a starting point, Kinmont provides a clear table showing how writers move from the focus on self to thinking about others, and through this to the final stage of recognizing aspects of reality. She combines this perspective with a cognitive developmental view moving from describing, through interpreting and generalizing to speculating, showing how affective and cognitive aspects are linked developmentally (Moffett, 1968; Kinmont, 1990). The ability to affect the reader brings in the idea of style in writing, and of adaptation to the purpose of the writing too, since both are linked. Adopting a particular style in writing is part of the adaptation to purpose. Kinmont points out that the selection of stylistic features involves both cognitive and affective aspects. Bereiter thinks that the mastery of stylistic conventions parallels the discovery that the reader can be affected by the writing. This stage begins to occur around the ages of 10 and 11, when there is a change in writing as pupils try to achieve their planned effects both by organization of content, and by the effort to improve the imaginative content through the use of vocabulary (Bereiter, 1980; Kinmont 1990).

The ideas of Moffett on cognitive stages were also taken up by Wilkinson *et al.* who added, in terms of affective stages, moral dimensions and the idea of style in writing (Wilkinson *et al.*, in Beard, 2000). This model is referred to as being only of a provisional kind, despite considerable research with children at ages 7, 10 and 13, but it is very interesting in its combination of the different aspects of development. These centre round the deepening awareness of others, the growing consciousness of this awareness, and how writing may reflect these changes. In terms of ages and stages, Beard believes that the journey through the use of stock language, conventional uses and stereotypes in children's writing, towards the achievement of autonomy, takes a long time. He suggests that writing expressed in individual ways, using original thoughts and ideas, may not even be reached by the age of 13 (Beard, 2000).

Content, Style and Form

The major genres, suggests Kress, are descriptive, scientific, technical, historical writing, and the creative writing of story forms (Kress, 1982). In this list of genres generally tackled in schools, he omits to mention poetry. He thinks that although children learn a lot about genres through their reading experiences and study of literature and other texts, this is insufficient for them to learn the forms and rules of a particular genre, without specific and direct teaching about these things, including adequate detail. Kress was writing two decades ago, before the inception of the Literacy Hour in primary schools generally, and although the text study components of the Literacy Hour do address these points well, with the modelling, instructing, demonstrating, displaying and discursive techniques used in reference to form and detail of the studied text, it is valuable to remember his point. On the other hand, Beard points out that to teach specific forms and ways of writing explicitly linked to particular genres can produce problems, of rigidity and inhibition of creativity, presumably. He concludes that in the educational context the term *genre* has a broader meaning than that of the usual dictionary definitions about style, and is more generally used in this context, to mean different kinds of writing in a general way (Beard, 2000). The NLSF and related documents prefer to use the term **text-type**, since it is true that some textual responses to different purposes for writing use characteristics from more than one genre.

Range of Purposes for Writing – a Taxonomy of Writing Categories

Exploring the range of writing, Collins suggests dividing the various text-types into the two broad categories of narrative (generally fiction) and non-narrative (generally non-fiction) (Collins, 1998). This is a common division as a first categorization of the different genres of text-types within the expected range of writing. The NLSF provides a pathway through the different kinds of writing expected at different ages. Returning to the distinction between empathy and impersonal writing, we may look at these as another way of categorizing purposes for writing and the different genres they require, with the more imaginative and creative forms of writing, including persuasive writing, demanding an understanding of feelings, while factual writing, description, using evidence and factual reportage require objectivity. There is a third major division that can accompany these two perspectives, that of study skills, the uses of writing for the writer's own learning.

1. **Personal writing (imaginative and creative writing)** – writing which involves empathy and use of imagination, eg narrative, characterization, biography/autobiography, writing in role, personal letters and persuasive writing.

2. **Impersonal writing** – factual writing, with an objective stance, often as children get older written in the passive voice, eg reportage (if without bias), description, arguments based on factual data, scientific reports, formal letters.

3. **Study skills** – writing to aid independent learning, eg note-making, selective note-making, summary, précis, learning patterns of discourse for essays, arguments, and reports etc, preparing notes for speaking.

The table on the ensuing pages provides a taxonomy of the main writing purposes, together with some defining features of the genres they warrant. This is just an overview, and more detailed, comprehensive lists pertaining to most sections are supplied in the relevant NC documents. These, in particular *Grammar for Writing* and *Developing Early Writing*, give very helpful summaries of the features of textual organization and language that are needed for the different text-types (DfEE, 2001/0107; DfEE, 2001/0055).

Exploring Some Text-Types

Discussing the range of purposes and genres used in children's writing, Beard provides a wealth of guidance for teachers to enhance children's understanding of genre and enhance their writing (Beard, 2000). Narrative is the genre with which children are familiar from early days, listening to stories, and as such it forms a basic pattern and foundation from which other sorts of writing can develop. Activities designed to aid the analysis of stories, and thinking about story, are represented with a range of story texts by Fisher, writing for teachers of younger children; such activities would support the use of story structure, both in recount writing and imaginative narrative (Fisher, 1999). Narrative may underlie texts written to entertain and amuse, explain, persuade, argue, and even some kinds of reportage.

Here is the start of a narrative, based on the idea of *Treasure Island*, by a Year 6 pupil:

Treasure Island

Over a 100 years ago, Captain Blackbeard and his fierce crew collected treasure from many different countries. They found a small deserted island, where they buried all their treasure. Overnight, another group of fierce pirates came to the island.

There was a horrible battle, and cowardly Captain Blackbeard hid somewhere secretly. In haste, he drew a map, for if he was ever to go to the island again.

Unfortunately his crew lost the battle and were all thrown into the shark-infested sea, Captain Blackbeard with the map in his pocket...

OVERVIEW OF CATEGORIES OF WRITING			
Categories	Essential Features	Comments	Knowledge, Skills & Understanding Required
1. **Fictional Narrative** Story Recount of Story Play Script	Basic story shape Central characters Action Resolution of situation created Chronological sequence	Lively characters Recognizable setting Possible dramatic use of dialogue Dialogue and stage directions	Imaginative use of experience (either personal or literary) Understanding of story structure and story language Knowledge of script format
2. **Non-fiction Narrative** Biography Autobiography	Account of experiences – 3rd person, impersonal Account of experiences made individual by personal comments, 1st person Generally chronological	Recollections, recount from primary or secondary sources Recollections of own experiences	Differentiate appropriately between 1st and 3rd persons Use past tense appropriately Sequence chronologically
3. **Reportage** News Diaries Reports	Factual, generally non-fiction, though in school may be pretending to be non-fiction Needs to be chronological if reporting an event, a process (eg in a science report)	Either personal or impersonal mode If personal, related as if author were an eyewitness – may have vivid recording, may be writing in role If impersonal, use of 3rd person and passive voice needed Reporting may be selective or biased, or may be designed to persuade	Able to sustain writing in appropriate person and voice throughout Is there flow, sequence and coherence? Awareness of the intended audience important Selection of appropriate vocabulary for purpose

4. **Letters** Personal Formal	Transactional communication, personal, in 1st person, or format; the latter may be in 1st person, or mainly in 1st person with both 1st and 3rd used, and may incorporate use of both active and passive voices.	Personal may include fictional, writing in role, as with diaries, above. Formal letters need to consider the purpose and audience for which they are written – may be for persuasive ends.	Content and style need to relate to purpose and audience Knowledge of conventional format and phraseology needed for formal letters
5. **Description** Chracterization Scene-setting Description of object Classification	Non-narrative Awareness of nature of the subject and degree of detail required Accuracy if description is observational	Ability to focus on aspects of detail which have relevance to the purpose Precise use of vocabulary, including adjectives and sometimes adverbs Use of sensory information	Understanding the effect of precise use of vocabulary and employment of verbs, adverbs and adjectives for effect Subject specific vocabulary Ability to question to self, perception of relationships, differences and similarities
6. **Argument/Discussion** Essay Evaluative report Review	Must have two points of view, or pros and cons These need to be weighed against one another They can be weighed against an initial hypothesis, or one may be generated subsequently A conclusion needs to be drawn: conclusive, inconclusive, or personal opinion, according to content and purpose.	Structure may be a mashalling of points for one side first, and then the other, followed by a conclusion OR A point by point statement relating opposing pairs of pros and cons before arriving at a resolution of some sort	General use of impersonal mode, though opinion, if stated as opinion, may be given in evaluation Clear understanding of main issues Able to represent both sides Able to present a conclusion

7. Persuasive Writing Advertisement Propaganda Inducing empathy	Writing very much adapted to purpose- eg if advert, short zippy slogans may be best, whereas to create empathy in a novel or a letter pleading for a charity may need longer, descriptive passages Use of emotive vocabulary	May be profitably linked to studies of bias and adverts, and also appreciation in novels Identifying the emotive and value-laden words in such passages can heighten awareness	Clear awareness of purpose and intended audience Models studied in reading prior to major attempts Use of verbs, adverbs and adjectives with some precision
8. Instruction and Explanation Instructions (How to...) Explanations	Instructions are chronological in nature, so sequence is important Clear presentation	Economy of words, clear organization, may need bullet points or numbered phrases, sentences or paragraphs	Awareness of reader Clear understanding of content Knowledge of how to structure and organize
9. Labelling Labels Captions Headlines Titles Lists Rotas	Clear succinct message Economy of words	Sentences not always required Punchy phrases for slogans and headlines Correct inclusions for lists and rotas	Understanding of purpose Knowledge of different modes of presentation, eg use of appropriate fonts in ICT
10. Poetry Different forms of poem, eg ballad, Haiku, sonnet, limerick etc	Sense of pattern Sense of breadth of meaning encapsulated within a few words Sense of freshness and originality	Achieved though: ■ Rhythm ■ Cadence ■ Resonance ■ Alliteration ■ Rhyme None of these are alone essential, but all or any may make a contribution Vivid imagery often produced through perceived resemblances Evocative language, may use recalled experiences Personal response oftcn	Understanding of verbal patterning and cadence when text is spoken (May lead to knowledge of stresses, feet, in analysing poetic text for more able at the top of the primary school) Precise use of verbs, adverbs, adjectives Maybe use of simile and metaphor

11. **Poetic Prose**	Same attributes as poetry but looser form, less patterning	Imagery important Precise use of vocabulary for intended effects	Planning and drafting really important here, to achieve intended effects to optimum levels Need to know about metaphor and simile
12. **Study Skills I Note-making** Note-making Selective note-making Note-making for speeches and debates	Above all, needs to be selective Clear Economy of words	Note-making from more than one source aids understanding of selective nature of note-making	Understands use of phrases, shortened words, need for economy and selectivity
13. **Study Skills II Paraphrase and Summary** Précis Summary	Selection of main points	Succinct expression	Prepare with exercises in finding main points, eg using Main Idea Analysis
14. **Study Skills III Review, Analysis and Hypothesis**	As above Suggesting an idea to test or assess Formulating an opinion or conclusion	Careful thought needed Weighing evidence	Able to analyse, list points, generate ideas
15. **Study Skills IV Essays**	May involve characteristics of argument and discussion, or of review	Need to prepare an organized plan, and write to plan, using more flowing, discursive style	Must be familiar with planning and drafting Need to be familiar with argument, discussion or review, according to purpose of essay

Table 7.1 ■ Adapted and extended from 'Categories of Writing' table in *Becoming a Writer*, 1984, KCC.

See the Summary of the Range of Work for Each Term, pages 66–8, given in the National Literacy Strategy: Framework for Teaching, DfEE, 1998, for a varied range of text-types which are subsumed by the above categories, eg diary and journal, which would be within the non-fictional narrative section, and would be autobiography. Also many types are listed in the text column of the technical Working Vocabulary List in the same document, starting on page 69, such as *sequel*, which would be in the fictional narrative section. Some text-types are additionally to be found in the Glossary of the NLS, such as the interesting example of *kenning*, an old Anglo-Saxon bi-word phrase naming an object in a punning mode, sometimes forming a structure for poetry and verse.

Here are excerpts from a version of the story written as a newspaper report by a pupil in the same class. What differences of style are there between reporting and writing the narrative version on page 94?

> *Double Death Trouble!!!*
>
> *Early in the evening of the 27th of April 1781 I went to investigate a shocking incident which happened in the village inn.*
>
> *The curtains were ripped and it seemed a lot of things had been thrown around. It was the work of saboteurs who were in here not long ago. They had been looking for something, ending in 2 peoples' death...*
>
> *Later that evening I spoke to Jim, a teenager who witnessed the incident. He recalls: 'It was quite scary, I think they were looking for something but I don't know what...*

Here is quite a different type of factual report, written by Kyle, in Year 7:

> *A Life in the Day of Kyle*
>
> *At roughly 7.30 am I get up in a pair of shorts and a t shirt. I run downstairs to go and have my breakfast.*
>
> *I run back upstairs and run into my bedroom and get on my dirty shirt, and find my trousers on the floor under my bed. I realise I've put on my really dirty shirt so I have to change really quickly.*
>
> *I have about 3 minutes to get down to the bus stop. I put on my tie but I never get it right so I'm there for about 4 minutes. When I have done my tie it is about 8.40 am and I just get into school on time.*

Discussing reportage, Crowhurst offers a range of interesting ways of presenting reports, to enliven the communication of factual information (Crowhurst, 1993). Children generally find writing non-fiction more difficult and less appealing than fiction, but there is a gender difference here; boys more often prefer factual writing, and its terseness or succinctness, as opposed to the building up at length of descriptions about people, relationships and feelings which become involved in later fiction writing.

After detailing the intention to build a chime frame and beater to make a musical instrument for a Year 5 design technology study, Alex continues:

Materials Needed
I will need a lot of wood for the frame, 9 curtain hooks to hold the pipes up, a toy wheel and a stick to make the beater, a rell of fishing string and a container.

Tools and Equipment
I will need for equipment and tools a drill, a malat, a little screwdriver, a hack saw, a pair of scissors and glue.

Intended method of Construction
I will drill holes in the bits of wood first in half of the pieces... so they can slot in with the others to make a square. Then I will screw the hooks in and tie a bit of fishing string to them. Next I will attached the pipes to the string getting smaller. Then I will put the rice in the container to make a shaker at the end.

Intended Finish
I will paint the base, sides and top of the frame. I will also paint the pipes and spray paint the fishing string and put coulered paper on the container.

The final evaluation mentions that the copper pipes had to be polished instead of painted. Although the method section doesn't detail this, an accompanying diagram shows how the different lengths of copper piping make different notes for the chimes, and each one is measured out in centimetres to the first decimal point, indicating this on the octave plus one range planned.

In a survey of attitudes towards writing at the ages of 11 and 15, done in the eighties by the Assessment of Performance Unit, imaginative writing was the most popular choice at both ages, though slightly less so at 15 than at 11. At both ages, boys showed preferences for factual writing greater than those expressed by girls, while girls more often stated that they were interested in letter writing and poetry. At 15 the same differences were observed, but by and large, the differences between boys and girls had become rather more marked (White, 1986). Findings by HMI about raising boys' achievements in English showed that boys tended to write shorter pieces of text than girls, make less use of school libraries, read less fiction than girls, and were less interested in poetry than girls (QCA, 1998 /081). From this we may conclude that boys need more help with the imaginative and creative genres of writing, while girls need more assistance in writing in more impersonal and succinct ways.

For older children, the use of writing frames is often mentioned in connection with factual writing; they have been found to be helpful, and though overuse is too rigid and inhibitory a technique, they are valuable as initial scaffolding (Bearne, 1995; Beard, 2000; Wray and Lewis, 2001; Lewis and Wray, 1996). They are particularly valuable in helping older pupils with English as an additional language who are at an early stage of acquisition.

Here is an example of a Year 5 pupil who, recently arrived, is only at an early stage of English acquisition, writing a piece for *The Secret Diary of Henry VIII* with the assistance of a writing frame:

> I woke up early today and went for walk around my grand palace. My beautiful second wife, Ann BolEyN joined me in the garden of Henry Court… This afternoon some important ambassadors came to discuss matters from abroad. We had a short meeting afterwards. We listened to some music they played. Music I had written.

He has substituted the wrong word beginning with *H* for *Hampton Court*, but this shows us something about his strategies for the completion of sentences in his frame. He has also not kept his eye on '*Boleyn*' when copying it from the board or elsewhere, but this shows he is moving towards trying to remember spelling patterns for himself. The rest of his insertions are correct and make sense, and the frame enables him to turn in a piece of work which will not look very dissimilar to those of his classmates, which is important for his self-confidence. Compare it with an extract from another pupil's work on the same task in the same class, without using a frame:

> It's a very important day today. We are going to visit my favirite place Hampton Court. Hans Holbein is going to send a picture of me. At Hampton Court we are going to play my favourite sports. I hope there will be lots of food. My wife Anne is coming. I just finished my breakfast. It was a plate of chicken. Hans Holbein is here now. I told him to make me look wise, strong and powerful. He said I already looked like that…

The latter writing, without the frame, has more immediacy and naturalness. Monitoring the language used in writing frames and matching them appropriately to ages and stages is important. Wray and Lewis also make the valuable point that planning needs to take account of development beyond writing frames, to ensure that their use as mere props is not being perpetuated. Perhaps, however, writing frames need to be developed for the more imaginative types of writing, to give boys a better start in these text-types. For boys, too, more awareness on the part of the teacher that they find the personal and decentring aspect more difficult than girls can produce more attention to this issue, with increased modelling and discussion. The same needs to hold good for girls in relation to the factual impersonal mode.

While persuasive writing is often referred to as factual, because it frequently deals with factual data, it does include an emotive element, the persuasion factor, and is not intended as objective writing. It mirrors the recognition of bias in the reading process, in fact. Here is a text-type which includes aspects of two genres, factual reporting of information with emotive opinion. Where there is an obvious transactional value to persuasive writing, as in the creation of blurbs, posters and advertisements, boys may be more interested in this than in the type of persuasive writing of a more emotional nature, dealing with persuasion in narrative, as part of the development of a character in a story, for instance. A good example of the latter was seen in a Year 6 lesson, when pupils had been noting textual references exemplifying the character of Mary in the opening parts of *The Secret Garden*. They were asked to rewrite some short scenes with Mary as an attractive character rather than a sour, introspective one, thus persuading the reader that the heroine was a pleasing personality (Hodgson Burnett, 1994). Sometimes writing in role has persuasive elements, too. To sum up, persuasion involves analytic thinking, and also demands an empathic element. Consider the following two examples, for which close models were seen in school.

Year 3 writing

Dear Pope,

I want to divorce the Queen and get married again to a new wife, and if you won't let me, I'm going to start my own church.

Love,

Henry

Year 6 writing

To our high and mighty sovereign lord and majesty, King Henry,
from his humble and dutiful servant, Sir Richard Pomeroy

My Liege Lord,

I pray you to devote but a moment of your majesty's attention and time to this message, so you may learn of the arrival at the Royal Dockyard of your new master architect of ships, Master Robert Sugg. I make supplication to your majesty and ask you to bestow upon him your good regard, and sufficient monies that he may set in hand the work of building your new warships in the new designs you have commanded.

Your obedient servant, Commander of the Royal Dockyard
Written this day 19th March in the Year of our lord 1541

The prototype of the first was seen in an exercise book, as an exercise in writing in role during a history topic on the Tudors. As an exercise in persuasion, the writer has grasped the very persuasive tool of threat, but the understanding of the writer about the period is limited, evident both in the baldness of the statements and the inappropriate use of language, using it in the way a modern child would speak, including the way of finishing the letter by saying '*Love, Henry*'. The writer is too young and immature to be able to write in role in an appropriate style for the Tudor time-scene, and it would have been better to ask for a simple statement, and if writing in role were to be required, to use a task nearer to the child's level of experience. Writing in role is not a demand for Year 3, in the NLSF, in any case, although letter writing is, and letters using content from other subjects is suggested. Recalling the evacuee letters mentioned already, Year 4 pupils here were able to write in role, and their own language was appropriate.

The prototype of the second example was found on the floor of a school hall, following an open evening, where Year 6 pupils were acting in role as guides to displays of work about the Tudors, including the use of a walk-in 'facsimile' of a Tudor quayside inn. It was written in a flourishing hand, on old wallpaper, with torn and deliberately tea-stained margins, rolled up and tied with a piece of red wool or string. It came from a group of boys who had become very keen on the tactics of the Armada, followed by an interest in a study of Henry's new ship, the *Mary Rose*. They had read some extracts from original accounts of naval warfare in Tudor periods, and could name many of the commanders. This was the spontaneous writing of someone in the group, a secret and personal role-play with his friends. Notice the use of archaic language and forms of address. The writer here has really become involved in imagining himself in the part he would like to play, adopting a subservient and somewhat begging attitude to the king. He can produce suitable expressions and language from his reading, and is able to use both thinking and feeling with adequate maturity in this piece of writing. In this piece, letter writing, writing in role, and the integration of history with English were spontaneously and successfully achieved.

Here is an excerpt of two portions taken from the draft, written in role by a Year 4 pupil, for a Prime Minister's speech to Parliament on the occasion of the victory of the Battle of Trafalgar.

Trafalgar

We are here today to thank those that fought for us in the battle. They have done there duty for us. The familys of our brave men should be very proud of them. The wounded and dead people will be remembered in centurys to come...and the death of Admiral Lord Horatio Nelson. I won't let France or Spain conquer us because I'm British. I love Britain. I proudly announce we are safe.

This has vocabulary and phraseology suitable to the occasion for which this pupil is writing; although it is not consistent in maintaining the style appropriately throughout, the writer has captured some good elements of an oratorial mode which are apt indeed.

Elizabeth, in Year 6, writes a letter from Brighthelmstone, supposedly in the year 1754, while staying at the Old Castle Inn on The Steine, then a very fashionable area to stay for a seaside 'cure'. Her letter format is impeccable and her work well paragraphed. Here are some excerpts from her letter home.

> Dearest Mama,
>
> I know that you will be relieved to discover that I have arrived safely in Brighthelmstone, although I am sorry to say that the journey was not without incident.
>
> Firstly the coach got stuck in the mud, so cattle had to come and pull us out. Next I had to get out of the coach to walk up the hill because these coaches cannot get up the steep hills.
>
> Morning brought my visit to Doctor Richard Russell's house to get my prescription. To my surprise I had to bathe in the sea as well as taking the seawater cure to which a lobster pill was added. Dr. Russell's house is quite close to the sea, so off I went to bathe in the sea.
>
> I had to get changed in a bathing machine; the horses pulled the machine into the sea. Martha Gunn (the queen of dippers) then dipped me in and out of the water which I must add was very cold. The sea water cure was strange but I hope it will make me better... ... ...

Elizabeth's letter evokes the scene for us well. There is an interesting use of the word *cattle*, which in that period was used to indicate both horses and oxen, as well as cows. Judgement needs to be used in setting in-role writing tasks in terms of the cognitive, empathic, and knowledge demands upon the writer.

Poetry, as we have seen, is also a genre which boys find uninteresting, but they can become enthused, if approaches are geared to attract their notice and engage their interest. In these poems, scientific knowledge, derived from science lessons incorporating experiments, is used as the subject matter.

Alex's poem:

> Friction is a force,
>
> Rougher surfaces, more friction,
>
> I can rub my hands together to gain friction,
>
> Can you think of a way to gain more friction?
>
> Together, my hands can keep me warm,
>
> I can skid on the floor,
>
> Oh! My skin is burnt!
>
> Nothing much to worry about, Ouch! Maybe it is!

Lourentina's poem:

Gravity keeps us on the floor

Rain FALLS down without a sound

Apples fall off a tree

Vertical force, it seems to be

Its very strong,

That powerful force

You must know it, its gravity!

Although a very simple device is used to structure these poems by Year 6 pupils, the subject matter is at an appropriately challenging level of understanding, particularly when there is the discipline of encapsulating it into a few small statements. Boys like challenges, though, and are competitive in responding to them, and they also prefer terse and succinct writing, on the whole, to lengthy descriptive or explicative writing. This sort of combination of science and poetry may be a lead-in to having a go at poetry writing, and poetic prose is more likely to be tackled with enthusiasm after some enjoyable experiences with poetry.

Listening to, discussing and reading poems is an essential part of coming to an appreciation of the patterning of language, in different ways, which is at the heart of poetry, together with the appeal to the reader in forms of imagery. Here is a poem written collaboratively by a pair of Year 6 pupils, as an extension in the ballad style of a poem called *The Listeners* by Walter de La Mare, which the class had been studying, showing, for age, a good sense of mood, style, rhythm and word patterning (De La Mare, 1979, in Webb). The first two lines are from the actual poem, and then Katie and Katherine's work continues:

And how the silence surged softly backward,

When the plunging hoofs were gone.

The listeners still felt his presence

As the headless traveller came back;

The horse was tired and weeping

His head was in a sack.

Even though he was present

The forest whistled alone,

The eerie sence crept up on him

As he let out an echoing mone.

The trees waved impatiently

As the house started to shake,

The voice of the headless traveller

Made the lonely listeners wake.

The horse rised his head

To see this awful sight

The listeners had become angry

On this continuous night.

In another Year 6 class, pupils had been studying sonnets, and looking not only at the metrical rhythms involved, and the rhyme patterns, but also at the kind of language used in some of them. Using the number of syllables in a line, to form a pattern, is called **quantitative verse**, and using metrical feet, where the patterns are composed of stressed and unstressed syllables, is termed **accentual verse**. Different patterns of stressed and unstressed syllables form the different types of metrical feet. Some Shakespeare sonnets were in the selection studied by this class, written in a metric form called **iambic pentameter**. Iambic pentameter is five iambic feet (metric feet, in terms of syllable and rhythm, that is), or five feet to a line, *mostly* iambic. An iamb is a foot made up of two syllables, first an unstressed one, and then a stressed one. A sonnet is usually 14 lines, with an end-stop rhyming pattern like a b a b, c d c d, e f e f, g g. It always ends with a rhyming couplet, whatever the pattern of rhymes before, and the couplet is supposed to encapsulate or resolve the thoughts expressed in the major part of the poem.

Shakespeare's *Sonnet XXXIII* starts like this:

Full many a glorious morning have I seen

Flatter the mountain-tops with sovereign eye,

Kissing with golden face the meadows green,

Gilding pale streams with heavenly alchemy;

Following their studies of several sonnets, the class were asked to make a first draft of some lines for a sonnet about springtime, and one boy began to write, slowly but steadily and with much thought, the following lines:

> Slowly the golden orb of sun doth rise
>
> Above the hill where meadows lie in dew,
>
> And slumbering sheep do newly open eyes
>
> On this glad world of spring....

Even for a final draft, he had got the feel of all three aspects, metrical rhythm, rhyme pattern and rather archaic language, very well indeed.

As a useful source book about many different types of poetry, Lennard's *The Poetry Handbook* is valuable (Lennard, 1996). It is not intended as an education book, but will provide the information needed for a comprehensive range of forms. Younger children find attending to both rhythm and rhyme difficult, comments Sandy Brownjohn, giving a detailed account of the thought processes involved in making rhymes (Brownjohn, 1995). In a previous publication she gives a range of word games to use as strategies supporting the development of the ability to rhyme, using the imagination within the game framework (Brownjohn, 1994). Children's poetry, she says, usually tends to employ what she calls '**end-stop rhyming**', and thus children are most familiar with this, but they need to know about other patterns of sound, such as **alliteration**, **assonance** and **consonance**. For older children, oral presentation of their own written poetry is often encouraging, and Ellis includes this aspect in her work on poetry, as well as features of listening to poetry (Ellis, 1995).

Turning to the major category of study skills, both Collins and Barrs have taken the position that writing for learning is just as important as those purposes for writing where writing is intended as communication to others. Collins gives an apt quotation from Perera: 'Writing is not merely a way of recording speech, but a different form of language in its own right which can lead to different forms of thinking.' (Collins, 1998; Perera, 1989.) Some authorities refer to note-taking, while others use the term note-making; Neate suggests that note-taking refers to the activity of taking notes at a meeting or lecture, while note-making is more descriptive of the skill in the context of using notes to study texts or research information (Neate, 2001, in Evans). The importance of the latter is clearly stated by Bristow *et al.*, who emphasize its value in Key Stages 3 and 4 particularly, and point out that it is crucial to note as a priority points or pieces of information which are important and possibly complex. This, they add, is to reduce the memory load (Bristow *et al.*, 1999). They also remind us of the value of using icons, of noting the meanings of unfamiliar words, and of the necessity of writing in phrases rather than full sentences all the time, for efficiency in terms of time. They also advocate a web or flow diagram type of approach, where suitable; this is sometimes referred to as **mind mapping**. Neate provides substantial guidance for beginning note-making with young children, while Moline expands on the use of graphic organizers as forms of planning notes for writing, something that older pupils will find helpful, and which will appeal, too, to boys (Neate, 2001, in Evans; Moline, 2001, in Evans).

Note-making is a selective activity, and this often makes difficulties for children, particularly in the early stages of acquiring the skill, or later when dealing with difficult and complex texts. They tend to start off by writing too much, and too fully, and the temptation is to copy too much of the actual text, rather than summarizing in their own words the main points and most important details. This temptation is more attractive when the notes are being made from only one source, as there is no competition to force a choice for inclusion or elimination. Using multiple sources impels selections to be made, and is therefore a better way of getting children to think carefully about what they will include and what they will leave out. A group of Year 5 children engaged in a topic on the Ancient Egyptians were given the task of making notes from three sources about the procedures used in mummification. The texts provided were from a children's book about the Egyptians, an adult text from a museum guide, and a print-off from the CD ROM. As a subject, mummification held huge appeal, and furthermore as the content was about a procedure, the final product needed to reflect a chronological order. The latter factor, together with the need to discard some of the information where it became redundant, provided a strong structure for the exercise.

Poor organization, due to poor verbal memory, say Bristow *et al.*, is characteristic of students later in the secondary school who have difficulty with essay writing. Organization of information is crucial, and it needs to be taught. Planning, in the form of a written plan to support the content and the detail, tabular and graphic organizers can all help. One useful format is to divide the page into three sections, with the labels 'What I know already', 'What I want to know' and 'What I have found out'; this is based on the ideas of Lewis and Wray, using their Know, Want, Learn (KWL) grid (Wray and Lewis, 1997). Brainstorming can be a useful and galvanic start (Bristow *et al.*, 1999). Patterns can be provided for essay structure, which may be either the type where a logically reasoned thread is followed through from its antecedents to its conclusion, or the discursive type where an argument needs to be presented before coming to a final conclusion.

Cross-Curricular Uses of Some Text-Types

While the NLSF makes it clear that other time must be used for some writing, apart from the Literacy Hour, it is difficult in today's curriculum-crammed timetables for schools to find adequate time for all the additions needed to the basic Literacy Hour, whether in speaking and listening, practising of skills, drama or in actual writing on any basis that allows more than short compositions. There are some strategies which can aid writing in an extended mode, and still utilize shorter sessions to produce the work. Character descriptions and scenarios, even dialogues, can be written on separate occasions, and then plugged into the basic plot of narratives. This allows freshness and originality to come to the fore, with good levels of concentration on the job in hand, without having to keep in mind the picture of the whole conception all the time, reducing the cognitive load. Again, when more detail and elaboration is required of a descriptive sort, pupils can go over their first draft with the intention of inserting adjectives, double adjectives, adverbs, better verbs, metaphors and similes. This also reduces the cognitive load while working out the basic line of the writing, and allows special untrammelled attention to the use of imagery in the writing.

Using **insertions** to apportion time economically as well as to focus separately on different aspects of a composition, reducing cognitive load and maximising attention on elaboration can be done by operating on the following features; some will be insertions of whole paragraphs, others occasional single words:

■ Character descriptions

■ Scenarios

■ Adding adjectives

■ Changing verbs for better verb variety

■ Adding adverbs

■ Using metaphors and similes.

A major way, however, in which time can be saved and utilized for writing is the employment of cross-curricular opportunities, killing two birds with one stone. While using cross-curricular opportunities demands considerable organization on the part of teachers at all ages, it is probably harder to achieve in the secondary school with its different subject specialisms than in the primary school where one teacher takes the class for all or most subjects, but the benefits in time saved and the extent of useful writing opportunities are great. However, this way of working for some of the writing objectives is recommended by both the NLSF for primary schools and the SFTE for Key Stage 3. It is difficult to get started, but planning with colleagues is essential, and in the secondary school, planning with colleagues from the different subject departments. A starting point would be to log the text-types needed for writing for the year group in question, and use these as column headings or sideways-on row prompts. A grid can then be prepared showing the subjects which are likely to utilize writing in certain text-types against the entries for the English requirements. An example is provided as follows, although it does not refer to any specific year group and is merely to display the method:

Starting to make a cross-curricular action plan					
DESCRIPTION Chronological/ non-chronological	REPORT WRITING	LETTERS	BIOGRAPHY and autobiography	ADVERTS (persuasive)	NOTES
Thing, process or event	Report format	Fictional or real	Fictional/real	Fiction/real	For study/ presentation
Geography	Science	History (in role)	History (fact)	PSE	
Science	ICT		History (fictional)	CZ	
DT	Maths	PSE/CZ		GG (eg green issues)	All
Art	DT	GG (eg environmental issues)	Art		subjects
History			Music		
			RE		

Following this stage, the different subject departments need to consider their study topics for the year, and then meet again to search for common meeting points which could be easily and/or effectively co-ordinated. Once time has been taken to plan with colleagues a cross-curricular project or theme, the structure can stay in place for re-use, even over years, so that over time the workload investment is not uneconomic. As long ago as 1989, the National Writing Project was advocating this mode of working, and the report of the team on writing and learning includes some useful examples for subject-integrated writing at Key Stage 3 (NWP, 1989). One such co-ordinated programme of work instances was a study of 'The Plague', carried out in biology, history and English subjects, in the first year of the secondary school. Work included: historical 'newspapers', diaries in historical role, experiments in data-handling using statistics from information about the great plague, posters, charts, notes for pupils' own spoken presentations to the class, maps and other materials. Combinations of writing with stimulus from art or music are perhaps easier to orchestrate, but as boys' interests so often fall within science and technology, the incorporation of some aspects of these subjects within an integrated theme would be very likely to enhance their engagement in writing tasks. Furthermore, evaluative writing could be practised in such subjects, as well as factual reporting, as a run-up towards the demands for this type of skill at GCSE level, in some subjects such as design technology. The opportunities afforded by residential study trips in the secondary school are fertile ground for cross-curricular writing projects.

■ Chapter Summary

1. Sufficient maturity to be able to use empathy is necessary for some writing genres, as well as the cognitive skills needed to organize and structure the work.

2. Different kinds of thought processes are demanded by the different text-types, also, as part of the cognitive effort, including recollection and speculation.

3. Text-types relate to the purposes for the writing, and sometimes incorporate features of more than one genre.

4. Text-types may be first divided into Personal writing, Impersonal writing and Study skills.

5. Children need direct teaching about the features needed for different text-types.

6. Cross-curricular opportunities can facilitate a better use of time and a better application of writing skills across the curriculum.

■ Teacher Activity

Bring two or three pieces of cross-curricular work from your class and share these with your colleagues. (Choose the 'best' pieces!) Together make a simple grid for all your pieces of work under the different subjects and/or start a portfolio of good cross-curricular examples. If you have not yet done any cross-curricular work and you are in a secondary school, talk to a colleague from another department, and try to make an action plan together for just one piece of writing. Or, analyse a chosen poem by rhyme and metric feet; list imagery contained in verbs, adjectives, adverbs, similes, metaphors and onomatopoeia. Write a quick critique and share with colleagues.

For following up further interests

Beard, R., (ed.) (1995) *Rhyme, Reading and Writing*. London: Hodder and Stoughton.

Bristow, J., Cowley, P. and Daines, B. (1999) *Memory and Learning – A Practical Guide For Teachers*. London: David Fulton.

Brownjohn, S. (1980) *Does It Have to Rhyme?* London: Hodder and Stoughton.

Crowhurst, M. (1993) *Writing in the Middle Years*. Markham, Ontario: Pippin Publishing.

Evans, J. (2001) *The Writing Classroom*. London: David Fulton.

Fisher, R. (1999) *First Stories for Thinking*. Oxford: Nash Pollock.

Graham, J. and Kelly, A. (1998) *Writing Under Control*. London: David Fulton.

Lennard, J. (1996) *The Poetry Handbook*. Oxford: Oxford University Press.

Weeks, A. (1992) *Your National Curriculum Planning and Integrated Theme*. London: New Education Press.

8 | Basic Strategies for Extending and Enhancing Self-Generated Writing

■ Sequence, Elaboration, Focus and Enrichment

Composition and review – Sequencing – Elaboration and economy – Focusing – Enrichment and exploration – Chapter summary – Teacher activity

Composition and review

Composing incorporates assembling ideas, shaping them and presenting them, but intimately involved in the shaping process is the concept of review. This is the third of Beard's components of writing: composition, transcription and review (Beard, 2000). Review is not necessarily something you do at the end of a piece of writing, it can be part of restructuring at an earlier point in the writing than the final polishing and proof-reading, and it is integral to the creative process of self-generated writing. Review is re-reading to assess aspects of the text already written, to see if the writing meets the expectations of the task in its purpose and for its audience. It is important to get over to children that it is part of the process of constructing a piece of writing, and not merely correcting spelling and tidying writing, just at the end, to produce a final draft. It needs to be seen as part of the ongoing process of producing a finished or extended piece of writing, unless, of course, the task is to be a one-off piece of writing written in a specified time period. Frank Smith has referred to the latter as 'only-one-chance' writing, as opposed to the kind of writing where draft is allowed (Smith, 1982). Of course, both types are necessary: one-off writing is needed as practice for speeding up, and for practising for tests and examinations, while writing utilizing draft is needed to extend the writer's ability to compose and to express ideas effectively. Editing is an active part of the review process, which itself enables the writer to think carefully about the writing, in a phase of relief from the burden of transcription. Competences for this may differ at different ages and stages, but the pattern of the process remains similar:

■ Planning, including assembling of ideas and planning the structure of the piece

■ Drafting

■ Shaping, including reviewing and re-drafting

■ Presenting.

When preparing to plan, brainstorming is sometimes a useful preparation, although very often this can be part of a joint or shared activity in the preceding phase of a lesson, where the sequence is from teacher input to joint activity and then to independent work, as often is the case in the Literacy Hour. Planning for writing will be less frequent for younger pupils, and the planning will be more skeletal; for instance, to begin with, children cannot cope with thinking about more than 'beginning, middle and end' parts to a story, and Kinmont refers to the need for appropriate sequencing in a story even at the 7 year-old stage (Kinmont, 1990). Later, they are able to write descriptions, set scenes, describe characters, and elaborate plots, and use insertion techniques to enhance their writing.

To aid the writing of extended pieces of narrative, the insertion of characterizations, scenarios and dialogues has already been mentioned, thus elaborating the writing but allowing concentration and focused attention on these descriptive parts without detracting from the thread of the story. At later levels, a draft can be worked through and additions made in terms of adjectives, adverbs and a range of different verbs, even metaphors and similes, to increase the word power for creating imagery, and to improve the cadences of the expression in the sentences. With other text types, different sections can be worked on at different times, if there is not a sufficient time for the length of the intended piece in one session, or if particular attention is needed to specific aspects of the task. For instance, in a discursive task, all the 'pros' could be written up from a list, and then the 'cons', and where there are matching pairs of 'fors' and 'againsts', these can be interwoven later into the argument pattern. In a report of an experiment or survey, it is easy to divide into parts, with the aim and the method beforehand, and the outcome written later. The shaping of the whole, however, needs to spring from a conception of the writing as one piece, with a coherence and cohesiveness that gives this impression, and this is part of the drafting technique too, noticing and eliminating unnecessary portions of writing, or rambling 'off-beam' episodes, as well as enhancing by additions.

To introduce or reinforce the notion of dynamic reviewing and editing, teacher modelling is helpful, especially with younger children. Sparks Linfield discusses her use of it with Year 4 pupils, where she found modelling and discussing revision paid dividends and improved attitudes, especially when marking schemes were discussed and peer evaluation and marking was introduced (Sparks Linfield, 1995, in Bearne). Although with older writers some reviewing is likely to be done independently by the writer, collaborative reviewing is very effective, and is commonly used in many schools at upper Key Stage 2. This may be either in a small group, or using the response partner mode, where suggestions may be made and good points commented on. Pupils generally enjoy this and see its value as a reciprocal activity. Occasionally, the drafts done by some pupils may be discussed by the class, and helpful critiques received. Using collaborative modes makes the writing process seem real to the writers, bringing their sense of audience to the fore. Revision of the writing can still be difficult, however, and sometimes prompts are useful, either at first draft stage or redraft stage. There are three types of prompt that can be used:

- ■ Reminder prompts – 'Don't forget to...'

- ■ Scaffolding prompts – 'Think carefully about...'

- ■ Exemplar prompts – 'Would you like to use any of these ideas?'

There is an example of a reminder for working with a response partner in the Appendix.

What else can be done to help children review and revise their writing? In researching answers to this question with children aged 8 and 10, Chanquoy found that postponed revisions were more effective, both in frequency and depth, than immediate revisions (Chanquoy, 2001). The postponed revisions were done the next day, the immediate revisions in the same session as the original writing. While both groups made revisions to the meanings expressed, the younger group made more surface revisions than the older group, yet the older pupils made more revisions overall. This looks as if meanings are more attended to than transcription errors as pupils mature, and it may be that they make fewer transcription errors anyway. Interpreting the results of this study, the focus on meanings and how they are adapted to reflect the intended expression appears to become more salient with age.

■ Sequencing

Focusing, sequencing, enrichment and exploration are four teaching and learning strategies highlighted two decades ago in an in-service training package for teachers (KCC, 1984). In the light of subsequent concerns about writing, however, these useful ideas will now be explored and updated. Enrichment and exploration will be surveyed under the umbrella term of enrichment, while elaboration and economy will be added as a fourth dimension dealing with expansion and reduction together as opposite dimensions. Since sequencing is probably the strategy for which there is the earliest need, in terms of age of pupils, this will be discussed first.

Sequencing a text is part of its coherence, and coherence is one of the important criteria for evaluating a piece of writing, together with cohesion. The QCA document *Improving Writing at Key Stages 3 and 4* defines coherence as 'the underlying logic and consistency of meaning of a text.' Cohesion is described as 'the underlying grammatical logic and connections within a text, achieved through such functions as the use of pronouns, reference and repetition.' (QCA, 1999/392.) Thus the consistency of the threads of meaning that run through a piece of text are essential to coherence, while the logical connections are the cohesive quality fastening together the ideas expressed.

The ability to place ideas expressed in sentences in an appropriate sequence is probably a function of the cognitive maturity of the child. At the ages of 4, 5 or even 6, children may still be thinking intuitively rather than logically, and may home in on the bits of remembered experiences or stories that appeal or seem salient to them. Events may not be seen as developing, nor may cause and effect necessarily be connected in their view of things. At the approach stage of the skill, and even at the early stages of independent writing, children write down ideas as they come to them, stimulated often by something in the previous sentence, or by a sudden thought. There is no particular plan, and no thoughts of ordering statements in a chronological succession. Consider the following:

> *I liked it at Bodiam castle it had hiy walls and a moat round it. We went on the coach and we took our lunch and on the way we saw a train and I saw people in it. When we got to the castle I went up the tower with Lucy and it was nice. I got a pencil and a rubber in the shop with my pocket munny. The shape of the tower was a square shape and it had kehole windows.*

Help in redrafting from an adult would enable a chronological sequence, putting together the pieces about the tower would also add cohesion to that portion of the writing, starting perhaps with a discussion about what happened first, and then demonstrating how to put it together in a different way. At Key Stage 1, the use of instructional tasks, often done perhaps as a shared writing task, can demonstrate clearly a chronological sequence, such as how to make pancakes, for instance, or clean out the rabbit hutch. Other sequences relating to children's experiences may be talked about and displayed, making a visual impact of sequencing using pictures and paintings, together with labels, such as the class listening walk, monitoring the growth of bulbs, or the life cycle of a butterfly.

Here is a well-sequenced piece of instructional writing, by Rebecca, a Year 6 pupil:

> <u>Dress to Impress</u>
>
> How to: Dress to Impress when you're going to a party.
>
> You will need:
>
> Dress/top & skirt/trousers
>
> Make-up
>
> And a lot of dance knowledge!
>
> Step 1: The day/week before the party:
>
> Practise your dance routines.
>
> Do the first coat of nail varnish and wash your hair. Newly washed hair is very hard to style.
>
> Step 2: Party Day:
>
> Have a long relaxing bath. Afterwards put on body crème and talcum powder. Do your nails and make sure your clothes are ready. Get dressed and style your hair. Apply make-up, but not too over the top (eg.: bright red lipsticks and black eyeshadows are a no-no.) Put on jewellery and wait.
>
> Step 3: the Party:
>
> Enjoy yourself and don't be afraid to mingle.
>
> Have Fun!!!

Discussing sequencing of texts read, and citing poetry, Phinn has pointed out the value of sequencing tasks, where a jumbled series of sentences, lines, or stanzas have to be sorted into a logical order (Phinn, 2001, in Evans). Making sense of prose or poetry texts in this way is a sort of verbal jigsaw puzzle that can be enjoyed. It is most valuable when done collaboratively, for alternative views may be put forward making speakers bring forth justification for their views, aiding the development of reasoning. This sort of task, although actually reading, has a spin-off in terms of the understanding of sequencing in writing, and can be adapted to challenge any age from the start of fluency in reading, whether achieved in Year 2 or Year 3, right up to an adult level. For younger children, it is the sequence of the sentences which will need concentrating on, but for older pupils and students it is the contents of the paragraphs, and in particular the starting and ending sentences of paragraphs as well as their main ideas. This exercise, at paragraph level forces attention upon the shifts of meaning or emphases, and the drift of the piece as a whole: the coherence and cohesion of the text.

Reference has already been made to the cut-and-stick operation for paragraphing work in an appropriate sequence when Year 4 pupils were writing letters in role as evacuees. This is a good way of helping children to come to terms with the part paragraphing plays in organizing and sequencing the stream of ideas and expressions in a piece of writing, because the physical nature of moveable sections means they are able to try out different combinations and see what is best. If ordering is to be left to another session, remembering Chanquoy's findings, then the paper strips could easily be placed in an envelope till the next time. After one or two experiences of doing this, children will be able to take the further step of just numbering their sentences, or indicating with arrows or colour coded marks, how they will join up their sentences differently to make better sense. Untrammelled by trying to think about what goes together at this stage, pupils are able to concentrate on getting ideas down first, and organizing them afterwards.

By Year 6, when paragraphing becomes habitually used by the majority of pupils, the awareness of the unity of meaning encapsulated in a paragraph, and the awareness of the unit of meaning in the thread of the meaning of the whole text, like beads upon a string, become the challenge for the next steps in learning about structure and sequence. These twin aspects are the defining features of paragraphing, and are crucial to a clear understanding of where the text is going and how to get there. These concepts are represented in the links and shifts between paragraphs, and how these are handled and introduced. Such a clear view of the paragraphing concept takes a lot of time and experience to achieve, and will still be developing through the Key Stage 3 years for many, if not most, pupils. Where more mature extended writing is concerned, the chapter becomes a unit to be considered, with the same perspective on a larger scale as that of the paragraph – how are the chapters strung together to carry forward the planned plot or drift of meaning? Finally, the use of cliffhangers and twists in the tail can be looked at; these appeal to writers of all ages, the surprise and often the humour of them, in leading the reader up the garden path for so long before the denouement, is a secret enjoyment for the writer – but, do they hang together with the plot when all is at last revealed, and were there *some* clues at least? Even the twist in the tail has to own relevance and be believable within its context.

In Elizabeth's (Year 6) horror story about a murder she has two twists. Her story starts with this paragraph:

> It's strange because people always thought I was so together, so stable. But then something like this happens and totally blows everything out of proportion. The day started well. There was no dark clouds or weird violin music. Just a strange feeling…

After a sinister chase and being incarcerated in a locked room, it's a struggle to the death between the 'writer' and his opponent:

> 'I'm not going to die today, you are.' I knew immediately what to do. As John approached me, I grabbed a pocket knife I always kept in my shoe. I straightened up to see John moving towards me slowly, the deadly blade clasped in his filthy hand, ready to kill…
>
> Well, that was it. It was done. I killed him. He was dead. The pathetic cry of John's pitiful death gave me strength. My clothes were stained with blood.

With further almost unmentionable horrors the nightmarish adventure continues, until:

> I opened my eyes slowly, my head was pounding. I was in my bed. It was a dream. I relaxed a little. I turned over curiously. I felt damp, kind of squelchy; and what was that weird smell?
>
> There, silhouetted against the light, was the outline of a boy. Not just any boy –
>
> 'John!' I gasped. My eyes glanced towards his right hand. Firmly clasped in his palm was the knife. I slammed my eyes shut. But I could still see his face; still see his eyes flashing evilly.
>
> 'Now it's my turn.'
>
> 'You died, you're not real,' I whispered to myself.
>
> 'You did kill me, but I'm very real.' I felt his cool breath on my face, he raised his knife, 'Not even death can save you from me.' A pain shot through my chest of such I have never felt before. Then nothing…

Elaboration and Economy

While sequencing is important for all categories of writing, in one way or another, elaboration is mostly concerned with the imaginative and creative types of writing. It is not merely the amount of detail, but the kind of detail that allows the reader to visualize the messages intended by the writer. Adding elaborative words or phrases to a partially constructed text reduces the cognitive load of what needs attending to at any one time. These insertions may be different parts of the whole plot or scheme, or they may be descriptive pieces, such as characterizations, scenarios and dialogues. Further, at later stages, work can be gone over by the writer in order to change verbs for more expressive ones, to add adjectives, sometimes by the end of Key Stage 2 or in Key Stage 3, double adjectives and adverbs. In particular at the later levels with older pupils, the use of simile and metaphor can be inserted to pack a real punch.

Simile is used to good purpose in this excerpt by Teresa from a Year 5 prediction exercise; the class have been studying a text about wildlife in the mountain vastnesses, sharing the reading and discussing the text, and now they are asked to prepare their own ending, and to include in the final piece some use of descriptive language and similes and/or metaphors:

> Down, down, down, the owl flew, through the blinding snow – landing unfortunately on what he thought was prey. He dug his talons deep into the wolverine. The animal spun round, burning with anger, hatred bubbling like a potion in a cauldron. The pain – worse than fire, blood absorbed in the snow, like water to a flannel. Carcajou sunk his fangs deep into a defenceless wing. The owl pecked viciously at Carcajou's right eye. He roared with pain. He slashed at the owl, but it was too late, the owl had seen the paw and successfully dodged it. He then risked his life and flew – talons first – into the wolf. He had succeeded, dinner was served!

Here is a 9 year-old using simile extensively in a poetic format, taken from Curtis' ideas about the moon:

> The moon is like a ball of wool
> spinning through our solar system
> untangling itself.
> The moon is silky and white
> making light throughout our galaxy.
> The moon is like a spoon scooping up
> light from the sun.
> The moon is like a marble
> rolling through space.
> The moon is like a gem
> floating around us.

In the factual genres, succinctness is a virtue, but it still has to allow the expression of an adequacy of meaning. Skeletal writing that misses out important parts of the information needed is no good. Although economy may be more valuable in factual writing than in imaginative and creative writing, nevertheless there is often a place in these kinds of writing, too, for some economy. This can be achieved through the clause and phrase structure of sentences, as well as by checking for redundancies, the over-repeated pieces of information. Recall the embedded clause, where a phrase, even sometimes as small as a couple of words, actually represents a whole dependent clause, and the clause, of course, is a reduction from a sentence, which might previously have been a separate sentence or a part of a compound sentence. The formation of subordinate clauses is a first step to economy of expression through structure, and the use of embedded clauses as phrases is a second step. While children naturally use these formations in their spoken language, and gradually replicate them spontaneously in their writing, a conscious awareness of clause and phrase structure is difficult to reach, and must come later than the unconscious usage.

By Year 6, however, pupils are able to grasp the concept of forming subordinate clauses from separate simple and/or compound sentences to make complex sentences, and to begin playing around with the placing of such subordinate clauses for maximum effect as well as for economy. The use of a subordinate clause to begin a sentence, as we have already seen, can have impact. Even more impact may be produced if an embedded clause is used, and children need to study phrases to be aware of these embedded clauses. The value and impact of such constructions comes from the economy of expression in terms of words used, whilst retaining the most powerful words, in terms of imagery and/or meanings. Finally, phrases, and even clauses, can sometimes be represented by one word, an adjective or an adverb:

> *Paint a picture and make it beautiful. Paint a picture so it's beautiful. Paint a beautiful picture.*
>
> *Present your work and arrange it in a table. Present your work in a table. Present your work tabularly.*

Economy and elaboration are two sides of the same coin in this respect, where impact is desired, for packing a punch, the use of expressions that maximize meaning or imagery, and minimize the more colourless 'carrier' words which would normally structure the others into a sentence.

Hayley is in Year 6. Her poetic description of stained glass shows economy in the use of words, but elaboration in the choices she has made to produce vivid imagery recalling thoughts and feelings:

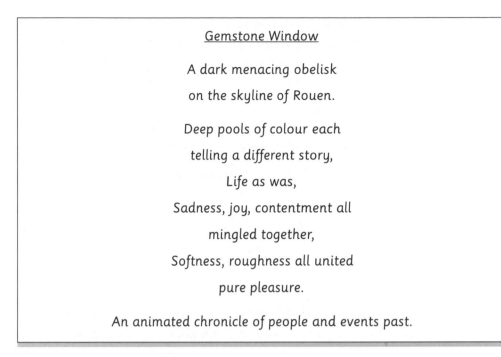

Gemstone Window

A dark menacing obelisk

on the skyline of Rouen.

Deep pools of colour each

telling a different story,

Life as was,

Sadness, joy, contentment all

mingled together,

Softness, roughness all united

pure pleasure.

An animated chronicle of people and events past.

In a way, Hayley is also focusing sharply on one object: the cathedral window.

■ Focusing

The notion of focusing is to do with the noticing and recording of detail with precision, setting down sufficient observational information to represent effectively an object, a creature, or a person. Michael Rosen has called attention to the use of an object as a helpful stimulus for writing (Rosen, 1998). The focusing strategy is particularly devoted to describing a single item; it is narrowing down the scope of the vision, but expanding the acuity of the perception, rather like looking through a microscope. This may, in the face of an unfamiliar subject, or a familiar one photographed from an unusual angle, include speculation as to an object's function, or a person's activities, for instance. Things like a plant, a mechanism such as a clock, an antique artefact, a pet, a real person, or an imaginary person such as a witch or an ogre, for instance, make good targets for focusing tasks.

Sometimes comparing a couple of variants of the same kind of thing may be a help in bringing the focus down to very minute detail: try comparing two potatoes (mainly shape differences, probably), two apples (mainly colour differences, probably), two leaves (shape, texture, colour, size), or two sea-shells (shape, texture, colour, size, and sound if you put them to your ear). What do the potatoes remind you of? If they are unusually shaped ones, they may be evocative of something else, eg a tortoise, an egg, a baby's bottle. Further, a collection of items used for a class topic may yield rich opportunities for a selection of items which could be written about in a focusing exercise, with pupils selecting their own object to describe. A collection of model boats, for instance, could be stimulating, or even something as mundane as a collection of shoes including Wellingtons, ballet shoes, trainers, brogues, high heels, old winkle pickers, plimsolls, jellies and sandals. What would you wear these for, do you think? Listening to each other's descriptions can be fun.

The skills practised in focusing tasks will come into play for insertions, and for writing in general, where description is called for, and will gradually be transferred to the general writing skill repertoire.

Here is a Year 2 child describing her teacher:

> Ginger beard, blue eyes, ginger hair, black glasses, and sometimes he even sticks half his tongue out. Orange shirt. Black and grey jacket keeps fiddling with his pen black trousers with silver buttons on. Gold round ring freckles ginger whiskers

This is well focused, but lacks appropriate sequencing. Another Year 2 pupil comments on a brass rubbing brought in by the teacher:

> Sir Roger de Trumpington died in 1289 and died with his pet dog at his feet Sir Roger de Trumpington went to the east to fight in the crusades on his left foot he has got a spur to keep his horse going fast Miss X brought him he has got a chain By the side of him His shield has six crosses on it and two trumpets on it too. He is laying on a carpet and his head is laying on a drum his eyes are open he has a surcoat over his chain mail

Two short descriptions also showing focusing follow. Both are by Year 7 pupils: first, Georgia's dog, and then Jon's pizza:

> My Dog
>
> My dog's eyes are the most beautiful. Inkey black with that mischievous glint. Her nose is almost perfectly round and the same colour as her eyes. Most of this adorable face is covered in a browny-Gray fur, as is the rest of her body. It's really rough and wiry to touch. Her ears are perfectly triangular, but quite large for her breed. She has a really scruffy bottle-brush tail, which is constantly wagging. Her stubby legs are covered in a thick hedge of that rock-coloured fur, but her left-hind leg is covered in a lovely golden fur, which is found nowhere else on her body.
>
> My Favourite Food
>
> The hard crunchy crust of golden brown bread and the blood-red tomatoes. On top of all that sat an array of pepperami disks. Hooks of green, scrumptious peppers with brown, pin-like mushrooms. My insides exploded with excitement. MMM!

Notice the use of adjectives in both these examples.

Here is another focused description: the following is a character description written for a 'Wanted' notice as if from the police, produced by Laurie (Year 6) in an extended writing session where vocabulary was discussed and prepared before writing:

> We are looking for Michael Pink. On the 21st of August 1999, he allegedly broke into a house, setting it alight, killing a ten year old girl and her Mother, who was 35. he was last seen wearing a big backpack, dirty blue jeans, sandals and a long green T-shirt which doesn't match the jeans. On the jeans and T-shirt it looks like there are holes that have been burnt away by fire. That could just be holes from where he dropped cigarettes. He has long grey hair, a beard, and is of slim build. If you see him, please call the police before approaching him for he is said to be armed and dangerous. The police are offering a reward of £200 if you find him. He was last seen in the area of Hastings. If you have any information please call 01424...

Lucy, in Year 6, wrote a poetic description of a scene she had seen on a walk in a wood, as part of a writing project called 'Messages to the Future'. It begins:

> Saw poppies swaying in the half-wild fields
>
> Took photographs of ruined rusty cars
>
> Puddles of paint forming slowly on the ground
>
> And a crane came to take the cars away
>
> Underfoot glass smothered the ground
>
> Litter sprayed all around
>
> Spectacular views surround.

Enrichment and Exploration

The idea of enrichment includes that of exploration, the latter being perhaps a more active, searching form of enrichment. Enrichment may come from reading and text study experiences, from listening to stories and novels, from the enjoyment of poetry, from using the library to read and to browse, from video and CD ROM, and from hearing about the writing of others in the class. Or it may come from sources generally external to the classroom such as author or poet visits to school to read their work or conduct workshops, or visits by pupils to museums, art galleries and other places of interest. The residential visits enjoyed by some year groups which may include explorations of geographical or scientific interest are all part of enrichment experiences. Finally, topic work or an integrated theme within the work of the class, but often linked with 'external' experiences, has an important part to play in stimulating writing of good quality at every stage. Themed input as stimulus for writing poetry has been explored by Rosen, and Bristow *et al.* have pointed out that remembering is better when information is presented in an outstanding or even a bizarre way, and this is patently the case, reminding us that for outstanding writing, we need outstanding input (Rosen, 1998; Bristow *et al.*, 1999).

Input may be in terms of understanding, or of information, or it may be visual, or enactive. When a class topic or theme combines all these aspects and is exciting to pupils, then the best writing will result. An important aspect of such a topical or themed experience is the way experiences are presented and sequenced. Time is part of this aspect, since time is needed for ideas and information to sink in, to become internalised, reinforced, retrieved and re-remembered. Recall again Chanquoy's research: recalling work anew seems to facilitate the thinking and learning process (Chanquoy, 2001). The first part of the input needs to be some direct exposition on the part of the teacher, and perhaps some reading aloud of relevant texts, followed by some independent research studies on the part of the pupils, note-making perhaps. Next in the sequence there needs to be some active experience, people to visit the school and speak, present information, give a workshop, the fieldwork opportunities, visits to sites, museums and so on. Following this, art, design and technology techniques enhance the learning. While painting, drawing, or making models, study-focused talk will ensue between pupils about their various creations and representations. This is not an adjunct to the work, it is an integral and valuable part, since doing and making, with visible and concrete means, helps to create better defined memories of the information through remembered images, while the talk and conversation reinforces and deepens the impressions already received. A thoroughly explored theme may be built up over several weeks, while other smaller topics can be shorter. Finally, the writing should come at the end, and after reading about the topic or aspects of it from several sources.

Of course, this kind of build-up to enrich writing would be impossible to utilize every time a piece of writing is needed, but it is an occasional luxury which can be planned into the programme, for the production of the best work, enriched, and deepened by the experiences and the levels of understanding. Remember the Year 6 boys playing at being at the Tudor court of Henry VIII? That spontaneous piece of writing, a throw away gesture almost, was the product of an enriched topic, which engaged the imagination. The sequence for this kind of special enrichment follows.

A sequence for enrichment through a topic approach

1. Direct teacher input – introduction.

2. Shared reading – background information.

3. Independent reading and note-making – greater depth of information.

4. Experience/activity – enriching knowledge and understanding at first hand.

5. Representations through art, design, technology (active reinforcement).

6. Conversations while producing representations (active reinforcement).

7. Final writing – expression of ideas.

Such an approach, involving as it does the integration of different subjects, can be more easily planned in the primary school, but it is harder in the secondary school with separate subject teachers. However, the use of integrated cross-curricular theme work, like the example of the work on The Great Plague, can be achieved sometimes, with the spadework of pre-planning carefully with colleagues from different subject departments. In another example, in Key Stage 3, cross-curricular work took place very successfully within a week of celebration of multicultural heritage, including music, dance, drama and food technology with pupils writing reviews about aspects which had interested them most. Again, a residential visit to Exmoor proved fertile ground for secondary cross-curricular studies, incorporating with English the subjects of geography, history, information and communication technology, and physical activity, giving rise to writing in a wide range of text-types. A night walk and exploration of places related to haunting events of the past were highlights of this visit. Hannah, in Year 8, describes the moor as a geographical feature, a habitat, and an experience:

A Prose Description of Exmoor

Exmoor is lonely, secluded and remote. If you stand still and listen, all you can hear is the sound of whistling wind, streams trickling down the hillside and maybe an animal roaming the vast space. If you close your eyes you worry what will face you when you open them again, and as you walk, your eyes water, your hands become numb and shivers run down your spine in the cold, desolate surroundings. It is mostly uninhabited but the few that live there like to keep themselves to themselves. They know the moor like no-one else does and they know the secrets that it keeps, as do the trees that rustle in the breeze, the rivers, the rocks and the creatures. They won't tell you though, because some secrets are to be kept and not told. We will never know what the moor hides, what it knows that we don't. Not all elements of the moor are lonely. Some have historical meaning and attract tourists, but a lot of the moor, no-one knows exists. We haven't seen every dale, every hill, every spring but they are all there, watching us.

Moors may seem bland, boring and have a lack of life, but if you look closely, you will see that they are beautiful, mysterious, exquisite and magnificent. The new life in spring, the lush green of summer, the crisp leaves in Autumn and the skeleton trees of winter all form different pictures in our minds. Exmoor is full of life and activity if we look beyond the obvious.

Years 5 and 6 in a village primary school went to Wales on a residential visit, where they enjoyed their activities, including some walking in the hills where they observed waterfalls cascading down from the ridges into the wooded valleys. Back at school, there was much discussion about the waterfalls, after looking at photographs pupils had taken of them, and a great deal of conversation about how to express evocatively the children's ideas and thoughts. The experience certainly made an impression, and from their own descriptions they made many poems of good quality. Here is Beth's (Year 6) poem:

> _From rain to rage_
>
> As morning casts its pale light across the horizon,
> As the darkness becomes distinct,
> As the world becomes conscious, once more,
> A smooth sound becomes faint to the ear.
>
> Casting a magical appearance upon the Earth,
> Intruding the peaceful calm,
> Steering its way through its path.
> Meandering. Slowly. Gently.
>
> Gathering speed, overtaking time,
> Tearing with a streak of fury,
> Rampaging like an angry bull,
> Running and launching off his rails.
>
> Rebellious against the tranquillity of the earth,
> Breaking through its skin,
> Revenge from the bottom of his heart,
> Upset from deep within.
>
> The world shall take notice of his glory,
> He shall make the world cry out in shame!
> Until he makes the fact clear,
> He will be noticed.
>
> Shadows creeping through the clouds,
> Night has drawn its curtain.
> The next morn's events will be different,
> The waterfall has spoken.

It is interesting that she writes personifying the waterfall in parts of her poem.

Art and music can often be starting points for enrichment, and a music lesson for Year 6 in an East End primary school utilized both, together with language, in creating an atmosphere of thought and feeling in which to create some musical compositions. Pupils worked in groups of four, and each group had a very large reproduction print of a well-known painting, each group having a picture from a different school of painting. First they had to discuss among themselves and produce some descriptive phrases about the features in the paintings. Then they had to chat again, and produce some statements about the kind of feelings the pictures engendered in them, capturing the mood of their painting. Following that, they linked mood words with the timbres of various instruments, and began to work on their simple scores. The words and phrases used were thoughtful and reflective, and would have made very good starting points for written work.

In another school, Year 6 visited the Monet exhibition at the Royal Academy, and on their return to school, after discussion and looking at the prints and postcards, and even plastic shopping bags covered with the water lilies they had bought, they began to make some poems.

Michael wrote:

> Capture yourself
>
> In one of his paintings,
>
> Walking in the poppy field,
>
> Standing on the Japanese bridge
>
> Sitting on the bank of the lilly pond.
>
> Looking at the pine tree with the sea behind it,
>
> Walking through his beautiful garden,
>
> Running free.

Gemma also wrote about Monet, after a visit to his garden at Giverny on a Year 6 residential visit to France:

> <u>Out of Sight, Yet the Influences Remain</u>
>
> I materialise to see
>
> What has become of my sanctuary
>
> My inspiration, my tranquil haven,
>
> My home, devoid of me but not of my memories
>
> Invaded by all and sundry,
>
> Probing my pictures, examining my art
>
> I creep across the bridge,
>
> Gazing at what has transformed,
>
> Standing in the middle
>
> Eyes upon the blooms,
>
> Fresh fragrances I breathe into my
>
> Decayed body
>
> Aromas from blood red roses and
>
> Liver coloured poppies.

These examples showing enrichment have all been of poetry or poetic prose, but that is not necessarily the case – enrichment can enhance a variety of different genres and text-types, of course. A study of iron-age life was part of a primary school history programme, and a hut typical of the age, replicating exact methods, was built in the school grounds. This was an exciting project, and most enriching experience. Alex wrote a ghost story which drew on his experiences of archaeology connected with the project. Here is an excerpt from the beginning of his story:

> Archaeologists were digging in their pit. Behind some trees they saw a ghost, with creepy eyes. Chris spotted it first and told everybody, but nobody believed him, as when they looked it had vanished. Despite it disappearing Chris saw the ghost again. Everybody then believed him as they saw it that time. Frightened, everybody looked away and pretended it wasn't there. Ghosts then popped up everywhere, scaring everybody in the pit. Hurrying along, everybody ran away to get away from the ghost.....Kicking stones out of the way, the ghosts started to catch them up. Long arms reached out to the people.....

Emily imagined life as a pot, centuries ago, using a pottery shard as a stimulus. Her story begins:

> I was living in the Bronze age. I was used to stew fruit, meat or vegetables, so that my masters could enjoy a tasty meal. Sometimes they would eat rabbit, sometimes a deer, depending on what they could hunt with their flint spears. My house burnt down through a tragic accident. My master dank too much mead and knocked a burning log against the wooden house. Soon the fire thatch roof was alight...

In a different primary school, Years 5 and 6 had been to visit the local supermarket, and had done some in-depth study about how products were promoted and displayed. As part of their work, in small groups or pairs, they had to create a new (imagined) product, design and produce the packaging in their art lessons, write a text for a presentation to retailers to persuade them to stock the product, and then make their presentation to the class. This is an interesting example of persuasive writing which is the culmination of a topic approach, yet which deals with a factual type of content. Both the packaging and the writing were enhanced by the visit, the discussions and the designing and making of the cartons. The live presentations were done with verve and enjoyment. Here is one text:

> I am here to present to you our new classical cereal, Carob Explosives from that wondrous cereal producer Ructoggs.
>
> Our edible breakfast product is aimed at the age group 5 and up. Survay shows not only is it popular with the age group, adults also recommend the fabouls health aspects of the sugar free, carob tasting cereal.
>
> To add to the mass selling of the product we have included a compotition with the fabulos chance to win a ticket to Alton Towers to stay in one of the lucsurious themed rooms at the Alton Towers Hotel with free admission to the park.
>
> The reason for promoting our product and not others is that ours has exceedingly, wonderful quality and fine texture and not that unplesant powder lurking at the foundation of the box.
>
> I would like to draw to your mind that now even more parents will buy this because the children with alargeys don't need to worry because our product has no sugar, no artifical colours, flavours, additives, preservatives and no chocolate just carob.
>
> All in all you will receive MASS amounts of profit to make your pocket bulge with money.
>
> Thanks for spending some time with me and I hope you will sell my product in your store.

Although the writers of this particular effort have some aberrant spellings and are economical with commas, they have caught the flavour of persuasion in a commercial context well. They have tried hard, and succeeded, in selecting suitable vocabulary to embroider this persuasion.

■ Chapter Summary

1. Review is an essential part of writing and includes editing and redrafting as part of the production process when a special piece of work is to be produced and the writing is not of the 'only-one-chance' variety.

2. Insertion techniques can be used to extend writing, and to relieve the load of thinking about all the parts of the writing at one time.

3. Certain teaching and learning strategies can be used to extend and enhance children's writing. These include:

   ■ Sequencing

   ■ Elaboration and economy

   ■ Focusing

   ■ Enrichment and exploration.

■ Teacher Activity

Try both a focused and an elaborated writing activity with your class; bring two or three of the best examples of each to share with your colleagues. Discuss the context for the writing, and tell each other some details of the input given to the children before they began to write.

For following up further interests

Beard, R. (2000) *Developing Writing 3–13*. London: Hodder and Stoughton.

Bearne, E. (1995) *Greater Expectations – Children Reading Writing*. London: Cassell.

Evans, J. (ed.) (2001) *The Writing Classroom – Aspects of Writing and the Primary Child*. London: David Fulton.

Rosen, M. (1998) *Did I Hear you Write?* Nottingham: Five Leaves Publications.

9 | Using Reading to Enhance Writing

■ Novel News

Higher level reading skills – Cloze procedure – Prediction and sequencing – Characterization and scene setting – Awareness of bias – Style and form – Summarizing and main idea analysis – Comprehension and the Barrett taxonomy – Approaches to the class novel – Chapter summary – Teacher activity

Higher Level Reading Skills

Reading is part of the enrichment discussed in the last chapter. Kinmont stresses the importance of the interdependence between reading and writing, emphasizing the need for children's literary experiences in developing their awareness of links between the two language modes (Kinmont, 1990). Both listening to stories and reading them for oneself are part of this, but text studies, as in the Literacy Hour, are also vital in learning about different kinds of text and of enjoying literature. Directed activities related to text are sometimes referred to as DARTS; these are often text study activities based on stories, but also can be utilized with non-fiction genres. Stories lead to knowledge of the narrative form, but also provide a basis for other kinds of learning. They help children to understand that the written word is an important medium by which experience can be extended. Reading texts in different forms also enables children to become familiar with a range of text-types, which they can emulate in their own writing.

Greater use of reading can be made to improve writing when reading is more skilled, and therefore more can be done to further the link between the two strands of literacy at Key Stage 2 than at Key Stage 1, and more even at Key Stage 3 than Key Stage 2. However, despite this it is important for the whole staff in a primary school team to share in knowing about the whole progression as a context for each stage, while early forms of some of the higher reading skills can be done orally with younger children, ensuring firm roots for later development. In Key Stage 1, seven main oral approaches can be used to form such roots:

■ Reading to children – the influence of literature, with its capacity for vocabulary extension, its range of grammatical usage, its displaying of story or poetic forms and its imparting of stylistic features, is crucial.

■ Asking children to give a resumé of what they have read, or stopping to ask them to make a prediction extends their thinking about texts and their contents. In group prediction situations, it can be demonstrated that more than one idea is possible, encouraging imagination and originality.

■ Asking questions about the texts children have just read.

■ Oral cloze activities from reading or talking to children.

■ Teacher's silly talk – a quick activity to fill the odd minute – children have to spot the oddities, eg things in the wrong order, like 'I put on my shoes, and then my socks...' (an idea taken from Gahagan and Gahagan, 1970).

■ Sharing big books, and then following this with shared writing, using simple sentences and sentence completion tasks.

■ Group reading – involving discussion of happenings, explanations of vocabulary, looking at spelling patterns, identifying punctuation, modelling expressive reading and responses to print and punctuation, and the use of different 'voices' to represent roles in dialogue.

Other approaches to story and reading, not necessarily limited to use in Key Stage 1, include the use of story aprons or capes by teachers and storytellers, where small items, notes or labels are hidden in a multiplicity of little pockets. Pupils may choose something from these which acts as a stimulus or motif for storytelling, such as a bean for *Jack and the Beanstalk*, a toy snake for Kipling's *Just So Story* about the *Elephant's Child*, or even a brightly coloured plastic fish to select *Deep Trouble* in the *Goosebumps* series by R.L. Stine (Kipling, 1994; Stine, 1994). Ingenuity can vary the range for selection from time to time and according to age. Story sacks are another idea, where children can borrow to take home a bag containing a fiction book to share or read, a toy or game connected to the story, and a non-fiction book on a related theme. The inclusion of the toy or game is a brilliant notion, since it is liable to stimulate speaking and listening too (NSP for Storysacks, website, see Bibliography p. 201).

Fluent reading may be used in a variety of ways, integrating both reading and writing and enhancing both. This can develop awareness of vocabulary use, grammatical structure, organization and style. Until fluency is reached, however, and the watershed is passed, the cognitive load involved in operating upon text is too much, as a general rule, especially in unsupported work or using unfamiliar texts. Once children attain Level 3 in their reading, they can begin to devote some of their working memory capacity to thinking about the meanings of a text and operating upon it, and this ability grows as more working memory capacity is released by the advancing rapidity of automation in reading. However, the matching of the level of the text to be worked on is still important, since with difficult texts even fluent readers tend to revert to low gear decoding. Remember the levels of reading accuracy proposed by Betts referred to in Chapter 5 (Betts, 1957). This is especially relevant, perhaps, in Years 3 and 4, and with less able pupils in the upper Key Stage 2 years, while at higher levels of ability in Key Stages 2 and 3 the avid and expert reader uses vocabulary, phraseology, style and aspects of plot spontaneously, to form the shape and style of independent and original writing. The value of the general reading background and the literary diet in contributing to learning to write cannot be stressed too much.

However, there are some specific skills in the repertoire of higher reading skills, for pupils at intermediate and higher stages of reading, that are particularly pertinent to the stimulation of aspects of writing, and these, over time, come to enhance independent writing skills. Some of these promote closer looks at vocabulary, others support the growth of understanding of structure and sequence in texts, including the cohesive aspect of paragraphing as well as the shifts involved between paragraphs, support the development of deduction and reasoning in using language, or aid study skills. Among the higher reading skills to be examined in this context will be cloze procedure, prediction and sequencing tasks, different types of comprehension exercises, the promotion of awareness of bias, and technique in making summaries.

▪ Cloze Procedure

Cloze procedure was designed to assess the readability of texts, but soon became more used for the assessment of children's comprehension of passages of text (Taylor, 1953; Southgate *et al.*, 1981). Taylor argued that readers can complete a broken text by apprehending the author's meaning, provided the text is suitable for the competence of the reader (Taylor, 1953). A cloze text is thus a text from which a number of deletions have been made, taxing the thought processes of the reader and focusing on the need to understand meaning accurately, in order to guess the missing word. The idea is based on the notion that skilled readers use context cues to aid their uptake of meaning from the page, both in forward and backward acting ways. It is aimed at both tapping and promoting children's abilities to reason logically in responding to such cues, of both syntactic and semantic types.

There are two main approaches to the deletions in making a cloze text. One is a numerical method, where every 'n'th word is removed, eg every tenth word, or every fifteenth word, say. This means the deletions will be random choices as far as syntactic and semantic representations are concerned. Increasing deletions raises the level of difficulty of the cloze task, and one in eight or one in ten rates of deletion are more common than higher rates, such as one in six. This method is termed regular deletion. The second way is to delete certain categories of words, in order to focus pupils' attention upon a particular kind of word usage, such as deleting every tenth adjective, for instance, if trying to promote children's use of adjectives. This is called specific deletion, and is more versatile than regular deletion. The gap left by the deleted word is usually a standard length of ten letter spaces, since to vary the space length according to the actual word may give the reader a clue which is not particularly apposite to the task, in terms of the search for meaning. Words chosen by the readers in completing a cloze text may often be the ones used by the author in the original text, or they may not be, yet prove to be just as suitable. Provided the words inserted are suitable, there is no 'right or wrong' answer in a cloze text: it is a matter of aptness for the context. This needs to be made clear to pupils, who may come up with several words, or different words from their peers. Spelling should be disregarded in this kind of exercise, since children must not be inhibited from selecting unusual yet appropriate words. Finally, it is better if there is a run-in to the task, with the first sentence, at least, not subject to deletions, and to round off the text, no deletions in the last sentence either.

The most productive way of using cloze procedure is to use a collaborative mode, so that discussion ensues about the suitability of different suggestions, with proponents having to justify their choices to others. This stimulates even more the reasoning element in the task. Small group or pair work is suitable. Hutchcroft, in her seminal book *Making Language Work*, describes how she used to have small groups working on this type of activity in a quiet area, perhaps outside the classroom somewhere, and the children taped for her their conversations as they proceeded with the task, so that later she could tap into this to hear their arguments and reasons for choices (Hutchcroft, 1981).

Here is a text completed by Charlotte and her group, in Year 6, working on their own and coming to an agreement about their insertions; the words substituted by them are underlined:

The Gods

The gods <u>promised</u>. By their word they made heaven and earth and clothed the earth with trees and grass, with all kinds of <u>animals</u> and plants. <u>God</u> made animals to live on the earth. But the animals did not know how to <u>please</u> their maker, <u>they</u> could only howl and hiss and <u>growl</u> and croak and cackle, they could <u>not</u> speak the name of God.

The gods said, <u>because</u> they are not able to praise <u>us</u>, they shall rend each other with tooth and claw and shall feed off each other's <u>flesh</u> for ever.

<u>So</u> the gods took clay and fashioned <u>Man</u> from that. But these men <u>could</u> not move or speak, they were too soft to stand <u>upright</u> or to turn their heads. When the rains fell their <u>bodies</u> melted <u>clay</u> was clay again. So the gods made men from <u>flesh</u> instead, and they moved and danced and spoke and reproduced <u>themselves</u>. But they had no <u>heart</u>, no souls, and not knowing who had created <u>them</u>, did not <u>praise</u> their creators; <u>so</u> even they fell on all <u>fours</u> <u>and</u> walked like beasts.

This text was not regularly deleted, nor was it aimed at one particular part of speech. The deletions appear to be random, but the teacher who created it may have wished to include a range of different syntactic word uses. Charlotte's group have got the gist of the text quite well, but there are one or two substitutions which sound a little odd. They have not maintained the plural *the gods* throughout, and use the singular in two places. Apart from this, however, the syntax of their chosen words is correct. Structure words, in fact, are easier to predict than content words.

Arnold has pointed out strongly that children's knowledge of idiom and convention in spoken language is often called upon in completing cloze texts, and that sometimes younger children have not acquired the necessary familiarity with certain phrases which are second nature to adults. She adds that children under 9 do not always scan very far forwards or backwards, but tend to be triggered by words close by, sometimes resulting in some amusing responses (Arnold, 1982; Southgate, 1983). Many 7 year-olds completed the sequence

'Mr Brown had been carefully nursing a huge...' with the word *baby*, triggered by the verb *nursing*, when only two sentences previously Mr Brown was talking about his vegetable marrow, and the sentence in which the deletion falls continues 'which he intended to enter for the vegetable show'. They generally used the word *put* instead of *pricked* in the sentence 'Paddington pricked up his ears...'

It must be stressed again that cloze procedure, because of the need to look forwards and backwards and consider meanings, should not be used as an unsupported written exercise until fluency is achieved, and the text must be suitable. It should always be used with a focused aim in mind for development, and not merely used indiscriminately as a time-filler.

Prediction and Sequencing

Prediction may be used as an individual activity or done as a group. Where appropriate, the latter mode is very useful, as it engenders discussion and supports reasoned thinking as well as imagination. Both of these, of course, are features of cognitive activity which are needed for improving writing. It is easily done orally. While reading to a class or group, stopping to ask what might happen next and to receive ideas from pupils is a stimulus point for further discussion and the use of questioning techniques to extend reasoning and ideas: 'Why do you think that?' 'Which part of the passage indicated that?' It is also easily done when listening to or sharing reading. With older children, there should be encouragement to refer to the text within answers, as justification for suitable imagined scenarios. As well as oral questioning about prediction, written responses can also be used in this way, such as writing another verse of a poem, or the last part of a story. The purposes of prediction are to facilitate the generation of ideas and to promote the use of reasoning. Here is Katie's prediction for the end of the wolverine story; like Teresa's, which we saw earlier in Chapter 9, it does use imagery as required for the task, though one simile is more apt than the other, but her ending is quite different from Teresa's, showing the originality of both predictions.

> *The owl banked down at the moving object not knowing it was putting its life at risk. He grabbed the thing in his talons struggling to see. He did not know it was Carcajou. A ferocious attack was about to appear out of the sky. The owl sank its talons into Carcajou's coat.*
>
> *Carcajou's fang snapped as he bit into the owl's leg. Pain poured down the owl and he screeched. The owl ripped flesh like tearing paper. The blood poured like larva from a volcano. Then all of a sudden Carcajou lashed with a bleeding and sharp claw and tore the owl's wing, leaving it half-skinned. Then out of all the excitement the owl could not stand it any longer and fell to the ground with one wing half skinned, a bleeding leg and the poor thing was blinded. Carcajou picked up the owl in his fangs and slid away.*

We have already seen the importance of sequencing in writing as a strategy, at sentence and at paragraph levels as well as in the organization of a whole text. Using a text activity to practise sequencing aids this development, promoting the awareness of appropriate ordering of elements of a text, by focusing on thinking about the sequence of a plot, or the logical presentation of information. The activity can be done collaboratively, leading to discussion perhaps, in upper Key Stage 2 and in Key Stage 3, about the unity or shifts or ideas indicated by the paragraphing. The main focus will be on looking at the beginning and ending sentences of each paragraph, to see how they fit together. Use a text from a book, newspaper, or instruction text to make a sequencing task suitable for the age and stage of the readers.

Characterization and Scene Setting

Studying texts together, looking for words used to describe a character, including the verbs used to describe actions and those used to contextualize dialogue, eg screamed, shouted, sniggered, etc, are part of the exploration of these aspects of reading and writing. Use of coloured pens or highlighters is most useful here, and makes for a much speedier exercise than noting all the words. If needed, they can be copied later, or selections made, as necessary. Pupils can also write their own description of a character or a short dialogue, and here the use of response partners working in collaborative mode is again helpful, evaluating each other's suggestions and making contributions. The purposes of such activities are to heighten the awareness of ways to characterize roles, to describe scenarios and to enliven dialogue. Pupils can use simple note-making techniques to record textual references for later compilation of a character study or a scenario.

Here is an example of just such an exercise, done by a Year 6 boy, first using a highlighter to mark the pieces he wanted in the text, and then noting them down for his compilation later. The text was from Dickens' *Oliver Twist* and the pupil has used a bullet point format:

Oliver Twist

The children's food and drink and appearance in the workhouse

- Oliver Twist's Ninth birthday found him a pale and thin child
- Been locked up therein for atrociously presuming to be hungry
- Just a leetle drop, with little cold water, and a lump of sugar
- A piece of bread and butter, lest he should seem too hungry
- All poor people should have the alternative of being starved by a gradual process
- Given three meals of gruel a day
- One or two women ladled the gruel at meal times

■ Awareness of Bias

The use of persuasion in writing has both legitimate and artistic purposes; it includes texts where bias is used, in order to capture the feelings of the reader. Where appreciation of character is an aim, including identification with a main character, and understanding of motives, writing may include emotive language and descriptions of feelings. Advertisement is also an area where the persuasion of the consumer is a specific goal. Zimet looks at the way print and words can be used to create bias or prejudice, and Williams explores the effects of verbal messages and advertisements upon the consumer (Zimet, 1976; Williams, 1977). Where bias is used to persuade, though, an impartial report is not being presented. To drive this important message home to pupils, activities may make use of different reports of the same incident from different sources, eg historically, or a modern incident from different newspapers, to illustrate the different points of view. Reports of a football match can be compared, looking at the local paper's reporting of the home team and one serving the area of the opponents, or a survey of the way three or four newspapers of differing styles carry a prominent story. The use of highlighters or underlining is a quick way of finding the words that carry the persuasion, emotion, or bias. Pupils can follow some activities like this with their own attempts at writing empathically or persuasively. The exciting examples in connection with an advertising project following a visit to the local supermarket have already been described. Another useful type of task is to rewrite a text narrated in the third person from the first person point of view, increasing the sense of empathy. The use and detection of bias and persuasion hinges on the distinction between fact and emotion, thinking and feeling.

■ Style and Form

Text studies may focus on looking at the writing of the same story or report done in different styles, again looking at the vocabulary choices and the grammatical structure used. Writing in different styles is a useful exercise, and Alston includes a useful examination of logical, stylistic and expressive features of writing (Alston, 1995). Pupils need exposure to a variety of texts in different genres and styles to be able to do this; they need to be able to ask themselves questions about texts, in terms of stylistic features that they meet. Stylistic features may include the following:

- Form – as in the appropriate format for a letter, poem, report, or story, the way the writing is organized and set out.

- Syntax – the type of grammatical structure used.

- Vocabulary – subject specific vocabularies, modern, old-fashioned or archaic words, imagery, onomatopoeia and so on.

- Voice – active or passive.

- Person – narrated by first or third person.

Old-fashioned language, stilted language, modern language, dialect and slang are all part of the necessary experience here. Again, in text study, highlighters are useful, and make for ease and speed in identifying the words or phrases that produce the particular character of the piece. Later work can make use of this experience, as in a lesson for a Year 6 class, where Dickens was being studied, and pupils were asked to write a description of the character of Scrooge, using modern terms and leaving out any old-fashioned words. Another lesson, in Year 5, used a similar task, but pupils were rewriting a short paragraph from Jane Austen. Old-fashioned or archaic expressions enliven writing and give it character and period flavour. Pupils enjoy and savour the language in stories of King Arthur's Knights of the Round Table, for instance, just as they enjoy also the modern idiom in books such as *A Very Wicked Headmistress*, by Margaret Mahy.

Look at the language used in this excerpt from *Morte d'Arthur*, Vol. One, by Sir Thomas Malory, who died in 1471:

> After this, Merlin departed from his master and came to King Arthur, that was in the castle of Bedegraine, that was one of the castles that stood in the Forest of Sherwood. And Merlin was so disguised that King Arthur knew him not, for he was all befurred in black sheep skins, and a great pair of boots, and a bow and arrows, in a russet gown, and brought wild geese in his hand, and it was morn after Candlemas day; but King Arthur knew him not. 'Sir,' said Merlin unto the king, 'will ye give me a gift?' 'Wherefore,' said King Arthur, 'should I give thee a gift, churl?' 'Sir,' said Merlin, 'ye were better to give me a gift that is not in your hand than to lose great riches, for here in the same place where the great battle was, is great treasure hid in the earth.' 'Who told thee so, churl?' said Arthur. 'Merlin told me so,' said he. Then Ulfius and Brastias knew him well enough, and smiled. 'Sir,' said these two knights, 'it is Merlin that so speaketh unto you.' Then King Arthur was greatly abashed, and had marvel of Merlin, and so had King Ban and King Bors, and so they had great disport at him.

It is not only vocabulary that is archaic, some syntactic forms are also: '*King Arthur knew him not...*', '*King Arthur...had marvel of Merlin...*'.

Compare the vocabulary and grammatical constructions of that passage with the next, from Margaret Mahy:

> There was a wicked headmistress called Miss Taffeta who ran a select school for girls. She had had a mixed but very adventurous career before she went into education, beginning as an aerial trapeze artist and going on to considerable success as Consuela, the Human Cannonball. She thought nothing of being fired out of a cannon wearing a smile and a bikini, and occasionally, when too much gunpowder was used, only a smile.
>
> (Mahy, 1984)

Pupils can also write about a modern character and place this person in a different time period, even a time-warp, or they may write in role as an historical person – we have already looked at some examples of this and at the disciplines needed to carry it out effectively.

Summarizing and Main Idea Analysis

Summarizing, which includes note-making, is part of the study skills category of writing. Its purposes are the identification and selection of relevant information, and the development through these of the skills of summarization. There are basically three forms of summarization.

■ Single source note-making

■ Selective note-making using more than one source

■ Making a précis or summary.

Where single source note-making is concerned, the tendency is to copy a considerable amount of material. Where more than one source is used, the redundancies have to be ironed out, and this is helpful as it forces attention on the process of selection. Children need to be taught note-making skills, and the point of selectivity needs making strongly. We have already looked at some issues to do with note-making, so these will not be repeated here.

Making a précis or summary is also a very selective process, and most people find this hard until they become used to ways of doing it. The tendency is to write too much, and to write in full sentences, when sometimes bullet points are appropriate. Here is the beginning of some note-making by a Key Stage 3 pupil, summarizing information about AIDS, and using bullet points appositely:

<u>The Hard Facts</u>

■ Aids is a worldwide epidemic of HIV infection that already effects millions of people. Most of these affected carry the Aids virus without developing the full range of symptoms; but all of these people who do develop the full symptoms eventually die.

■ So far, the death toll in the United States and Europe is less than 20,000 – very small when compared with earlier illnesses or viruses such as the plague (the Black death) or the flu epidemic at the end of the First World War, which claimed 20 million victims. But nobody has really counted how many people are dying in Africa, and the virus is spreading rapidly everywhere.

■ Aids can be avoided. It is not very easy to catch...

An interesting way in to the start of understanding the process of selectivity was seen in a Year 4 lesson, where the teacher had prepared a text containing a number of statements, some of which concerned information about the Vikings, a current topic, and others which were fairly obviously irrelevant. Pupils had to sort out those that were about the Vikings, marking these and later copying them out to make a 'summary' about the Vikings. The first example was done in a shared reading episode, to introduce the idea. The teacher planned to continue by giving the class more texts to sort into relevant and irrelevant information, with the latter getting closer to the relevant over time, so that summarizing became more real and less artificial. Pupils were certainly able to do the sorting task they were given using a simple text of ten sentences, of which five were about Viking runes, the subject of the summary, while the others were irrelevant statements intermingled with these. Among the latter, to be eliminated, were sentences about bones at the butcher's shop, and where to find writing materials when shopping today.

Another idea for learning how to make a summary is called **Main Idea Analysis**. Here, using a pen or highlighter, as each paragraph is studied, the sentence within it which most reflects the meaning of the paragraph as a whole is identified. Later, these sentences are copied out to make a neat précis. To begin with, much discussion is needed about the **kernel sentences**, and the process is best carried out as a shared activity, modelled at first by the teacher and then done collaboratively. As a later enhancement, once the précis is achieved, the question can be asked as to whether there is any piece of really vital information that has been missed by this method, and any such item can then be added, irrelevancies deleted and sentences conjoined to make a seamless representation.

Here is part of a text from a historical source, SRA Text Blue 2C/15, designed for schools, about the Great Fire of London:

> <u>The summer of 1666 was a hot and dry one for England</u>. There had been no rain for months. The great town of London lay gasping under hot blue skies. The River Thames, which flows through the city, was quite low. People slept with their windows wide open at night. But the air that came into their wooden houses was hot.
>
> About two o'clock on the morning of September 2, things got much hotter. <u>A fire broke out in a baker's shop in Pudding Lane near London Bridge</u>. In a few minutes it had spread to all the houses in the lane. In a few hours a large part of London was on fire.
>
> People awoke that day to see great clouds of smoke pouring into the sky. Then they saw the great sheets of fire leaping from house to house. The wood was so dry! <u>The fire moved almost as fast as a person could run.</u>

The sentences underlined were chosen as the most representative of these first three paragraphs. The whole summary ran as follows:

> *The summer of 1666 was a hot and dry one for England. A fire broke out in a baker's shop in Pudding Lane near London Bridge. The fire moved almost as fast as a person could run. A strong east wind made the fire burn even faster. Store houses of oil by the river burst into flame. People were frightened and ran away or went to the river. Some people were nearly burned trying to save their riches. Soldiers made a fire break by destroying some houses. The great fire burned for four days. Finally the greatest fire London had ever seen died out.*

Original text: 420 words approximately; précis: 104 words.

Comprehension and the Barrett Taxonomy

Here we are trying to look at how much the reader understands, and his ability to reflect upon what he has read, but again the comprehension exercise if used well can focus attention on the way ideas and information are expressed. Understanding needs to develop as to how some information is packaged within the text, thus not only reading the lines, but hinting at and providing nuances for making inferences, sometimes called reading *between* the lines. Colley emphasizes the fact that text may include the implicit as well as the explicit, and comments that the intended message of the author may go well beyond that which is the apparent message in terms of its representation in words, at a surface level (Colley, 1987, in Beech and Colley). Comprehension is, therefore, a problem-solving approach to text study, and as such demands dynamic investigative methods on the part of the reader, rather than mere regurgitation.

Oakhill outlines a number of skills involved in comprehension: understanding the structure and the main point of the text, monitoring an ongoing process of comprehension as reading takes place, and the making of inferences (Oakhill, 1995, in Lee and Das Gupta). She goes on to say that comprehension skills do not develop automatically and thus they need to be rehearsed and practised, and discussed. It is important that fluency has been achieved in reading (Level 3) before unsupported written comprehension exercises are given. Working memory is involved in making inferences, and in the ongoing monitoring of comprehension as reading progresses. Bristow *et al.* state that recent research has indicated the crucial involvement of phonological working memory in making inferences. In comprehension, they say, the key element is the ability to manipulate in an active way the spoken words that correspond to the written words of the text, in the verbal working memory (Bristow *et al.*, 1999). Maturity is involved here, with the need for working memory capacity to be sufficient to devote to the reflection on textual meaning, in order to solve the problems posed by the text.

In a controlled experiment using a large sample of 7 year-olds, Latham found that a teaching programme to promote the use of succeeding cues in reading, employing a specifically directed cloze procedure technique, increased such usage. This increased ability would certainly enhance comprehension skills, taking in information later in the sentence or paragraph, to utilize the maximum data available for making sense of the text (Latham, 1983). The same programme also improved textual recall, suggesting increases in the focus upon reading for meaning. Further, recall performance was positively correlated with memory span (Latham, 1983). In another experimental study, with young children, Demont and Gombert found that metalinguistic abilities, including syntactic knowledge, were positively linked to performance in comprehension (Demont and Gombert, 1996).

While early comprehension tasks may involve just the use of literal responses which are within the texts, full comprehension demands more. Children need to be able to pick out ideas, recognize an author's drift, reorganize material, understand cause and effect, make judgements about truth, fiction and opinion, appreciate style and use feeling and empathy to identify with characters. They need to be able to answer thought-provoking questions. Bristow *et al.* suggest that efficiency can be aided in comprehension by encouraging pupils to underline key words, while for pupils with poor verbal memory function they recommend more time being allowed for re-reading, together with the selection of texts with short rather than long sentences (Bristow *et al.*, 1999). This means that the choice of texts in creating comprehension exercises is crucial. *Choosing Texts for the National Literacy Strategy* is helpful for the primary school (Lazim and Ellis, 2000). For the secondary school, texts from prescribed books, plays and poems, together with literature up to adult level, will provide a rich and varied source.

In a QCA report analysing educational resources at Key Stages 2, 3 and 4, in 1997/8, dissatisfaction with commercial materials for comprehension was reported by schools at Key Stage 2, both in terms of exercises integral to general English courses and of free-standing skills materials. Furthermore, at Key Stages 3 and 4, many reading tasks were found to be highly fragmentary and occasionally even trivial (QCA, 1998/247). Although many commercial resources for English do incorporate questions of a problem solving nature in their comprehension tasks, there is sometimes an emphasis on literal comprehension, with only occasional forays into the realms of using inference, organizing material or appreciating style. Some products are better than others, and teachers need to be aware of the range of comprehension types on which such work should be based. Obviously it has to be scaled according to ages and stages, but some types of comprehension question can be used in simple and more elaborate forms. First the text needs to be suitable for the understanding of the readers, and then the questions need to pose appropriate levels of challenge to develop thinking. The Literacy Progress Unit *Reading Between the Lines*, for Key Stage 3, focuses particularly on the making of inferences and predictions in studying text (DfEE, 2001/0476).

Several taxonomies or classifications of types of comprehension question have been formulated. One of these, arranged according to the thinking skills they involve, is the Barrett Taxonomy of Cognitive and Affective Dimensions of Reading Comprehension. Its title reminds us that feeling as well as thinking is once again involved (Barrett, 1967; Barrett, 1972, in Melnik and Merritt). It forms a useful system of classification of comprehension question types, and a good reminder or checklist for assessing the range of skills to be promoted. Naturally the more sophisticated categories (Sections 4 and 5) will not be used with younger children, and it is likely that the whole range is only able to be used with any great awareness by pupils in Key Stage 4, and the more able in Key Stage 3, but there are no hard and fast rules, and pupils at the top of Key Stage 2 will be able to deal with some of the aspects of Sections 4 and 5 if texts are suitable.

THE BARRETT TAXONOMY – SUMMARY OF MAIN CATEGORIES

1. **Literal Comprehension**

   a) Recognition (locate/identify)
      i) of details
      ii) of main ideas
      iii) of sequence
      iv) of comparison
      v) cause/effect relations
      vi) character traits

   b) Recall (i.e. from memory)
      i) of details
      ii) of main ideas
      iii) sequence, etc. as in a) above

2. **Reorganisation**

   a) Classifying
   b) Outlining
   c) Summarising

3. **Inference**

   a) of supporting detail
   b) of main ideas
   c) of sequence
   d) of comparisons (e.g. time, characters)
   e) of cause/effect relations
   f) of character traits
   g) of outcomes (prediction)
   h) of figurative language (interpretation)

4. **Evaluation**

   Judgements of:
   a) reality/fantasy
   b) fact/opinion
   c) adequacy/validity
   d) appropriateness
   e) worth, desirability, acceptability

5. **Appreciation**

   a) Emotional response to content
   b) Identifications with characters or incidents
   c) Reactions to author's use of language
   d) Imagery

Table 9.1 ■ THE BARRETT TAXONOMY
Cognitive and Affective Dimensions of Reading Comprehension
Reproduced by permission of The National Society for the Study of Education, University of Illinois, Chicago, from: Barrett, T.C. (1997) 'A Taxonomy of Cognitive and Affective Dimensions of Reading Comprehension', in Robinson, H.M. (ed.) (1968) 'Innovation and Change in Reading Instruction', *67th Year Book of The National Society for the Study of Education*, 7–29, Chicago: University of Illinois.

For an example of a comprehension exercise based on the Barrett Taxonomy, see 'The Strange White Bird' in the Appendix. For which age group would you think this is most suitable? How easy did you find this task?

■ Approaches to the Class Novel

We have already recognized the importance of reading in general, and the literary diet is particularly important for both reading and writing, needing to be wide, rich and varied. Barrs and Cork emphasize the value of reading aloud (Barrs and Cork, 2001). Reading stories or a short book to younger children on a regular basis is a recognized priority, but how about reading aloud, by the teacher or shared by pupils, at Key Stage 2, or in the secondary school? This has value, and the shared enjoyment and ensuing discussions are a crucial part of this communal experience. The use of a class book in this way can be extended to a spin-off of writing activities, providing further opportunities for enhancing progress in writing. With young children, such writing activities may need to be done in shared writing mode. With older pupils, the opportunities are greater, and there is a wide range of activities which can stem from the study of a book, in terms of speaking and listening or drama activities, themselves able to stimulate writing, as well as written activities too.

In the very first draft of the English National Curriculum for England, but not the version later accepted as the first 'Orders' for the English NC, was a list of activities that could be done as follow-up work to the reading of a shared class book. This was entitled 'Approaches to the Class Novel', and formed a most useful taxonomy of book-related activities (DES, 1988). It contains much useful information about strategies to use and practical activities to extend studies when using a class book as a serial. It disappeared from all subsequent versions of the English NC. However, it is too good a resource to lose, and permission has been granted to reproduce this most comprehensive and interesting list in this book and it is in the Appendix. Like cloze procedure and comprehension, the activities given in the list are suitable for both primary and secondary phases, as the level of challenge depends on the texts chosen and the way the tasks are structured. 'Approaches to the Class Novel' is a valuable tool for teachers.

■ Chapter Summary

1. Once fluency has been achieved, reading can be used to enhance and improve writing.

2. In general, there are strong influences coming from a pupil's reading into the writing.

3. Apart from the general literary influences, though, there are specific strategies related to higher reading skills which can be used to stimulate aspects of progress in writing.

4. These include cloze procedure, prediction and sequencing, looking at characterization and dialogue, and at style and form, using persuasion and detecting bias, and note-making and summarizing.

5. Comprehension skills are also included, and these need to be developed to cover a wide range of categories of comprehension, utilizing reasoning, the ability to reorganize material, the making of inferences, and the employment of empathy in appreciation of a text: thinking and feeling combine in these cognitive functions.

6. 'Approaches to the Class Novel' provides a taxonomy of strategies for extending text study through the use of a shared class book.

■ Teacher Activity

Prepare an adult cloze procedure and an adult prediction exercise, and give them to your colleagues to do, as a collaborative activity. Choose dramatic, interesting or racy texts to make it interesting and/or humorous. What did people find most difficult? Most easy? Now prepare similar exercises for your class.

For following up further interests

Alston, J. (1995) *Assessing and Promoting Writing Skills*. Stafford: NASEN Enterprises.

Barrs, M. and Cork, V. (2001) *The Reader in the Writer – The links between the study of literature and writing development at Key Stage 2*. Centre for Language in Primary Education (London Borough of Southwark).

Hutchcroft, D. M. R. (1981) *Making Language Work – A practical approach for teachers of 5 to 13 year old children*. Maidenhead: McGraw Hill.

Southgate, V., Arnold, H., and Johnson, S. (1981) *Extending Beginning Reading*. London: Heinemann Educational.

10 | Using Speaking and Listening and Drama to Stimulate Writing

■ Dramatic Dynamics

Oral communication and transitivity – Developing speaking and listening at different stages – Storytelling and narrative – Using drama lessons and theatre workshops – Shakespeare projects – Collaborative modes of working – Chapter summary – Teacher activity

Oral Communication and Transitivity

Looking once again at speaking and listening we return to the concept of transitivity, the understanding of the recipients in the communication process, and how effectively this has been transmitted by the originator of the message. If failures in transitivity are only occasional occurrences of non-comprehension of a word, then this is easy to remedy with explanations, examples and repetitions, and even with verbal grafting, using the new word alongside familiar ones. If, however, there are frequent misunderstandings or non-comprehension, more needs to be done, and both rematching of levels of challenge and a careful assessment followed by planning a programme of action to redress the situation as far as possible are required.

Here are three examples of children not knowing certain words during lessons, but they are symptomatic of limited vocabulary range for their ages and flag up the need for extending word use through oral techniques. This would include explanations about vocabulary before and after aspects of lessons where they are likely to occur, in the last two examples:

■ In a Year R class in a school where most children had very deprived backgrounds, both linguistically and experientially, the teacher was making an exciting game of extending children's vocabulary combined with first-hand experience, by taking a series of different vegetables out of a bag. Where there were fruits or vegetables they knew, she had craftily included a couple of specimens so that differences in shape or colour could be discussed as well as the names of the items, and the children were able to handle them all, too. Eventually she drew out of the bag a large field mushroom, rotund and pale, and as she held it by the stalk, a multitude of voices shouted '*beefburger*'. They had never seen or noticed a mushroom before, and thought it was the doughy bun top of an item of fast food, neither had they formed any concept of 'vegetable' which would be exclusive of other foods such as buns and burgers, despite the teacher's efforts to explain about vegetables at the start of the session.

■ In a Year 4 class, the children had been watching a video of a cartoon film showing a simplified version of parts of *Macbeth* in the library area. Returning to the classroom, children were chattering about what they had just seen, and a less able pupil was chanting to himself from the three witches' episode, but his version was '*Bubble, bubble, toilet trouble!*' The word *toil* was completely outside his understanding, yet he had struggled to make sense of the lines in the only way he knew. One can imagine what he thought the outcome of the witches' spell might be!

■ In a Year 6 class, a teacher had a very wide range of attainment to target in her literacy hour. With one or two likely to reach a Level 5 in the forthcoming SATs, and a few expected to achieve Level 4, the bulk of the class were at different stages of Level 3, but about a fifth of the pupils were only operating at Level 2. She had planned the lesson expertly, thinking carefully about what she expected each group of pupils could be expected to learn, and delivered it both sensitively and with good explanations. She made an excellent and dramatic presentation of an excerpt from Dickens' *Great Expectations*, using the passage where the convict leaps out at Pip from among the graves in the churchyard. While every pupil was gripped by the horror of the situation, and enjoyed the excitement, it later transpired that many pupils in the less able groups had no knowledge of what a tombstone or a grave was, or even a churchyard or graveyard. Thus, though these pupils appreciated the situation of the life-threatening onslaught upon Pip, they had no concept of the context of the episode, and were not able fully to visualize the scene.

Speaking and listening is crucial to the development of both strands of literacy, as we have already seen, and so effective development of children's oracy to meet the needs of their learning in literacy is vital and cannot be stressed enough. The range of vocabulary, the use of syntactic structure, the familiarity with idioms and conventional phrases, and the transmission of ideas are all part of this development. To ensure that progress in speaking and listening is given the impetus it needs, the evaluation and planning cycle carried out by teachers is the key mechanism. To back this up securely, a detailed scheme of work for speaking and listening is essential, showing some of the important differences to be expected at different stages, ordered within a developmental sequence. Too often, because the NLSF provides schemes of work for the core work in reading and writing, schemes of work for the areas of English outside the NLSF have been abandoned. Where this has happened, this is a misapprehension, because the NLSF itself points out the importance of these other areas, and most specifically of speaking and listening. Speaking and listening is still the required first strand of English in the National Curriculum for England (DfEE, 1999a).

The NC Level descriptors provide some guidance, but are too far apart to help gauge progress within the year at Key Stage 1 and across the two years expected for average progress between Levels at Key Stage 2 and the years within Key Stage 3. The Centre for Language in Primary Education produces and publishes *The Primary Language Record*, which includes the assessment and recording of talking and listening as well as of reading and writing, together with the related hand-book (Barrs *et al.*, 1988). This provides just one method of assessment among others, and Grugeon *et al.* discuss its usefulness and other ways of evaluating children's progress in speaking and listening (Grugeon *et al.*, 1998). They also give useful tabulations of observable features of talk from Level 1 up to Level 6, including, that is, the expected goals for Key Stage 3, in addition analysing the Level Descriptors from Level 1 to Level 6. The assessment of speaking and listening in the optional Year 4 tests is explored as well (Grugeon *et al.*, 1998).

Developing Speaking and Listening at Different Stages

Clear guidance for developing speaking and listening in the Foundation Stage is provided in the Stepping Stones sections of the Foundation Stage Framework, including attention to the role of adults in this process towards the Early Learning Goals (ELGs) expected for the majority by the end of the reception year (QCA, 2000/587). In the early years, **role-play** needs to be stimulated by provision in the 'pretend corner', using different focuses or themes for imaginary scenarios. These need to be changed to maintain interest and enjoyment, and to fit in with other themed work that is happening. The 'pretend corner' can be a witch's cave, a castle, the Three Bears' cottage, a space ship, a café, a post office, a surgery, a garden centre and so on. Appropriate selections of dressing-up clothes are important to the full extension of this play, which is supportive of co-operative play and thus generative of conversations. The writing table is often placed appositely near by, in the classroom, affording the incorporation of writing with the pretend play, whether pretend or emergent writing.

Questioning techniques, and in particular, open-ended questioning using starting words like *why, when, who, where, how* and *what*, are important at every stage, matching the content of the questions to the age and stage of the pupils. At the Foundation Stage and in Year 1, such questioning to encourage the extension of utterance length is crucial for the development of more complex syntactic structure as a later prerequisite for writing at Level 3 and onwards. 'Show and tell' sessions and the use of plenaries can be exploited in this way, and both shared writing and emergent writing can spring from the stimulus of such talk and play. Grugeon *et al.* have expanded on ways to maximize the use of conversation and speaking and listening games at this stage, and include the use of puppets, and, of course, storytelling activities (Grugeon *et al.*, 1998). Wyse has emphasized the importance of role-play and its links with emergent writing (Wyse, 1998). He includes such items of equipment as telephones, as well, and describes in detail the setting up of writing areas and role-play areas near to one another for this purpose of dovetailing the two types of activity in a variety of ways.

By Year 2, as well as role-play, perhaps rather more specifically stimulated, and story listening, reading and making, simple plays and puppet shows can be part of the scene. Question and answer sequences are more focused, and children take part in a more prolonged way in reporting back in plenaries and in presentation in assemblies. In Year 2, too, children begin to realize the importance of talk for learning, and can pose questions themselves about things they are interested in learning. Encouragement of fluency is important: speaking and listening has application across the whole curriculum.

In the lower years of Key Stage 2, children are able to prepare and give short talks to the class, like one-minute speeches, perhaps on the subject of a hobby or interest of their own, and to field extemporaneously questions about their talk from their classmates. The one or two minutes needed for this can easily be fitted in to an English lesson or other corner of the day, and done on a regular basis so that every child in rotation will get a turn, perhaps once or twice during the year. Preparation for such an activity is often undertaken at home, as part of homework, and involves planning the content, making notes, and checking time for the talk. Tim held everyone spellbound when he described his experiences at camp as a young junior army cadet, and the questions were thick and fast.

By the end of Key Stage 2, and in Key Stage 3, pupils should be able to take part in short debates on suitable topics, preparing their notes for proposing and opposing motions and introducing evidence from others. An effective debate in Year 6 took place as a role-play episode, where participants modelled parts as members of the local council and observing residents, debating an environmental issue about the park versus development of the area for more housing. In another school, Year 6 children were debating a similar issue, and the reports of the debate formed part of a real submission to the council from the pupils of the school. Such activities can lead to a deeper understanding of presenting a written argument, or an essay with two opposing viewpoints.

With older children, too, the device of preparing a radio programme to be taped and played to an audience combines both talk and writing. Questions prepared for interviews need to be written down, and parts of the programme scripted. Taking this further, scripting can be prepared for making creative video, and Parker has explored this in detail, linking it with the cross-curricular project approach as a way of using language for realistic purposes (Parker, 1988, in Maclure *et al.*). He takes a comprehensive look at the process of scripting, which he calls 'from talk to writing and back again', from experiences in working with classes of children at the ages of 8, 10 and 14. While the younger children are often unaware of the need for scripting and prompts in television, since it appears so natural when they watch it, by 14 pupils enjoy the notion of the studio and all it entails.

Exploring talk across the curriculum, Grugeon *et al.* suggest looking at the National Curriculum and highlighting in all subject programmes the places where discussion is referenced (Grugeon *et al.*, 1998). They also describe how children can come to an understanding of talk as a strategy for learning, and grow to value it, through plenty of opportunities for speaking and listening, including carefully planned and organized occasions, and from supportive attitudes which encourage confidence in speaking out and tolerance in listening to others. A whole range of ways of stimulating speaking and listening are listed, including the use of interactive displays, role-play, including 'role-play days' and visiting speakers or performers (Grugeon *et al.*, 1998). Corden also discusses comprehensively ways in which talk can be fostered purposefully, and how this can be used to stimulate writing. He also puts forward the idea of a 'talk audit', to evaluate how talk is used in the classroom, and within the school (Corden, 2000). He places a high value upon exploratory talk, where pupils can be encouraged to take an active part in interactive discourse, and suggests that the most productive kind of talk needs the teacher's ability not only to engage in skilful instruction, but also to develop the skills of listening to pupils and drawing them into a real exchange. He also shows how teacher-pupil conferencing can be used to improve writing.

Where children have restricted range in their linguistic uses, more specific techniques can sometimes help. Following research into language uses with young children, Gahagan and Gahagan developed some games and techniques for supporting the development of a wider range of talk, and in particular, the kind of specific use of vocabulary and syntax which is related to learning and the pedagogical situation (Gahagan and Gahagan, 1970). 'Teacher's silly talk' is related to this kind of usage, where children have to spot the illogicality or wrongly sequenced items. There is also the game where a screen is placed in front of one child, and, having identical items (for instance farm animal models) in an identical arrangement to start with, the other child moves his pieces and describes his moves. The responding child then moves his according to instructions, and at the end they see if the instructions have been sufficiently clear to enable a similar rearrangement. Before the former Inner London Education Authority (ILEA) was dissolved, a set of educational games for promoting just such specific language uses was produced under its aegis. Aimed at several levels, the use of the series was for primary schools, and included the cognitive challenges of comparison, enquiry and elimination of options through reasoning, of description in specific detail, and of discussion and coming to group decisions, where arguments need to be justified and backed up with evidence. These were active modes of learning which children found enjoyable, yet encouraged thinking through exercising and extending speaking and listening skills. Some of these games were based on stories. Although the ILEA publications centre no longer exists, most of these games are still available, having been taken over by another publisher (AMS Educational, 2001). There are a number of commercial resources available for games and activities to stimulate speaking and listening.

Storytelling and Narrative

Harold Rosen reviews studies of story form and analyses some different theoretical approaches to children's understanding and ability to reproduce or contribute to stories (Rosen, 1988, in Maclure *et al.*; Bauman, 1984). He thinks that much of the investigation into narrative tends to ignore naturally occurring narrative, including jokes and story-swapping, plays down oral narrative, and pays little or no attention to multiculturalism in terms of story. He concludes that there is a lack of much needed educational theory of narrative and its concomitant practice. He goes on to examine Bruner's work on narrative and stories, which he believes sets out a radical viewpoint suggesting that narrative is not merely a genre option, but forms one of two types of avenue for mental processes (Bruner, 1986). Bruner contrasts ways of understanding through story with its identification with the experiences of characters, and the structures of story with the alternative mode of reasoning and scientific enquiry. However, as we have seen, stories do include elements of logic and reasoning within them, so the dichotomy is not total. Rosen focuses also on Bruner's comments about cultural influences, but gives his opinion that this aspect was not truly integrated by Bruner into his ideas on narrative, despite his realization of the importance of such inclusion for the educational scene. Rosen proposes a perspective of narrative as including both reproduction and invention, the reception, the telling and the oral tradition, as well as the modifying and creation of stories. In this perspective, the multi-cultural heritage should be an integral part. Stories, he says, must not be restricted to the recitation of time-honoured tales, but need to be challenged, and retold as well, with both teachers and pupils as the storytellers (Rosen, 1988, in Maclure *et al.*).

The ability to listen to and comprehend stories, and to reproduce or produce them, does have a facilitative effect on cognitive processes, and upon personal development, too. Bruner has, after all, shown that the understanding of narrative involves very complex mental activity, and children who engage in listening to or reading stories on a wide scale are greatly enlarging their strategies for grasping meanings, their knowledge and understanding of the world around them and their imaginations (Bruner, 1988; Grugeon *et al.*, 1998). Through identifying with characters, the process of decentring is aided, and children also gain confidence through the fear resolution in many of the stories they experience, with the happy ending after the terrifying adventure. Bettelheim tells us 'The enchanted world of fairy tales, with its princesses and stepmothers, its magic forests and wise old kings, has been an integral part of childhood for hundreds of years. Worn smooth by time, these stories are not only extremely beautiful, but of great help to the child in dealing with the emotional turmoils of his early years.' (Bettelheim, 1977.) Sadness, trouble, terror, and anxiety become formalized in stories, and the meanings of justice, fidelity, love, and courage begin to be sensed, not as lessons, but as discoveries, experiences and pleasures. Stories form a priceless source of aesthetic pleasure and of moral sustenance.

In her exposition of storytelling *Traditional Storytelling in the Primary Classroom* Grainger addresses the planning of storytelling within the curriculum, and shows how stories can be exploited through linked activities as well as through role-play and drama (Grainger, 1997). The drama techniques and conventions she details are comprehensive, and are given clearly with interesting examples. Corden discusses the idea of story-making, and gives a range of ideas which can be used to help children in constructing their own stories, including the use of story frames, ways of using prompts for different features of a story, and the discussion which needs to go alongside these before the story can be produced (Corden, 2000).

■ Using Drama Lessons and Theatre Workshops

Drama lessons form a rich vein of imaginary experiences from which to write. Having imagined a sequence of action by taking part in it or by watching their peers take part, children have more imagery to call upon in terms of plot and content when they come to write. There are two aspects to drama: the first is the process aspect, where children are sharing a significant make-believe experience, and where their capacity for imagination is crucial, and the second is the aspect of performance, where acting and theatre skills are important in the presentation to the audience. From another perspective, pupils' experiences of drama can be seen within two other dimensions, that of creating and performing drama, and the further involvement in appreciating and appraising it. Pupils' achievements in drama need to include the extent to which they are able to accept and be involved in the use of imagination, in creating drama with concentration and conviction, and their ability to respond sensitively to their own work and that of others. They need to be able to develop the use of a range of dramatic skills and techniques, in order to express their ideas and feelings effectively, and to respond to, discuss and recall drama they have seen. Drama can help them to come to terms with the unexpected, and to have increased confidence in negotiating meanings and exploring ideas. Above all, in drama, pupils need to be able to co-operate with others.

While there are no actual Level Descriptors for drama in the English National Curriculum for England, expected goals in drama are given in the lists of expected knowledge and understanding for speaking and listening at each stage. This shows how skills are to be built up from the early role play and simple story-telling through the acting and sustaining of roles, and the devising and scripting of plays at Key Stage 2, to the improvisation of drama including the use of role, devising, scripting and performing of plays, and the reviewing of performance at Key Stages 3 and 4. Parker gives useful strategies for scripting, rehearsing and performing, and points out the complex processes involved in scripting (Parker, 1988, in Maclure *et al.*). However, scripting a play is quite a lengthy process, and culminates in a formal product, whereas mime, or improvisation done as an experience rather than as a performance can be more or less immediate.

Drama allows children to try on other characters, and temporarily step into their shoes, comments Grainger, thus rehearsing for the possibilities life may bring, through the symbolic potential that drama affords (Grainger, 1997). She talks about **storydrama**, the use of tales to support the steps into the world of make-believe that drama provides. In such storydrama, children can plan and question, challenging the ideas in stories, remaking new tales and new texts in the way proposed by Harold Rosen. It is active imagining, extending and transforming through symbolic representations children's understanding. As new tales, new versions and new texts are formed through the dramatic process, says Grainger, a real purpose and audience can be provided for pupils' writing. She shows excitingly how drama can be created from just a fragment of a story, perhaps the opening or even just the ending, and provides a useful list of extension activities for further development of a story both in drama and in writing (Grainger, 1997).

A Year 4 class had listened to the story of *Robin Hood and the Silver Arrow*, and went on to enjoy actively dramatizing it during a hall period. The next day, pupils were asked to write a letter in role about the scenario they had acted out. Here are some extracts from Josiah's first draft, after he had created a mind-map or web to note ideas for his letter.

> Dear Johnathan,
>
> You'll think you're dreaming. It all happened yesterday. I went to the archery contest you know the one everybody has been gabbiling about. I saved up 6 silver pennys amazing aye
>
> Well it was beautiful there were banners of all sizes and coulers...... There were kings huntsmen, kings champion, sherriff's archers and Robin Hood but he was disguised as a smelly, ragged old man. But the king's champion was much different he was posh with purple silk clothes. Robin Hood steped up to the fireuring line he hit the target straight in the middle, everyone cheered but not the king. The king's champion steped up to the fireuring line and he hit the arrow smack bang in the target everyone booed.

In another lesson in Year 5, children were building up a story of space adventure through a series of drama lessons, and creating both roles and community rules for living on another planet. In one episode a visit to earth was about to take place, and the 'space people' were expressing their fears and worries about the forthcoming exploration of the unknown. This was an interesting perspective, and threw up moral issues which were discussed. Group work was part of the drama, and each group discussed their next piece of improvisation and mime with both eagerness and thoughtfulness. Such imaginative development provides a wealth of ideas for the making of a written story, with the richness of shared initiatives.

Watching a play or taking part in a drama workshop provided by a visiting theatre group can be a vital source of inspiration, as can the visiting storyteller, poet, or dance group. In history, visitors dressed in costume and acting in role provide an impact, and in geography speakers from different places can also stimulate children's interest in a similar way. Visiting theatre groups very often involve some or all of the pupils in some aspects of the performance. Frequently the topics of such plays are designed to lead to discussion of important issues, so that speaking and listening is a naturally ensuing extension of the experience. Older pupils are sometimes taken to a local theatre to see a play, and this is an exciting event which will long be remembered. In another Year 5 class, pupils were being asked to discuss with a partner their plans for an imaginary outing, and then to describe the venue and give their reasons why it would be suitable for children. One pair were describing in excellent detail a visit to a theatre, with obvious knowledge of what a theatre is like; one of them had been to *The Lion, the Witch, and the Wardrobe* on the London stage as a Christmas treat, with her parents. She was so enthralled by this experience that she had imparted her enthusiasm to her partner, and it became the focus for this piece of persuasive written work.

Shakespeare Projects

Drama cannot be discussed without the mention of Shakespeare, an important part of the prescribed literary studies in the secondary school, but also the source, usually in simplified versions, of some work in the range of literary studies in Year 6, at the end of the primary phase, as suggested in the NLSF. In Year 6, such studies very often take the form of excerpts from certain parts of a Shakespeare play, or else a simplified story about the main plot and characters. Various versions of simplified stories of the Shakespeare plays exist, but the classic is *Lamb's Tales from Shakespeare*; these can aid studies of plot and characters (Lamb, 1995). In one primary school, Year 6 were studying *Macbeth*, and having enjoyed the story, made their own character studies or descriptions of scenes using quite dramatic language, and finished by presenting them as 'published' versions, using their own bookmaking techniques: covers were impressively eye-catching.

For those in the secondary years, writing becomes part of the repertoire of study skills needed to explore, investigate and get to know a literary text such as a Shakespeare play. Here are some excerpts from work by a secondary pupil studying *Twelfth Night*, showing thumbnail character studies of the main characters and an outline of the main parts of the plot.

> Olivia is a rich countess and loves Viola and later Sebastian. She is rather modest and a beautiful young woman and is one of the main characters in the story. At the end of the story, Olivia and Sebastian get married. Duke Orsino also gets married to Viola (after he has discovered that <u>he</u> is a she!) and the two happy couples have a double wedding.
>
> Sir Toby Belch is one of my favourite characters – and what a funny name! He is full to the brim with tricks especially to play on Malvolio and he enjoys teasing people as well. He is also Olivia's uncle and he finds Malvolio an easy target.
>
> Antonio is very nice, but can take advantage of you. So BEWARE. He is Sebastian's friend and a sea captain. Though I do feel he is taking advantage of Sebastian because he is always wanting money and gets very impatient if he does not get what he wants.

This pupil has a good grasp of the storyline of the play, and is able to describe all the main characters, not just in terms of the obvious characteristic, but also of their personalities, and the way they interact!

Fifield describes how he introduced Shakespeare to a Year 8 class, with many pupils with special educational needs within it, using *Romeo and Juliet* (Fifield, 1995, in Bearne). He also had a pupil with English as an additional language at an early stage, with Turkish as the mother tongue, for whom he was able to find a Turkish translation. He describes how he used a film version of the play, to aid understanding as the plot unfolded. He reports that used to happy endings, the class were shocked at the final denouement, which made a great impression upon them. They enjoyed studying the play, and though they used words simply and with economy, they produced some writing which encapsulated accurately the main events; a version written as a newspaper report really packed a punch!

In the last two or three years an exciting Shakespeare project has been taking place in Swindon, with collaboration in the scheme between many upper Key Stage 2 classes in local primary schools and their local secondary school. Drama has been a key factor in the whole process, culminating in a Shakespeare festival. Some of the pupils involved spoke on a BBC Radio 4 programme about their experiences, with obvious knowledge and understanding, and great enthusiasm. One of the local infant schools also joined in, and produced simple versions of scenes from *Henry V* and *The Tempest*. Using active means of taking part obviously had an effect upon pupils' understanding of the plays at every level, but here is a story with evocative use of words, about part of *The Tempest* by a Key Stage 1 pupil.

Kyra's story – Year 2

> Yellow striking thunder and lightning, Crash went the boat! The waves went thrash as the boat went crash. Rolling waves, broken boat. The storm was frightening. The people on the ship's deck wreck! The prince screamed as he was thrown overboard! The King shouted out his name, Ferdinand! "Papa" called Ferdinand, "I found an island, and I think its really near Tieland!"

Among many other opportunities for promoting studies of Shakespeare's work, Shakespeare's Globe Theatre offers workshops at the theatre, for both Key Stage 2 pupils and higher, starting from the age of 8 and going up to adulthood, on a commercial basis. Schools availing themselves of this service are able to select the play of their choice, pupils are involved, and the workshops specifically adopt a performance perspective. There are special practical SATs study days for Key Stage 3. Teacher courses are also run, and in addition there is a distance learning project on the GlobeLink website, which is password protected (Shakespeare's Globe Theatre, 2001).

■ Collaborative Modes of Working

Collaboration aids attention and perseverance in a task, supports the development of reasoning through discussion and argument, where evidence, reasons and justifications have to be brought forward, and also allows for evaluative comment on a reciprocal basis. Chang and Wells point out the value of peer group interaction, where status is one of virtual equality, yet the teacher-learner interplay can take place within this context, where both participants have a common goal in achieving the task and may change role to mutual benefit (Chang and Wells, 1988, in Maclure *et al.*). Shared understanding as a basis, though, is important. They argue that aspects of the process of becoming literate can take place within speech, when it uses the symbolic functions to aid awareness of thought processes taking place. In other words, the metalinguistic dimension is called into action behind the scenes of speaking and listening. Collaborative talk, they maintain, has the potential to support literate outcomes, either in spoken ways or using speech to produce writing.

Also exploring the relationship between talking and learning, Grugeon *et al.* give some ground rules for group talk, developed from children's own ideas (Grugeon *et al.*, 1998). These include the importance of taking turns and having equal chances to speak, respecting each other's ideas and contributions, and asking each member of the group for their opinions and for reasons backing up their opinions. Grugeon *et al.* have also commented on the rather general nature of the Level Descriptors for speaking and listening in the National Curriculum, as well as their breadth in terms of year groups targeted, making accurate assignment to levels not an easy matter. They provide some useful suggestions for assessing and evaluating progress in this strand of English.

Corden reports that the National Oracy project found gender differences in the patterns of discourse used, which confirms the findings of other research into the kinds of talk that characterize boys and girls (Corden, 2000). Summarizing a range of this research, Corden lists the following generalized differences:

■ Boys talk more and interrupt more, being more aggressive.

■ Girls are generally more tentative, and often defer to the ideas of others.

■ Boys are more challenging.

■ Girls are more consensus seeking.

■ Boys often deviate from the task.

■ Girls more often remain on task and are better at steering the group.

■ Girls use more abstract language than boys.

Corden goes on to provide some ideas for strategies to deal with some of these differences, and to promote collaboration rather than competitiveness. He also lists a number of strategies for paired and small group collaborative working (Corden, 2000). Again, as recommended in a previous chapter, the use of mixed groups and of structured tasks can aid the oral development of both boys and girls in collaborative talk focused on specific purposes.

■ Chapter Summary

1. The notion of transitivity reminds us of the importance of the matching of work level, in speaking and listening, and of the need to support some children in particular in developing their oracy.

2. Because of the way oracy skills support and can inspire and enhance writing, attention to the development of speaking and listening is a priority.

3. Schools need to have a developmentally sequenced scheme of work for speaking and listening.

4. Storytelling, story reading and story making are powerful learning tools, and narrative features are called upon in many writing genres.

5. Drama, in terms of both process and performance drama, including literary drama such as Shakespeare, develops the imagination and pupils' experience of the world around them, and can enhance and inspire writing in a variety of ways.

6. Collaborative modes of talk are valuable learning tools, whether used as small group discussion opportunities, or response partner pairs.

■ Teacher Activity

For young children, read a story, then put appropriate dressing up clothes and props in the pretend corner; note any play arising from the story – does it happen immediately, or is it a few days later? For older pupils, ask some pupils to prepare a one-minute speech on a favourite topic or hobby, and to be prepared to take questions from the class afterwards – how does it go? Discuss the results with your colleagues.

For following up further interests

Corden, R. (2000) *Literacy and Learning Through Talk – Strategies for the Primary Classroom*. Buckingham: The Open University Press.

Bearne, E. (ed.) (1995) *Greater Expectations – Children Reading Writing*. London: Cassell.

Grainger, T. (1997) *Traditional Storytelling – In the Primary Classroom*. Leamington Spa: Scholastic.

Grugeon, E., Hubbard, L., Smith, C. and Dawes, L. (1998) *Teaching Speaking and Listening in the Primary School*. London: David Fulton.

Maclure, M., Phillips, T. and Wilkinson, A. (eds.) (1988) *Oracy Matters*. Buckingham: The Open University Press.

Lamb, C. (1995, modern edition) *Lamb's Tales from Shakespeare*. Penguin Popular Classics, Harmondsworth: Penguin Books.

Epilogue
Improving Writing – An
Overview

■ Advances

Quality, flow and pace: a whole school approach – Bridging the primary/secondary divide – The three main strands of English – Gender and inclusion issues – A summary of pointers for improvement – An overview of writing in the twenty-first century – Summary – Teacher activity

Quality, Flow and Pace: a Whole School Approach

Though schools may wish to pay attention to raising achievement by the end of a key stage, at the top of the primary school, for instance, or at the end of Key Stage 3, standards in general rest on the quality, flow and pace of work through the school, or key stage, as a whole. While some extension and catch-up work can be done to boost performance, this is a short-term perspective which is more limited in what can be achieved, compared to a whole school approach to improvement on a long-term basis. Learning is incremental, and therefore maximum improvement comes from a whole school long-term perspective, although this should not prevent initiatives to extend pupils as much as possible at specific junctures or in later stages. Earlier intervention is likely, at any stage, to be more productive than later intervention, however. Early learning with the implementation of the match, or in other words the apposite use of the ZPD, applied at the best pace possible without failure of learning, will provide for optimum progress.

If work is not matched so that the zone of proximal development is not tapped, then faulty learning and even failure to learn will result. If the pace is too slow, optimum progress will not take place, and if teaching makes the pace too fast, that also is an edifice built for failure. The key to the whole process of the quality, flow and pace of learning is the appropriate use of the **assessment and planning cycle**. While this does need to incorporate formal assessment at certain periodic junctures, including analysis and evaluation of such assessment, it also needs to make use of informal ongoing assessment, on a day to day basis; this does not necessarily mean copious tick-sheets or note-making, but careful observation of the success of strategies used for teaching and learning, and adapting next steps accordingly, whether faster, slower, or the need to recycle work.

While the NLSF has greatly improved teaching and learning in the major strands of English in primary schools, and the whole-class teaching elements are at the core of this improvement, there are situations where the whole class element cannot provide effectively for appropriate matches of learning challenge across a whole class. Where there is not a fairly homogenous level of attainment across the class, and it spans several Levels, providing appropriate challenges for these groups within one whole class session can become a teacher's nightmare. This can happen in small rural schools where there are varied age classes, or in a few other schools with very diverse catchment sectors. In some cases, a Year 6 class may have a range of attainment stretching from Level 2 up to Level 5, with substantial groups at each stage; this is a teaching target range of five or six years in terms of capabilities. Although this situation is rare, it is not a non-occurrence. What has been called the 'one size fits all' text study session will not fulfil the demands of any strategy for optimum learning in these unusual cases. A compromise must be found, with occasional whole-class sessions, but more often using the alternatives of two separate groupings for text study, alternating perhaps between leadership of the teacher and the class assistant under teacher guidance.

Flow and pace are of paramount importance: flow is a useful word to describe the twin concepts of continuity and progression, depending as they do upon the assessment/planning cycle. Because of the incremental nature of learning, the best pace it is possible to maintain with success ensured will produce more and faster learning, and greater achievement. Whole school or whole key stage perspectives are important to flow and pace, as they inform teachers' awareness of the pre-requisites pupils need and the goals they will be progressing towards, outside the confines of their own year group viewpoints. A team outlook with shared understanding of pupils' development through stages of learning will enhance the work of individual teachers by aiding understanding of when to adjust pace, when to revise certain learning, when to introduce new learning of different kinds for best effect, and when to increase challenge for some pupils.

Bridging the Primary/Secondary Divide

The importance for progress in learning of continuity and teamwork brings us to the issue of the division between primary and secondary education. An essential divide, somewhere along the line, for a variety of reasons, but one which needs to be bridged in certain ways, rather than becoming a gulf to be leapt. *Building Bridges* is a document produced by the QCA as guidance and training materials for teachers of Year 6 and Year 7 pupils, and incorporates, as well as moving further on from, two previous publications by The School Curriculum and Assessment Authority (SCAA) in 1996 and 1997, entitled respectively *Promoting Continuity between Key Stages 2 and 3* and *Making effective use of Key Stage 2 assessments at the transfer between Key Stage 2 and Key Stage 3 to support the teaching of pupils in Year 7* (QCA, 1998/144). *Building Bridges* states that while the majority of pupils are well prepared for the primary/secondary transfer, especially in pastoral matters and issues of special educational needs, many pupils do not make the progress expected in Year 7. The document concentrates on ways to improve the common understanding of standards between teachers in Years 6 and 7, to improve the analysis and use of transfer data, and from this, to improve target setting for cohorts and individuals moving into Year 7. Crucial to all this is the meeting of teachers from Years 6 and 7, and the sharing of information about how they see standards, to reach a common understanding. As we have seen, Level Descriptors are not always sufficiently definitive in guiding assessment, and evaluation can be considerably subjective; this area still needs greater interactive agreement, and *Building Bridges* details the way roles and responsibilities of teachers in these two years can bring them closer together in structuring the transfer.

The coming of the Key Stage 3 Strategy for England, in both English and mathematics, is designed to help achieve this smoothness of flow between the two phases of education, and though there are some problems in grafting the new structure onto what are seen as the needs of Key Stage 3, when major glitches are ironed out the strategy will aid this smoothness of flow (DfEE, 2001/0019). The emphasis is on active engagement of pupils, which has always been evident in the best practice, and on supporting pupils to become independent in their learning. It also incorporates more explicit teaching of skills than is sometimes pursued, with more frequent revision of skills for pupils who are insecure in their understanding. Strengthening progression is one of the main basic principles.

The Three Main Strands of English

The three main strands in the subject of English, although often necessarily focused upon separately, are not in actuality discrete, and developments within them are often intertwined and interdependent. We have seen that speaking and listening are first order skills – that is sound symbols standing for meanings, while reading and writing, the obverse and reverse of the same coin, are second order skills – that is shape symbols acting as representations of sound symbols, in turn standing for meanings. Remember also that until overlearned and automated, second order skills carry a heavy cognitive load, and if too laborious, meaning is lost. Writing carries a heavier cognitive load than reading, too, because it is productive rather than receptive, and demands in addition secretarial skills. When mature, reading and writing skills are very fast indeed and the cognitive load lightens, allowing much more attention to meaning, and content becomes more salient. Young children, however, can focus on meaning within their speaking and listening skills and can practise the roots of some of the higher skills which will later be embedded in their reading and writing. At the levels of skills learning, aspects of reading and writing often need to be dealt with as separate subject divisions, but as the apprehension of meaning develops, integration of all three strands takes place virtually spontaneously, and does so particularly in the best teaching practice. Although the focus may be on one strand, the others are also involved to a well-integrated degree, and this is both a most natural and a most fruitful context for the learning of literacy as well as oracy.

In all of this, however, speaking and listening is of prime importance: it is the strand on which the other two depend. We have seen that the use of certain grammatical constructions in reading and writing depend upon their prior presence in children's speech, and therefore in their understanding when they listen as well, so that speaking and listening needs to go ahead of reading and writing. Since the inception of the NSLF schools in England have, understandably, concentrated greatly upon the two strands of literacy, and in some schools, speaking and listening has become de-emphasized. Speaking and listening is still the first strand of English in the NC orders. It is essential for schools to:

- Formulate a thorough and developmentally sequenced scheme of work for speaking and listening.

- Plan for short but regular occasions for speaking and listening tasks to be incorporated into the work of the Literacy Hour.

- Occasionally take time outside the Literacy Hour for specific formal speaking and listening or drama sessions.

- Sharpen assessment in speaking and listening, whether formal or informal.

It is also important to provide enriched input, including story and literature, drama and theatre, stimulus and themed approaches based on active experience.

Gender and Inclusion Issues

From the differences observed between the two genders, and some information about their origins in both brain structure and function and in social influences, we have been able to draw some conclusions about ways to try to reduce the gender gap found in achievement, and to enhance teaching and learning for both boys and girls. Boys will need far more structure in their approaches to writing, and in particular, to their narrative writing. Girls will benefit from being asked to do factual and concise writing, which boys enjoy more. The differences in reading choices need taking into account when using texts, but a balance between them is essential. In speaking and listening, boys will tend to answer more in class, but be less reflective in their answers, while girls tend to give way to the opinions of others more, although when they express their own, they are often very thoughtful. Careful questioning can encourage boys to reflect further, after having had their initial responses accepted, while girls need encouragement to speak their own inner thoughts. In collaborative work, mixed groups do better, since the enthusiasm and competitiveness of boys can be combined with the persistence and more focused approach of girls. This does not always hold good for mixed pairs, however.

Where pupils with English as an additional language are concerned, or those for whom the home cultures have grown from different ethnic minority traditions, care is needed in understanding and respecting those traditions, and how they may affect understanding and learning. Values may be different, and where English is an additional language, the native tongue and/or writing system may focus on different features in ways that contrast with those in English. Use of pupils' own writing systems and bilingual books are a part of celebrating what is valuable to these pupils and their families, and will help them to see the aspects of English literacy and oracy as similar, though with rather differing systems, instead of something alien.

Pupils with special educational needs are also part of the inclusion scene, but although their needs encompass a wide range of aspects of learning, structures and documentation are well in place in most schools to ensure effective support and help. The same priorities relate to the differentiation of work for these pupils as for all others, the importance of the match of work to provide sufficient challenge to draw their learning forward, but with sufficient familiarity from previous learning to ensure success. Success is the watchword here, as it displays that the match has been correct, firmly founded upon the assessment/planning cycle.

A Summary of Pointers for Improvement

Former HMI Graham Frater recently conducted a survey of writing in Key Stage 2, and has made some useful insights from this study (Frater, 2001). Drawing on his evidence, he shows that the schools which were most highly effective in teaching writing were characterized by several features, which may be summarized as follows:

- They gave the highest priority to text level work, using purposes that make sense to pupils.

- Teaching about word and sentence level skills was done in the contexts where it served the purposes of the text level tasks.

- They invited children to write frequently and at length.

- They gave significant time and attention to reading, and the extent to which reading fed into the written work was unusual.

- They read complete texts and whole novels, and also found that traditional tales from varied cultures helped with story structure.

- Lastly, they gave particular attention to the close assessment of pupils' progress in writing and took action as a result, particularly where underachieving boys were concerned.

The above indications add to, or underline strongly, many of the issues explored in this book. Putting these together, a list of ten priorities can be made which will guide schools towards their aims for improvement:

- Staff teamwork, with a shared outlook, over time

- Emphasis on developing speaking and listening, including drama

- Employing collaborative modes of working

- ■ Using opportunities to reduce cognitive load

- ■ Using strategies to maximise the potentials of both genders

- ■ Provision of opportunities for writing frequently and at length

- ■ Emphasis on text level work and meaningful contexts

- ■ Using reading well to influence writing

- ■ Enriching input and providing impact, for quality output

- ■ Improving the ongoing informal assessment/planning cycle and taking early action on the zones of proximal development thus identified for both groups and individuals.

An Overview of Writing in the Twenty-First Century

Reasons for writing have not changed much in essence, from the olden days when writing first emerged, up to our own times today. In the beginning, the market place, administrative and legal needs stimulated the emergence of writing in the Middle East in ancient times, and literary, spiritual and entertainment purposes rapidly developed. Although some of these could be displayed to the public, as in storytelling, the ritual of worship, or the appreciation of drama, communication between ordinary people was not really possible until the production of an alphabet. This allowed an economical level of learning to be invested in acquiring the necessary skills. Even then, literacy did not become widely available until the advent of printing. When this happened, and gradually literacy slowly grew to be virtually universal, all the original purposes for writing were advanced, and became more used on a widespread and often more personal basis. Letter writing and personal reading became the norm.

Today, what purposes do we have which would not fall into the old categories? Certainly there is a multiplicity of records of all kinds, and we might think for instance that medical records are something modern, labels and warnings on products, too. Newspapers proliferate, and also captions on television, but the electronic revolution of information and communication technology is the very big difference. In Britain the electric telegraph, a forerunner of the more sophisticated electronic means of communication of today, was in operation by 1850, enabling the transmission of messages quickly over time and space. Later, the telegraph system was taken to distant parts of what was then the Empire, and later the Commonwealth. When the 'singing line' was installed across Australia from Darwin to Adelaide, messages to Britain suddenly took only three days, instead of the three months needed for a letter to travel by boat. Today, global transmission can be almost instantaneous with e-mail, via satellite. Text-messaging on mobiles is a favourite pastime, even generating national competitions for very short poems, using the abbreviated coding now common for this kind of communication. We have come, some say, from clay-mail to e-mail, from the clay tablet to the electronic message. People are sometimes worried about 'netlingo', and fear that we will lose the ability to enjoy reading or take time to write properly, but reading and writing knowledge is still needed for netlingo, and people still enjoy a good read. For specific writing purposes they will still take time to write appropriately.

When we read what others have written, or write for others to read, we employ a vast range of purposes, some very ancient, and some newer or updated, but some may carry different priorities for us and for our lives. Writing a prescription, a medicine bottle label, an instruction booklet for machinery, or drawing up a legal document are types of writing which can have crucial consequences, one way or another. Making a subject action plan is also an important activity, in terms of the quality of teaching and learning it aims to provide, while a shopping list is a helpful aide-memoire of our domestic requirements. Writing a letter is often recreational, although it can be of crucial importance, too, and doing a crossword can be fun. Surfing the net, e-mailing, down-loading, creating a website, and text-messaging on our mobiles have created amazingly rapid forms of communication, which by their speed lead us to use them in rather different ways, although they may still belong in the broadest sense to the old categories. However, whatever the style of writing or the reason for writing by such rapid electronic means, the communication still depends on the age-old use of the alphabet, which has travelled to us over the millennia, from its dayspring amidst the foreign tongues of the East.

There have been three great leaps forward in time, from that early start, the beginning of writing: first, the arrival of the alphabet, second, the advent of printing, and third, the speed and technology of the electronic age. Hooker (1984) states '...the immense possibilities inherent in each individual's being able to read and write – to transmit and receive information at will – have yet to be exhausted even now, 4,000 years later.'

■ Summary

■ A whole school or whole key stage view is necessary for the smooth flow of progress.

■ Pace of progress depends on the match, with its exploitation of the zone of proximal development.

■ The three main strands of English are interwoven and interdependent, although for skills learning separate aspects may need to be focused on in the early stages.

■ Account needs to be taken of differences in brain structure and function, and of social influences, to cater for both boys and girls in improving writing and reducing the gender gap.

■ Awareness of features of native tongues is essential for teachers of pupils with English as an additional language, and ways of showing respect for the values of ethnic minority traditions and cultures need to be found.

■ Differentiation of tasks is essential for pupils with special educational needs, although the principles of effective teaching and learning are universal.

■ Purposes for writing have hardly changed in many millennia, but accessibility to literacy for all has been a great leap forward and made them more personal, while today the media and electronic transmission have produced amazingly fast communication.

■ Teacher Activity

Survey what you have learned from the book as a whole; what do you think has been the most important learning? Swap these ideas with your colleagues.

Appendix

EMAS (Ethnic Minority Advisory Service): Stages of Fluency in English

This item, showing stages of fluency in English for pupils with English as an additional language, is reproduced by kind permission of the Education Department of the London Borough of Lewisham.

The stages of fluency in English describe the acquisition of English *as an additional language*. These are broken down into five stages that are described below. These stages are intended to help teachers to identify where pupils are in the process of acquiring English as an additional language. This will enable teachers to plan appropriate intervention to help pupils progress to the next stage.

In deciding where on this continuum the EAL pupil is, it is important to remember that *this is in comparison with a monolingual child of a similar age and ability*. Therefore, teachers should consider the English they would expect monolingual pupils in the class to have developed.

Stage 1 'New to English'

- recently arrived from another country
- uses mostly a language other than English
- relies on non-verbal gestures to communicate
- is beginning to imitate language of peers
- may use greetings and short phrases in English.

Stage 2 'Demonstrates a growing command of vocabulary, structures and comprehension in English'

- is beginning to hold conversations with peers
- can understand more than can use
- combines simple phrases eg 'Where book goes?'; 'Put sand box'
- beginning to write simple accounts of activities, stories seen or been involved in *.

Stage 3 'Appears to be orally fluent in informal contexts but has difficulty coping with the academic language demands of the curriculum'

- ■ able to use more complex structures in a variety of situations eg 'We couldn't go because it was raining'

- ■ understands more complex structures in a variety of contexts eg 'What do think will happen if we put the spoon in first?'

- ■ writing shows evidence of a growing command of English grammar, a greater range of tenses, use of appropriate prepositions and a wider range of sentence connectives, eg After that; Finally; Instead of *.

Stage 4 'Confident user of English in most contexts'

- ■ still needs to develop full range of higher order language skills, such as those used in hypothesising, reasoning, presenting an argument, expressing emotions (at the appropriate level according to age)

- ■ able to read most age appropriate texts

- ■ writes with increasing confidence and able to use most structures and tenses. *

Stage 5 'Fully fluent user of English comparable to a monolingual child of a similar age and ability'

* = as appropriate to age and ability

■ A Comprehension Exercise

The text for this exercise has been formed from extracts taken from: *The Strange White Bird*, pp.186–190, in *More Boys and Girls of History*, by Eileen and Rhoda Power, published in 1936 by Cambridge University Press.

Permission has kindly been granted by Cambridge University Press to reproduce it here.

The Strange White Bird

Taniwha awoke later than usual. He rubbed his eyes and sat up. The room was empty. Bare feet were pattering excitedly up and down the verandah and there was a murmur of frightened voices. A woman cried, 'Someone has offended the gods and they are going to punish us!'

Taniwha's heart leapt. The pa, which was usually quietly busy at this time of day, was in confusion. Two or three of the Maori warriors were standing on the lookout platform which towered nearly thirty feet above the roofs of the huts. They were shouting and pointing towards the sea. In the middle of the pa, the chief and some of the most important tribesmen were seated in council.

They looked anxious and had evidently met hurriedly, for the chief, Te Pou, had forgotten his carved staff and had not even put on his head-dress of kiwi feathers, while the others were wearing their common flax mantles instead of the soft feather cloaks which they always wore at a council. Women were talking in groups and some of the girls were crying.

Taniwha ran across the verandah to some of his own friends, who were standing on tiptoe and lifting one another as high as they could. 'What has happened?' he asked. 'What are you looking at?'

All the little boys began to talk at once, pointing and gesticulating in the direction of the sea. 'A flying monster, sent by the gods!' 'A strange bird.' 'Great white wings!' 'A baby bird beside it!' 'So big, perhaps it will eat us.'

Taniwha stretched his neck and stood on tiptoe, but he could not see over the high palisade. 'Come down to the beach.' he cried, and the others followed, running headlong through the pa.

Once through the gate, they quickened their speed and sliding, scrambling, rolling, they stumbled helter-skelter down the cliff to the beach below.

Taniwha shaded his eyes with his hands, 'Oooh!' he gasped, 'its wings are as big as a house. And – it's coming nearer. Hide!' The boys darted behind some rocks, their little black heads peeping cautiously round the sides.

'Eeee! A canoe.' Taniwha popped up from the rock like a rabbit. Then he squealed 'There are goblins in it!' and with a terrified scuttle each dark head ducked down again.

The strange white bird with its little one was now quite close to the shore, but the canoe manned by the goblins was nearer still. Soon they had beached their canoe and were wandering up and down, talking to one another in a hard hissing speech. Taniwha watched them anxiously.

They looked so strange with their ugly three-cornered headdresses and their arms and legs and bodies covered in such an uncomfortable way. Suddenly one of them lifted a staff with a thin end and a thick top and pointed it at a cormorant which was sitting on a rock. There was a quick flash of lightning from the staff, a clap like thunder and the cormorant fell dead.

Screaming 'Goblins! Goblins with a magic stick!' all the little Maoris sprang from behind the rocks, scrambled up the cliff and fled, shrieking into the woods.

Some time passed before they dared to steal from their hiding place and creep home to the pa. Suddenly they stopped short and stared at one another in open-eyed amazement.

There was the Maori chief in his kiwi headdress and his best dog skin mantle lined with the minutest of blue, green and red feathers. There were the tribesmen, some in robes of woven flax with coloured borders and some in rough cloaks and waist mats. There were the women, with their babies slung on their backs, standing in a circle, silently staring. And there were the goblins sitting around a fire with the Maoris, talking, laughing and making the friendliest gestures.

Read the story of 'The Strange White Bird', then answer the questions given below. You may look back over the story when you are answering them.

1. What is the name of the boy in the story?

2. What do you think he looks like?

3. What was the name of the chief?

4. What is the pa?

5. How high was the lookout platform?

6. What was the Maori village like?

7. Why did the boys rush down to the beach?

8. What did the boys think of the strange object out at sea? What did they take it to be?

9. What do you think of the goblins?

10. How did they kill the cormorant?

11. What would you have felt like if you had been watching with Taniwha on the beach?

12. What do you imagine the beach was like? Describe how you see it.

13. Why were the boys surprised when they arrived back at the pa?

14. What were the special things the chief wore at the council?

15. How were the Maoris dressed?

16. What might have happened if the visitors had not been friendly?

17. How might the story end?

18. Where are the events described in the story supposed to take place, do you think?

19. And when?

20. Do you think the incident was fortunate or unfortunate for the Maoris?

21. What was the strange object on the sea with great white wings?

22. Do you think the story might be a true one, or is it imagined?

23. What questions would you like to ask the author?

Write as much or as little as you like to answer the questions.

Approaches to the Class Novel

Formerly published by the Department of Education and Science as Appendix 5 in the *Draft National Curriculum in English* in 1988 and reproduced here with the permission of the Stationery Office.

APPROACHES	METHODOLOGY/EXAMPLES	LEARNING FEATURES
Author's visit	Real visits arranged through 'writers in school' scheme, or imagined as in framing questions to ask the author or in correspondence with author.	Access to a professional writer. Seeing text in the writer's terms, readers communicating directly with writer, with texts as middle ground.
Reading logs	Exercise book or folder containing rough jottings, reflections, personal connections, reviews in relation to books read in class and in private.	Developing personal responses. Valuing the reader's judgements and insights into texts. Providing a cumulative record of reading experiences; developing learner's autonomy.
Cloze	An extract represented with deletions in text in order to focus on author's style and vocabulary. In group/class make suggestions about deleted words by drawing on their understanding of style and language used in text so far.	Highlighting stylistic linguistic features of text, drawing attention to syntax. Encouraging hypothetical/ speculative talk as well as problem-solving activity. Developing reflective awareness of how a text is constructed, encouraging awareness of selection and alternative.
Prediction	Formal: extract is 'cut up' into sections, groups speculate on what's going to happen in next section by reference to text in section before. Informal: breaking the reading in order to invite speculation on where the narrative is going.	Confirming and giving confidence in learner's existing sense of story. Developing logical sequencing skills. Encouraging close reading and awareness of contextual clues, to provide evidence from text.
Active comprehension	Groups frame their own questions about a passage and select key question to explore as a group or to offer to rest of class.	Developing ability to frame appropriate questions. Encouraging readers to adopt an active, interrogative attitude to the text.

Spider diagrams	To map out ideas, further questions – relating to key question, or factors affecting a key event; or relationship between central characters and other characters; or relating events to central theme.	Finding patterns and relationships of meaning in a complete text, drawing attention to structure and form; identifying themes and issues underpinning text.
Maps	Representing journeys or a particular environment – building, street etc. Whole wall maps with room for quotations, pictures, events to be pasted on to form spatial relationships.	Making the text concrete. Visualizing the text. Awareness or structure, developing sense of place. Tracking events. Matching events to places.
Family trees	Particularly when many characters are involved in narrative. 'Tree' may represent blood ties, may have themes to do with who knows who; how people have met; what interests they serve to promote etc.	Aiding the reader. Providing a structure to facilitate reader's progress with text. Holding the structure of the book; looking for relationships in text.
Storyboard for TV/film	Series of drawings representing the way the camera would portray an event or passage from the book – camera angles, close-ups, long shots etc.	Translating from one medium to another, working in familiar forms; selectivity of symbol. Matching images to event. Enabling reader to 'realise' perspective on text.
Advertisers	Promoting the book 'as if' the group were advertisers – choosing what to highlight about the book; target audiences, form of advertising, bookshop posters, jacket illustrations, blurbs etc.	Developing critical awareness. Highlighting concepts of audience, register, writer's intentions etc. Selecting appropriate symbols, images, quotations, 'marketing' literature, providing motivation and sustaining interest.
Illustrators	Working 'as if' illustrators to discuss or execute illustrations of text, jacket covers etc. Emphasis on matching form of illustration to sense of text.	Working as 'experts' rather than as learners. Emphasis on style and atmosphere of text. Selecting events or moments to capture. Justifying and making decisions in relation to how the text should be represented. Close reading.

Casting directors	What sort of actor would have the right 'image' for the character in the book – tall/short; assertive; young; deep-voiced, etc?	'Filling out' characters. Making inferences. Sterotypic/original interpretations. Collective image of how a character would appear. Dwelling on aspects of character.
News	Incidents from the story written as news, front pages with a composite of stories relating to central event. Emphasis on reporting from outside the event; what should be selected as 'news'.	Translating events into familiar forms. Popularising the text. Reporting and journalistic conventions. Creating a distance between characters' perceptions of events and the readers'.
Investigative journalism	In form of a documentary exposing an issue, or presenting an issue that is important in the book – maybe a number of related items drawing on background material beyond that offered in text, public inquiry, expose, etc.	Emphasising issues in book. Relating text to other material dealing with same theme. Presenting, selecting, arranging material. Authorial intention and bias. Airing values, making judgements.
Diaries or journals	Written 'as if' by characters in book reflecting their reactions to events of the narrative. Daily diaries, log of a journey, prison journals or extra instalments for journals and diaries that appear in the story.	'Personalising' the characters and events. Imagining what people and events would be like. As an aid to reflection, filling out the text. Active narrative.
Time line	Representing temporal relationships between events, places, characters etc as a linear sequence. Events in a character's life, frequency and proximity of events within time span of book.	Drawing attention to sequencing and structure. Establishing cause and effect relationships. Providing a framework of book's events for quick reference.
Alternative narrators	In groups, re-telling events from point of view other than that used by author – peripheral characters; third person, first person. Carrying on the retelling in a variety of different registers etc.	Highlighting characterisation. Offering fresh perspectives on story. 'Playing' with text. Demonstrating relationships between viewpoints and attitudes. Emphasising selectivity of style and language in the original form.

Costume/set design	Deciding on how a character, or groups of characters, should be costumed, including personal props. Or how a set should be designed for a particular event or place in the text. Designs discussed, illustrated, made, or written as notes.	Dwelling on aspects of character awareness of descriptive imagery. Making people and places more concrete and immediate. Attention to detail and contextual clues. Establishing a cultural context.
Correspondence	Writing letters from characters to imagined people outside the text, or between characters, or between peripheral characters about behaviour or personality of a central character.	Becoming actively involved with the people and events in text. Demonstrating comprehension of aspects of characters. Commenting on text as a reader but from viewpoint of the characters.
Waxworks/still images/photos	Group work to produce tableaux representing gesture, spatial relationships, body language at a particular moment, or to illustrate a quote; others can guess which moment or line is being presented and why.	Freezing action to allow discussion and reflection on the significance of the selected moment. Allowing a greater variety of forms of communication to represent group's 'meanings' beyond verbal forms. Develops iconic creativity and response.
Alternative chapters	Planning in talk or writing 'missing chapters' that fill out the original or foreground peripheral characters not present in the central events.	Developing sense of alternatives and emphasising role of writer. Matching new material to existing forms in text – vocabulary, syntax, register, conventions etc.
Spring boarding	Fiction is used as a starting point and focus for detailed analysis of an important issue. Fiction compared against factual material relating to the issue, or in comparison with other fiction which has an alternative bias on the issue.	Book used as a starting point for issue-based teaching. Story helps to personalise the issues and allows for effective response to issue. Developing empathy for characters faced with an issue from a different perspective to readers eg disability, race, gender, poverty etc.

Sound tracking	In groups, composing and performing sounds to accompany a sequence of action or to establish a sense of place.	Emphasising descriptive imagery. Matching non-verbal form to sense of text. Developing sense of 'atmosphere' and the 'environment' of the book.
Thought tracking	Creating 'interior speech' for each character at critical moments or in crucial passages of dialogue. Contrasting inner dialogue (what is thought) with other dialogue (what is said).	Encouraging reflective awareness of characters' feelings and thoughts. Recognising characters' relationships with others. Making inferences. Bringing readers into closer more active participation with events and characters. Encouraging readers' insight into character.
Visual interrogation	Drawing introduced as a means of making sense of a problematic passage. Building in image from clues in text. Accurately portraying textual description. Collective drawing. Representing negotiated consensus of how some thing, place, or person would appear.	Using alternative iconic form to gain access to the text. Discovering from others as a result of mutual activity. Matching intuitions and hunches to what's actually represented in the text. Accessible form for less able reader.
Starting in the middle	As a way into book or introduction to new section – a message letter or fragment of text is presented and group asked to build speculations as to meaning, context, consequence.	Motivating readers' interest prior to reading of whole text. Encouraging intuitive speculation about narrative, characters, style. Extending range of possibilities offered by text. Looking for clues, problem-solving activity.
Cultural contexts	Reconstructing and inferring a broader cultural context for characters or events, type of housing, likely occupations, cultural pursuits, class/gender attitudes – how far are the events and characters socially constructed? How would a change of cultural context affect the effects?	Identifying social and cultural pressures and influences on characters and events. Identifying cultural and social assumptions underpinning book. Identifying authorial bias, purpose and intention. Filling out the world of the book. Testing credibility of book's context, examining stereotype and social cliché.

Meeting/courts	Improvised re-enactments of crucial meeting in story, or imagined meetings to deal with issues or events in story, or as post-mortem to events or to establish motivations. Consequences as in court case.	Bringing readers into active participation with text. Examining pressures and conflicts affecting decisions in book. Examining cause and effect relationships.
Hot-seating	Individually, or collectively, taking on role of a character to answer questions posed by rest of group, who may also have a role, eg detectives, scientists, etc.	Highlighting character's motivation and personality disposition. Encouraging insights. Making readers participants in the action. Encouraging reflective awareness.

■ Example of Writing Partner Help Card

Writer:	Read your work to your partner.
Partner:	Listen carefully.
Together:	Say your favourite parts.
	Does the writing make sense?
	And say what you want it to say? Are some words repeated a lot?
	Can you make any improvements with better words or phrases?
	Could the beginning or ending be improved?

Reproduced by permission of Our Lady of Lourdes Catholic Primary School, Rottingdean.

| Glossary

Accelerated learning Ensuring optimum progress for all pupils, especially through thinking skills.

Accentual verse Use of stressed and unstressed syllables to form metrical feet.

Alliteration Word patterning using the same initial sound; adjacent words beginning with the same phoneme.

Alphabetic To do with or from the alphabet, or in the order of the alphabet.

Aphasia Inability to speak or disorder of speech function.

Appreciative reading Reading with awareness of author's intentions and devices used to pursue these – usually at Level 6 of the National Curriculum for England or above.

Articulatory loop A verbal feedback system in models of working memory.

Assessment and planning cycle Using assessment to guide and adjust the content of subsequent planning, then to access assessment again after implementation of planning.

Associative structure In children's writing each sentence is generated by association with the previous sentence, usually characteristic of Level 2 in the National Curriculum for England.

Assonance Repetition of vowel sounds in words.

Automation, automatization (alternative forms of the term) Indicating skill tasks performed almost without awareness, such as expert reading and writing skills.

Basic connectives Words, in general basic use, that join clauses, such as *while, so, so that, because, when, where, that, which, who.*

Bias Distortion in viewpoint – prejudice, or persuasion – may be intended, as in advertising or propaganda or persuasive writing.

Bi-syllabic Describes words of two syllables.

Blend Two or more phonemes fused together.

Blending Fusing phonemes into clusters, syllables and words.

Central executive The mechanism in overall control within working memory.

Cerebral cortex The surface layers of grey matter of the hemispheres of the brain.

Chaining In chained sentences each sentence is linked to, or formed from, ideas in the previous sentence, as in associative writing.

Characterization Description of a character or a character's attributes.

Clause A distinct part of a sentence containing a verb – can be main or subsidiary.

Cloze procedure An exercise using a text with deletions to be completed by pupils, by focusing on meanings.

Coarticulation Refers to difficulties in pronouncing isolated sounds with accuracy when they are not in words.

Coherence The underlying logic and consistency of meaning of a text.

Cohesion The underlying grammatical logic and links within a text.

Collaborative writing The production of a piece of writing by more than one person, working together.

Communicative writing Writing of text at the level where the writer is aware of the reader and tries to communicate with the reader, usually at level 5 and above, in the National Curriculum for England.

Complex sentence A sentence made up of a main clause and subsidiary clauses, sometimes called dependent clauses.

Composition The setting down of ideas to form a text.

Comprehension A level of understanding of text, for example literal, inferential, evaluative.

Compound sentence Two or more main clauses joined by simple conjunctions like *and* and *but*.

Conjunctions Words that join clauses or connect words within the same phrase.

Connectionism A theory of learning based on connections.

Connectives Conjunctions and relative words joining clauses together – include conjunctions, adverbs, pronouns and prepositional words and phrases.

Consonance In agreement.

Co-operative play Playing together to achieve a shared goal.

Corpus callosum A band of matter joining the two halves of the brain – allows sharing of information between the hemispheres.

Criterion-referenced tests Tests with a selected level of difficulty designed without reference to average performances for age and related distributions.

Cursive Joined up handwriting.

CVCs (cvcs) Words made up of a consonant followed by a vowel followed by a consonant.

Decentre Become less egocentric and more aware of others' feelings.

Dependent clause A clause which cannot stand alone as a sentence and which relates to a main clause.

Dialogue Speech as conversation between two or more people.

Digraph Two letters, or graphemes, representing a single phoneme – like *th*, *sh*, *ou*.

Dimorphic Adjective implying two distinct forms of the same item.

Dysgraphia Defective formation of words in writing due to brain disorders or damage.

Dyslexia Impairment of the ability to read, or to understand what one reads – often goes hand in hand with difficulties in spelling and/or writing.

Dyspraxia Poor physical co-ordination.

Early connectives Connectives used at an early stage in writing such as *and* and *then*, occasionally *but*.

Echolalia Repetition of sounds in very early stages of beginning to speak.

Egocentric Self-centred.

Egocentric play Playing alone for one's own aims and intentions, regardless of others.

Egocentric speech Words spoken to the self, not intended as conversation.

Elaborated code Formal and/or enriched uses of language.

ELGs Early Learning Goals – majority of children are expected to reach these by the age of 5 or the end of the year in which they become 5 – The Foundation Stage Framework for England.

Ellipsis Incomplete fragments of speech, that is not complete sentences or incomplete information made comprehensible by shared understanding and/or gesture.

Elliptic Language characterized by ellipsis.

Embedded clause A clause collapsed into a phrase.

Emergent reading A stage where decoding skills are being learned.

Emergent writing A stage where encoding skills are being learned.

End-stop rhyming Poetry with rhymes at the ends of lines.

Epistemic A term used by Bereiter, no doubt derived from epistemology a branch of philosophy investigating the nature and origins of knowledge/theory of nature of knowledge – a bit like metalanguage – for Bereiter, typified by personal search for meaning.

Exploratory talk Discussion between teacher and pupils, including active involvement of pupils in verbal discourse, exploring meanings and understanding.

Expressive reading Reading performed fluently and with expression – usually by Level 3 of the National Curriculum for England.

Genres Different categories of text type – see definition in the glossary of the National Literacy Strategy Framework for England, which gives good examples.

GPC Grapheme/phoneme correspondence.

Grapheme A symbol representing a sound – may be a letter or a digraph.

Grapheme/phoneme correspondence The system of links between sounds and their written representations in a writing system using speech symbolism.

Hemisphere One half of the brain, left hemisphere or right hemisphere.

HFCs High frequency clusters of letters in words.

High frequency clusters Groups of letters characteristic of the orthographic system of a language.

Holophrase Meaning encapsulated within the representation provided by one word – an early stage of speech acquisition.

Homophony Use of words sounding the same with different meanings.

Iamb A metrical foot made up of an unstressed and then a stressed syllable as a pair of syllables, in accentual verse. Also refers to a short syllable followed by a long one in quantitative verse, that is, not accounting for stress.

Iambic pentameter A poetic form using five iambic feet to the line.

Icon answers Using small pictures as rebuses when a word is not known.

Ideational fluency Easy and plentiful generation of ideas.

Inclusion The policy of including all pupils on a basis of full equality, for all types of opportunity, whatever their backgrounds, needs, or difficulties – particularly used in reference to such a policy within mainstream schooling.

Independent reading Reading performed on own without help, usually refers to word by word reading at Level 2 of the National Curriculum for England.

Independent writing Writing done on own without specific help.

Inductive process Reasoning from the particular to the general.

Inflections Affixes which alter words by changing tense, number, person and so on.

Informative reading Fluent reading well focused on the apprehension of information, usually achieved round about Level 4 of the National Curriculum for England.

Initial-letter shorthand Using initial letters to indicate words at an emergent stage of writing.

Insertions Later editions to a text already drafted or partly drafted and placed within that text.

Interactive journal Pupils write their own 'news' or information with the help/contributions of teacher or adult.

Interpretive reading Fluent reading that incorporates the ability to make use of inference, 'reading between the lines', usually well exercised round about the stage of Level 5 of the National Curriculum for England.

Intransitive A verb which has no object in the sentence such as 'they arrived', 'he played well'.

Inventive spelling Spelling as words sound – an early writing strategy.

Kenning A word pattern common in Old English and Norse poetry, using two words to describe one, often humorous or dramatic, such as 'night shiner' = moon. See the National Literacy Strategy Framework glossary for good examples.

Kernel sentences A term to use in Main Idea Analysis – a sentence from among other sentences within a paragraph which most represents the meaning of the paragraph.

Kinaesthetic Related to movement, sensations and action memory, as in kinaesthetic imagery.

Laterality Dominance of one hand, eye, foot over the other, that is, left or right overall, or mixed.

LCWC Look, cover, write, check. A strategy for learning spellings.

Lexical Pertaining to vocabulary or morphemes.

Lexicon a) vocabulary; b) in linguistics, the morphemes of a language; c) a person's own vocabulary store in memory.

Linguistic relativity hypothesis The theory that meanings and understanding are socially structured via word use.

Literacy Reading and writing.

Logographic Describes a writing system based on speech representation by use of morphemic units.

Long-term memory Storage in memory of all information on a basis of meaning – long lasting, and applies to anything stored beyond a few seconds as opposed to working memory. Often types of information are classified so that there are different kinds of memory designated, such as verbal, episodic, visual, kinaesthetic within the main long-term memory model.

Magic 'e' A spelling rule where final e changes the medial vowel value, such as *plan* changed to *plane.*

Magic line A spelling strategy where a line is used to complete a word when a pupil cannot spell it all.

Main clause The main section of a sentence, or the sentence itself if it is a simple sentence; it must contain a verb.

Main Idea Analysis The selection of a kernel sentence from each paragraph in a text to form a composite précis.

Memory span Number of items recalled in a memory test (words or digits) usually presented at one-second intervals and accessed by hearing or sight.

Metalanguage Language about language – linguistic and grammatical terms.

Metalinguistic skills Having the ability to think about and discuss features of language using appropriate vocabulary.

Metaphor Imagery where the writer writes about something as if it were something else.

Metrical feet Patterning of long and short syllables or stressed and unstressed syllables making particular rhythm patterns in poetry.

Mind mapping Jotting down ideas for a piece of writing in web or flow diagram form.

Modelled writing Demonstration of some text composition by teacher to pupils.

Monologue A commentary out loud for self alone.

Morphemes The smallest meaningful units in a language may be words, syllables or affixes.

Morphology The study of morphemes or the system of morphemes in a particular language.

Myelin A white fatty sheath covering nerve fibres.

Myelinization The formation of sheaths over nerve fibres.

NC The National Curriculum for England.

NC Key Stages See preface for details of Key Stages.

NC Levels Expected levels of achievement within the National Curriculum for most pupils of a certain age.

Neologisms Newly made words, original formations or new uses of words.

NLSF The National Literacy Strategy Framework.

Normal curve Normal frequencies of occurrence/performance, which when plotted as a graph form a bell-shaped curve.

NSFTE The National Strategy For Teaching English at Key Stage 3.

Onomatopoeia Words which when spoken own some resemblance to the sound their meaning represents, such as *buzz*.

Onset (as in onset and rime) The initial consonant, consonant blend or consonant cluster of a word (words beginning with vowels have no onset).

Open-ended questions Questions which demand full answers not just affirmatives or negatives and which can elicit more elaborate details.

Optic chiasma The place in the brain where optic nerves from both eyes cross over, so that each eye provides input to each hemisphere.

Optic nerve The nerve channel from the eye and on towards the brain.

Oracy Speaking and listening.

Organized structure The structure of a piece of writing envisaged as a whole, with an awareness of how the parts combine or will combine to make the whole – characteristic usually of Level 4 in the National Curriculum for England.

Orthographic Relating to correct spelling.

Orthography The correct spelling, or study or knowledge of correct spelling patterns of a language.

Over-extensions A feature of an early stage in the acquisition of speech where a regular rule noticed is applied incorrectly to an irregular form, such as 'he runned' instead of 'he ran'.

P Scales Assessment scales for stages below ELGs, and National Curriculum Level 1.

Parallel play A stage of early play development where children like to play alongside each other and address remarks to each other but still play for themselves alone and do not fully converse.

Performative Used by Bereiter – able to do, fulfilling requirements.

Persuasion In writing, trying to encourage a reader to accord with the opinion of the writer.

Phoneme A single sound.

Phonetic Pertaining to phonetics.

Phonetics A system of representation of one sound to one symbol, or the study of the sound system of a language and how it is written.

Phonic By sound, or sounding, sounded.

Phonics Learning to spell/decode by sound.

Phonographic A type of writing system where graphemes (or letters) represent the phonemes (or sounds).

Phonological To do with the discernment and use of sounds.

Phonological loop A verbal feedback mechanism in the model of working memory.

Phonological training Training in discerning, matching and using sounds and in using symbols which represent them.

Phonology Using sounds, study of sounds.

Phrase A group of words without a verb, that is therefore not a clause.

Pictographic Characterized by pictorial symbols.

Pivot grammar Two-word utterances where one word forms the basis of the meaning and the other modifies it – an early stage of speech acquisition.

Play writing Pretending to write, making marks on paper.

Polysyllabic Describes words of more than one syllable.

PPT Chomsky's principles and parameters theory – to do with syntactic rules.

Prediction Imagining or forecasting what might come next or eventuate in a story.

Principles and parameters Types of rule involved in Chomsky's 'principles and parameters theory'.

Production As in speaking and writing.

Prosodic Adjective referring to prosody.

Prosody Use of voice, pronunciation, stress, cadence and expression.

Purposes Reasons for writing, or aims in writing.

Quantitative verse In poetry, word patterns derived from counting syllables, whether stressed or unstressed.

Reception As in listening and reading.

Recount Retelling of a text or story.

Relational structure A characteristic structure of writing where ideas are related and are expressed often in complex sentences, usually reached around Level 3 of the National Curriculum.

Relative pronouns These introduce subordinate clauses in complex sentences. Examples of relative pronouns include that, which, who.

Restricted code A narrow language usage, probably restricted to one form, or informal/local forms.

Rhyme Words which rhyme contain the same rime in their final syllable.

Rime Part of a syllable or short word which contains the vowel and final consonant or consonant cluster, used as in onset and rime.

Role-play Pretending to be someone else, a character in a story or play.

Saccades Intervals or jumps between visual 'gulps' of words when reading.

SATs Standard Assessment Tests/Tasks for different Key Stages belonging to the National Curriculum for England.

Second order A second level or tier of organization or symbolism.

Scaffolding Providing a structure to help writers.

Scene-setting Description of place where action of a story takes place.

SCWC Say, cover, write, check. A strategy for learning spellings.

Selective note making Making notes from more than one text on a similar topic and thus being forced to select and eliminate information.

Self-generated writing Used as a term to include both fiction and factual writing of an original type, since the phrase 'creative writing' can imply fiction only.

Semantic Relating to meaning.

Semanticity Meaning.

Sensori-motor a) Feeling and moving actions; b) pertaining to the neural transit from a sense organ to a muscle.

Sentence markers Capitals and full stops.

Sequencing (reading) Identifying the logical order of segments of a text.

Sequencing (writing) Placing segments of texts in a logical order, or redrafting writing into a logical sequence.

Shared writing The writing process modelled by a teacher with children involved in making suggestions and comments: an interactive process.

Short-term memory A precursor model similar to working memory, but less detailed in some ways.

Simile The likening of something to something else, in order to increase imagery in writing.

Simple sentence A one clause sentence made up of a main clause standing alone.

Sophisticated connectives Use of a wider range of connectives beyond the basic, such as however, furthermore, nevertheless, finally.

Standardized tests Tests constructed according to age norms and the expected frequency of performance derived from these.

Storydrama Using drama to illuminate, create and/or extend story.

Streamers Lists of words on elongated posters written by children, as classroom wall word/banks.

Subordinated clauses Clauses elaborating a main clause, therefore depending upon it – sometimes called dependent clauses.

Syllabic To do with syllables.

Syllabification Dividing words into syllables.

Syllable Each 'beat' in a word; one-beat words like cvcs are monosyllabic.

Syntactic Relating to grammar.

Syntax The grammatical relationships between words, phrases and clauses.

Teacher/scribe An adult writing for children, at their dictation, before the children are able to write for themselves.

Telegraphic speech An early stage in language acquisition where short phrases or sentences are used consisting mainly of nouns, verbs and modifiers.

Text-types A term used often in the National Curriculum for England instead of always using genre, since some purposes for writing involve elements of more than one genre.

The theory theory A theory of language acquisition and use put forward by Gopnik, referring to the way children may be using their own hypotheses to form theories for themselves about their experiences and language interactions.

Transitive verb A verb with an object within the sentence, such as 'he hit the ball', 'she went to the shop'.

Transitivity A term notably put forward by Halliday, indicating communication of meaning between sender and receiver in the use of language.

Unified Used by Bereiter of his penultimate stage of writing within his stage scheme, where performative and judgemental or logically reasoned attitudes combine.

Visual memory span The amount of visual items recalled in a working memory recall task.

Visuo-spatial Of visual and spatial nature.

Visuo-spatial scratch pad A temporary hold for visual and spatial impressions within working memory.

Word banks Selections of words available in easily accessible form to aid children in choice of words and how to spell them.

Working memory A theoretically constructed model drawn from experimental findings indicating memory function for 'working things out' and as a temporary store.

ZPD (zone of proximal development) Vygotsky's idea that children can be helped to learn certain 'next steps' learning with adult help, which on their own they would be unable to do. Sometimes called 'the zone of potential development'.

| Bibliography

Alston, J. (1995) *Assessing and Promoting Writing Skills*. Stafford: NASEN Enterprises.

Altmann, G.M.T. (1997) *The Ascent of Babel*. Oxford: Oxford University Press.

AMS Educational Literacy 2001 (2001 Catalogue). Leeds: AMS Educational.

Arnold, H. (1982) *Listening to Children Reading*. London: Hodder and Stoughton Educational.

Arnold, R. (1997) *Raising Levels of Achievement in Boys*. Slough: National Foundation for Educational Research.

Arnot, M., Gray, J., James, M., Rudduck, J. with Duveen, G. (1998) *Recent Research on Gender and Educational Performance*. London: Department for Education and Employment, for OFSTED Review of Research.

Baddeley, A.D. and Hitch, G. (1974) 'Working Memory', in Bower, G.A. (ed.) *Recent Advances in Learning and Motivation*. New York: Academic Press.

Baddeley, A.D. (1976) *The Psychology of Memory*. New York: Harper and Row.

Baddeley, A.D. (1986) *Working Memory*. Oxford: Oxford University Press.

Baddeley, A.D. (1997) *Human Memory*. Hove: Psychology Press.

Bancroft, D. (1995) 'Language development' in Lee and Das Gupta, q.v.

Barnes, D., Britton, J. and Rosen, H. (1969) *Language, the Learner and the School*. Harmondsworth: Penguin Books.

Barnes, D. (1976) *From Communication to Curriculum*. Harmondsworth: Penguin Books.

Baron-Cohen, S. (1998) 'Is autism an extreme form of male brain?', in Carter, q.v.

Barrett, T.C. (1967) 'Taxonomy of the cognitive and affective dimensions of reading comprehension', in Robinson, H. M. (1968) *Innovation and Change in Reading Instruction*, 67th Yearbook of the National Society for the Study of Education. Chicago: University of Illinois, pp. 7–29.

Barrs, M. and Cork, V. (2001) *The Reader in the Writer – the links between the study of literature and writing development at Key Stage 2*. Centre for Language in Primary Education (London Borough of Southwark).

Barrs, M., Ellis, S., Hester, H. and Thomas, A. (1988) *The Primary Language Record – Handbook for Teachers*. Centre for Language in Primary Education (London Borough of Southwark).

Barrs, M. and Pidgeon, S. (1993) *Reading the Difference*. Centre for Language in Primary Education (London Borough of Southwark).

Bauman, R. (1984) *Verbal Art as Performance*. Prospect Heights, Illinois: Waveland Press.

BBC (British Broadcasting Corporation) (1997) *Dyslexia in the Primary School* (package for teachers). Weatherby: BBC Publications.

BDA (British Dyslexia Association) (2001) *XO2 – Dyslexia in Context*. British Dyslexia Association.

Beard, R. (ed.) (1993) *Teaching Literacy: balancing perspectives*. London: Hodder and Stoughton.

Beard, R. (ed.) (1995) *Rhyme, Reading and Writing*. London: Hodder and Stoughton.

Beard, R. (2000) *Developing Writing 3–13*. London: Hodder and Stoughton.

Bearne, E. (1995) *Greater Expectations – Children Reading Writing*. London: Cassell.

Beech, J. and Colley, A. (eds.) (1987) *Cognitive Approaches to Reading*. Chichester: John Wiley and Sons Limited.

Bereiter, C. and Scardamalia, M. (1987) *The Psychology of Written Composition*. Hillsdale, N.J.: Lawrence Erlbaum.

Bereiter, C. (1980) 'Development in Writing', in Gregg, L. W. and Steinberg, E.R. (eds.). *Cognitive Processes in Writing*. Hillsdale, N.J.: Lawrence Erlbaum Associates.

Berger, P.L. and Luckman (1967) *The Social Construction of Reality*. Harmondsworth: Penguin Books.

Bernstein, B. (1960) 'Language and Social Class', *British Journal of Sociology*. 11: 271–276.

Bernstein, B. (1971) *Class, Codes and Control*. London: Routledge and Kegan Paul.

Bettelheim, B. (1977) *The Uses of Enchantment: the Meaning and Importance of Fairy Tales*. London: Thames and Hudson.

Betts, A. (1957) *Foundations of Reading Instruction*. American Book Company, UK.

Biddulph, S. (1997) *Raising Boys*. London: Thorsons.

Booth, D. (1994) *Story Drama, Reading, Writing and Role Playing Across the Curriculum*. Ontario: Pembroke.

Bowerman, M. and Levinson, S.C. (eds.) (2001) *Language Acquisition and Conceptual Development*. Cambridge: Cambridge University Press.

Bradley, L. and Bryant, P.E. (1983) 'Categorizing Sounds and Learning to Read – a Causal Connection', *Nature*, 301: 419–421.

Bremner, J.G. (1999) 'Knowledge of the physical world in infancy', in Messer and Miller, q.v.

Brierley, J. (1976) *The Growing Brain*. Slough: National Foundation for Educational Research.

Bristow, J., Cowley, P. and Daines, B. (1999) *Memory and Learning – A Practical Guide for Teachers*. London: David Fulton.

Brown, R. (1976) *A First Language*. Harmondsworth: Penguin Books.

Brownjohn, S. (1980) *Does it Have to Rhyme? Teaching Children to Write Poetry*. London: Hodder and Stoughton.

Brownjohn, S. (1994) *To Rhyme or Not to Rhyme*. London: Hodder and Stoughton

Brownjohn, S. (1995) 'Rhyme in Children's Writing', Beard, R. (ed.) *Rhyme, Reading and Writing*. London: Hodder and Stoughton.

Bruner, J.S. (1966) *Towards a Theory of Instruction*. Oxford: Oxford University Press.

Bruner, J. S. (1985) 'Vygotsky: A Historical and Conceptual Perspective', in Wertsch, J.V. (ed.), *Culture, Communication and Cognition, Vygotskyan Perspectives*. Cambridge: Cambridge University Press.

Bruner, J. S. (1986) *Actual Minds, Possible Worlds*. Cambridge, Mass: Harvard University Press.

Bruner, J. S. (1988) 'Life as Narrative', *Language Arts*, 65:6.

Bryant, P. (1989) 'Nursery Rhymes, Phonological Skills and Reading', *Journal of Child Language*. 16: 407–428.

Bryant, P. (1993) 'Phonological Aspects of Learning to Read', in Beard, R. (ed.) *Teaching Literacy: balancing perspectives*. London: Hodder and Stoughton.

Bryson, B. (1990) *Mother Tongue – The English Language*. Harmondsworth: Penguin Books.

Byrne, B. (1998) *The Foundation of Literacy – the child's acquisition of the alphabetic principle*. Hove: Psychology Press.

Carroll, J.B. and Casagrande, J.B. (1958) 'The Function of Language Classification', in Maccoby *et al.*, (eds.) *Readings in Social Psychology*. New York: Hold, Rinehart and Winston.

Carter, R. (1998) *Mapping the Mind*. London: Phoenix Paperbacks, Orion Books Limited.

Chang, G.L. and Wells, G. (1988) 'The Literate Potential of Collaborative Talk', in Maclure *et al.*, q.v.

Chanquoy, L. (2001) 'How to Make it Easier for Children to Revise their Writing: a study of text revision from third to fifth grades', *British Journal of Education and Psychology*, 71: 15–41.

Clark, E. V. (2001) 'Emergent categories in first language acquisition' in Bowerman and Levinson, q.v.

CLPE (Centre for Language in Primary Education) (1999) *Finding Yourself in a Book*. Centre for Language in Primary Education (London Borough of Southwark).

CLPE (Centre for Language in Primary Education) (2000) *The Primary Language Record*. Centre for Language in Education (London Borough of Southwark).

Colley, A. (1987) 'Text Comprehension', in Beech and Colley q.v.

Collins, F. (1998) 'Composition' in Graham, J. and Kelly, A., *Writing Under Control*. London: David Fulton.

Coltheart, M., Patterson, K., and Marshall, J.C. (eds.) (1980) *Deep Dyslexia*. London: Routledge and Kegan Paul.

Conrad, R. and Hull, A.J. (1964) 'Information, Acoustic Confusions and Memory Span', *British Journal of Educational Psychology*, 86: 429–432.

Conrad, R. (1972) 'Speech and Reading', in Kavanagh, J.F. and Mattingly, I.G. (eds.) *Language by Ear and Eye*. Cambridge, Mass: MIT Press.

Corden, R. (2000) *Literacy and Learning Through Talk – strategies for the primary classroom*. Buckingham: Open University Press.

Coulson, M. (1995) 'Models of memory development', in Lee and Das Gupta, q.v.

Craik, F. M. and Lockhart, R.S. (1972) 'Levels of Processing: A Framework for Memory Research', *Journal of Verbal Learning and Verbal Behavior*, 11: 671–684.

Crowhurst, M. (1993) *Writing in the Middle Years*. Markham, Ontario: Pippin Publishing.

Crystal, D. (1982) *Child Language, Learning and Linguistics*. London: Arnold.

Crystal, D. (1990) *The English Language*. Harmondsworth: Penguin Books.

Crystal, D. (1997) *English as a Global Language*. Cambridge: Cambridge University Press.

Das Gupta, P. and Richardson, K. (1995) 'Theories in Cognitive Development' in Lee and Das Gupta (eds.) *Children's Cognitive and Language Development*. Oxford: Blackwell.

Davie, R., Butler, N. and Goldstein, H. (1972) *From Birth to Seven – The Second Report of the National Child Development Study*. London: Longman.

De La Mare, W. (1979) 'The Listeners', in Webb, K., *I Like This Poem*. Harmondsworth: Puffin Books, Penguin Books.

Demb, J.B., Boynton, G.M. and Heeger, D.J. (1998) 'Functional Magnetic Resonance Imaging of Early Visual Pathways in Dyslexia', *The Journal of Neuroscience*, 18: 6939–6951.

Demont, E. and Gombert, J.E. (1996) 'Phonological Awareness as a Predictor of Recoding Skills and Syntactic Awareness as a Predictor of Comprehension Skills', *British Journal of Educational Psychology*, 66: 315–332.

Department for Education and Employment (1990) *Teaching and Learning of Drama*. London: HMSO.

Department for Education and Employment (1998) *The National Literacy Strategy – Framework for Teaching*. London: Department for Education and Employment Publications.

Department for Education and Employment (1999a) *The National Curriculum for England – English – Key Stages 1–4*. London: The Stationery Office, for The Department for Education and Employment.

Department for Education and Employment (1999b) *The National Literacy Strategy: Phonics – Progression in Phonics: Materials for Whole-Class Teaching*. London: Department for Education and Employment Publications.

Department for Education and Employment (2000) *Curriculum Guidance for the Foundation Stage*. London: The Qualifications and Curriculum Authority.

Department for Education and Employment (2001, rev.) *Supporting and Target Setting Process*. London: Department for Education and Employment Publications.

Department for Education and Employment (2001/0019) *Key Stage 3 National Strategy for Teaching English – Framework for Teaching English: Years 7, 8 and 9*. London: Department for Education and Employment Publications.

Department for Education and Employment (2001/0055) *Developing Early Writing*. London: Department for Education and Employment Publications.

Department for Education and Employment (2001/0107) *The National Literacy Strategy: Grammar for Writing*. London: Department for Education and Employment Publications.

Department for Education and Employment (2001/0473) *Key Stage 3 National Strategy for Teaching English – Literacy Progress Unit: Writing Organisation*. London: Department for Education and Employment Publications.

Department for Education and Employment (2001/0474) *Key Stage 3 National Strategy for Teaching English – Literacy Progress Unit: Information Retrieval*. London: Department for Education and Employment Publications.

Department for Education and Employment (2001/0475) *Key Stage 3 National Strategy for Teaching English – Literacy Progress Unit: Spelling*. London: Department for Education and Employment Publications.

Department for Education and Employment (2001/0476) *Key Stage 3 National Strategy for Teaching English: Literacy Progress Unit – Reading Between the Lines*. London: Department for Education and Employment Publications.

Department for Education and Employment (2001/0477) *Key Stage 3 National Strategy for Teaching English – Literacy Progress Unit: Phonics*. London: Department for Education and Employment Publications.

Department for Education and Employment (2001/0478) *Key Stage 3 National Strategy for Teaching English – Literacy Progress Unit: Sentences*. London: Department for Education and Employment Publications.

Department of Education and Science (1988) *Draft National Curriculum for England – English: Appendix Five – Approaches to the Class Novel*. London: Department of Education and Science.

Dickens, C. (1940s edition) *Oliver Twist*. London: Collins Pocket Classics, Collins.

Donaldson, M. (1978) *Children's Minds*. Harmondsworth: Penguin Books.

Downing, J. and Leong, C.K. (1982) *Psychology of Reading*. London: Collier MacMillan.

Drozd, K.F. (2001) 'Children's weak interpretations of universally quantified questions', in Bowerman and Levinson, q.v.

Ehri, L. (1979) ' Learning to Read and to Spell Are One and the Same Almost', in Perfetti, C., Rieben, L. and Fayol, M. (eds.) *Learning to Spell: Research, Theory and Practice Across Language*. Mahwah, NJ: Lawrence Erlbaum.

Ellis, A.W. (1984) *Reading, Writing and Dyslexia: a cognitive analysis*. Hillsdale NJ: Erlbaum.

Ellis, S. (ed.) (1995) *Hands on Poetry – Using Poetry in the Classroom*. Centre for Language in Primary Education (London Borough of Southwark).

Engle, R.W., Kane, M.J., and Tukolski, S.W. (1999) 'Individual differences in working memory capacity and what they tell us about controlled attention, general fluid intelligence and functions of pre-frontal cortex' in Myake, N., and Shah, P. (eds.) *Models of Working Memory*. Cambridge: Cambridge University Press.

Evans, J. (eds.) (2001) *The Writing Classroom – aspects of writing and the primary child 3–11*. London: David Fulton.

Fawcett, A. J. and Nicolson, R. I. (eds.) (1994) *Dyslexia in Children: multi-disciplinary perspectives*. Brighton: Harvester Press.

Fawcett, A.J., and Nicolson, R.I. (1996) *The Dyslexia Screening Test: Nonsense Passage Reading*. London: The Psychological Corporation.

Fawcett, A. J., Nicolson, R.I. and Dean, P. (1996) 'Impaired Performance of Children with Dyslexia on a Range of Cerebellar Tasks', *Annals of Dyslexia*. 46: 259–283.

Fernald, G.M. (1943) *Remedial Techniques in Basic School Subjects*. New York: McGraw-Hill.

Fifield, P. (1995) *Love at First Sight? Children who have special needs working on Romeo and Juliet*, in Bearne, q.v.

Fisher, R. (1999) *First Stories for Thinking*. Oxford: Nash Pollock Publishing.

Fontana, D. and Evans, M. (1980) 'Mode of Stimulus Presentation and Short-Term Memory Efficiency in Primary School Children', *British Journal of Educational Psychology*, 50: 229–235.

Frater, G. (2001) *Effective Practice in Writing at Key Stage 2*. London: The Basic Skills Agency.

Frith, U. (1980) *Cognitive Processes in Spelling*, London: Academic Press.

Frith, U. (1985) 'Beneath the Surface of Developmental Dyslexia', in Patterson, K.E., Marshall, J.C. and Coltheart, M. (eds.) *Surface Dyslexia*. London: Erlbaum.

Frith, U., referred to by Oakhill (1995) in Lee and Das Gupta, q.v.

Gahagan, D.M. and Gahagan, G.A. (1970) *Talk Reform*. London: Routledge and Kegan Paul.

Gathercole, S.E. and Adams, A.M. (1993) 'Phonological Working Memory in Very Young Children', *Developmental Psychology*, 28: 887–898.

Gathercole, S.E. and Pickering, S.J. (2000) 'Working Memory Deficits in Children with Low Achievements in the National Curriculum at Seven Years of Age', *British Journal of Educational Psychology*, 70: 177–194.

Gentry, J.R. (1982) 'An Analysis of Development Spelling in GNYS AT WRK', *The Reading Teacher*, 36: 192–200.

Gillborn, D. and Mirza, H.S. (2000) *Educational in Equality – Mapping Race Class Gender – a synthesis of research evidence*. London: Office for Standards in Education.

Gopnik A. (2001) 'Theories, language and culture: Whorf without wincing' in Bowerman and Levinson, q.v.

Goswami, U. and Bryant, P.E. (1990) *Phonological Skills and Learning to Read*. Hove: Erlbaum.

Goswami, U. (1995) 'Rhyme in Children's Early Reading', in Beard, R. (ed.) *Rhyme, Reading and Writing*. London: Hodder and Stoughton.

Graham, J. and Kelly, A. (eds.) (1998) *Writing Under Control – Teaching Writing in the Primary School*. London: David Fulton Publishers.

Grainger, T. (1997) *Traditional Story Telling – in the Primary Classroom*. Leamington Spa: Scholastic.

Grainger, T. (1998) 'Drama and Reading: Illuminating their Interaction', *in English in Education*, 32(1): 29–36.

Gravelle, M. (ed.) (2000) *Planning for Bilingual Learners – an inclusive curriculum*. Stoke on Trent: Trentham Books.

Gredler, G.R. (1987) 'Severe reading disability – some correlates' in Reid and Donaldson, q.v.

Greenfield, S.A. (2000a) *Brain Story*. London: British Broadcasting Corporation Worldwide.

Greenfield, S.A. (2000b) *The Private Life of the Brain*. Harmondsworth: Penguin Books.

Gregory, E. (1996) *Making Sense of a New World – Learning to Read in a Second Language*. London: Paul Chapman.

Grugeon, E., Hubbard, L., Smith, C. and Dawes, L. (1998) *Teaching, Speaking and Listening in the Primary School*. London: David Fulton.

Gurney, R. (1973) *Language, Brain and Interactive Processes*. London: Edward Arnold.

Habib, M. (2000) 'The Neurological Basis of Developmental Dyslexia – an overview and working hypothesis' in *Brain*, 1–3: 2373–2399.

Halliday, M.A.K. (1969) 'Relevant Models of Language', in Williams A.M. (ed.) *The State of Language*. Birmingham: University of Birmingham School of Education.

HCC (Hampshire County Council) (1997) *SIDNEY*. Winchester: Hampshire County Council.

Henry, J. (2001) *Help for the Boys Helps the Girls*. London: *The Times Educational Supplement* (1 June 2001), TSL Educational.

Hodgson Burnett, F. (1994) *The Secret Garden*. Harmondsworth: Puffin Books, Penguin Books.

Hooker, J.T. (ed.) (1984) *A History of Writing from Cuneiform to the Alphabet*. London: British Museum Press.

Hulme, C. (1987) 'Reading and Retardation', in Beech and Colley q.v.

Hutchcroft, D.M.R. (1981) *Making Language Work – A practical approach to literacy for teachers of 5–13 year old children*. Maidenhead: McGraw Hill.

Hutt, C. (1972) *Males and Females*, Harmondsworth, Penguin Books.

Johnson, M.H. (1997) 'The Neural Basis of Cognitive Development', in Damon, W., Kuhn,. D. and Siegler, R.S. (eds.) *Handbook of Child Psychology*. New York: John Wiley.

KCC (Kent County Council) (1984) *Becoming a Writer* (in-service package for teachers). Maidstone: Kent County Council.

Kinmont, A. (1990) *The Dimensions of Writing – studies in primary education*. London: David Fulton.

Kipling, R. (1994 edition) *The Just So Stories*. Harmondsworth: Puffin Books, Penguin Books.

Kress, G. (1982) *Learning to Write*. London: Routledge and Kegan Paul.

Lamb, C. (1995 – modern edition) *Lamb's Tales from Shakespeare*. Harmondsworth: Penguin Popular Classics, Penguin Books.

Latham, D.S. (1983) 'Memory Span and the use of Context Cues in Young Children's Reading', unpublished M.A. dissertation, University of Kent at Canterbury.

Laurita, R.E. (2000) *Latin Roots and Their Modern English Spellings*. Maine: Leonardo Press.

Lazim, A. and Ellis, S. (2000) *Choosing Texts for the National Literacy Strategy*. Centre for Language in Primary Education (London Borough of Southwark).

Lee, V. and Das Gupta, P. (eds.) (1995) *Children's Cognitive and Language Development*. Oxford: Blackwell.

Lennard, J. (1996) *The Poetry Handbook – a guide to reading poetry for pleasure and practical criticism*. Oxford: Oxford University Press.

Lewis, M. and Wray, D. (1995) *Developing Children's Non-fiction Writing*. Leamington Spa: Scholastic.

Lewis, M. and Wray, D. (1996) *Writing Frames – scaffolding children's non-fiction writing in a range of genres*. Reading: University of Reading, Reading and Language Information Centre.

Lyons, J. (1970) *Chomsky*. London: Fontana/Collins.

Macintyre, C. (2000) *Dyspraxia in the Early Years*. London: David Fulton.

Maclure, M., Phillips, T. and Wilkinson, A. (1988) *Oracy Matters*. Buckingham: University Press.

Mahy, M. (1984) *The Birthday Burglar and The Very Wicked Headmistress*. London: Magnet Books.

Malory, Sir Thomas (1471) *Morte d'Arthur, Vol. One* (1946 edition). J.M. Dent and Son.

Marcel, T. (1980) 'Surface Dyslexia and Beginning Reading – a revised hypothesis of the pronunciation of print and its impairments', in Coltheart et al, q.v.

McPhillips, M., Hepper, P.G. and Mulhearn, G. (2000) in *The Lancet*, 355:537–541.

Melnik, A. and Merritt, J. (1972) *Reading: Today and Tomorrow*. London: University of London Press for the Open University.

Mercer, N., Edwards, D. and Maybin, D. (1988) 'Putting context into oracy: the construction of shared knowledge through classroom discourse', in Maclure *et al.*, q.v.

Messer, D.J. (1999) 'The Development of Communication and Language', in Messer, D.J. and Millar, S. (eds.), q.v.

Messer, D.J. and Millar, S. (eds.) (1999) *Exploring Developmental Psychology*. London: Arnold.

Messer, D.J. (2000) 'State of the Art: Language Acquisition', in *The Psychologist*, The British Psychological Society, Vol. 13 No. 3, March 2000, 138–143.

Millard, E. (1997) *Differently Literate – Boys, Girls and the Schooling of Literacy*. London: Routledge Falmer.

Millard, E. (2001) 'Aspects of Gender: how boys' and girls' experiences of reading shape their writing', in Evans, J. (ed.) London: David Fulton.

Miller, G.A. (1956) 'The Magical Number Seven, Plus or Minus Two: Some Limits of Our Capacity for Processing Information', *Psychological Review*, 63: 81–97.

Miyake,N., and Shah, P. (eds.) (1999) *Models of Working Memory*. Cambridge: Cambridge University Press.

Moffett, J. (1968) *Teaching the Universe of Discourse*. Boston: Houghton Mifflin.

Moir, A. and Jessel, D. (1989) *Brainsex: The Real Difference Between Men and Women*. London: Michael Joseph.

Moline, S. (2001) 'Using Graphic Organisers to Write Information Texts', in Evans, J. (ed.) *The Writing Classroom*. London: David Fulton.

Morse, B. (1995) 'Rhyming Poetry for Children', in Beard, R. (ed.) *Rhyme, Reading and Writing*. London: Hodder and Stoughton.

Morwood, J. and Warman, M. (1990) *Our Greek and Latin Roots*. Cambridge: Cambridge University Press.

NWP (National Writing Project) (1989) *Writing and Learning*. Kingston-upon-Thames: Thomas Nelson and Sons.

Neate, B. (2001) 'Notemaking Techniques for Young Children', in Evans, J. (ed.) *The Writing Classroom*. London: David Fulton.

Nicolson, R.I. (1999) 'Reading Skill and Dyslexia', in Messer and Millar, q.v.

Nicolson, R.I. and Fawcett, A.J. (1990) 'Automaticity: A new framework for dyslexia research', *Cognition*, 35: 159–182.

Nicolson, R.I. and Fawcett, A.J. (1996) *The Dyslexia Early Screening Test*. London: The Psychological Corporation.

Oakhill, J. (1995) 'Development in Reading', in Lee and Das Gupta, q.v.

Oakhill, J. and Garnham, A. (1988) *Becoming a Skilled Reader*. Oxford: Blackwell.

Office for Standards in Education (1998a) *The National Literacy Project*. London: OFSTED Publications.

Office for Standards in Education (1998b) *Recent Research in Gender and Educational Performance*. London: HMSO.

Office for Standards in Education (1999) *Raising the Attainment of Minority Ethnic Pupils – School and LEA Responses*. London: OFSTED Publications.

Office for Standards in Education (2001/HMI/326) *Managing Support for the Attainment of Pupils from Minority Ethnic Groups*. London: OFSTED Publications.

O'Sullivan, O. and Thomas, A. (2000) *Understanding Spelling*. Centre for Language in Primary Education (London Borough of Southwark).

Ozawa, F., Matsuo, K., Kato, C., Nakai, T., Isoda, H., Talehara, Y., Mariya, T. and Sakahara, H. (2000) 'The effects of listening comprehension of various genres of literature on response in the linguistic area', an fMRI study, *NeuroReport*, 11: 1141–1143.

Parker, S. (1988) 'Scripting for creative video: from talk to writing and back again' in Maclure *et al.*, q.v.

Perera, K. (1989) 'Grammatical Differentiation Between Speech and Writing in Children Age 8–12', in Carter, R. (ed.) *Knowledge About Language and the Curriculum*. London: Hodder and Stoughton.

Peters, M.L. (1967) *Spelling, Caught or Taught?* London: Routledge and Kegan Paul.

Peters, M.L. (1985) *Spelling, Caught or Taught? A New Look*. London: Routledge and Kegan Paul.

Phinn, G. (2001) 'Responding to poetry through writing', in Evans, q.v.

Piaget, J. (1959) *The Language and Thought of the Child*. London: Routledge and Kegan Paul.

Pinker, S. (1994) *The Language Instinct*. Harmondsworth: Penguin Books.

Porter, M. (2001) Column by Dr Mark Porter, 21st April 2001, *Radio Times*, London: British Broadcasting Corporation Worldwide.

Power, R. and Power, E. (1936) *More Boys and Girls of History*. Cambridge: Cambridge University Press.

Qualifications and Curriculum Authority (1998/052) *The Grammar Papers – Perspective on the Teaching of Grammar in the National Curriculum*. London: QCA Publications.

Qualifications and Curriculum Authority (1998/081) *Can Do Better – Raising Boys' Achievement in English*. London: QCA Publications.

Qualifications and Curriculum Authority (1998/144) *Building Bridges – Guidance and Training Materials for Teachers of Year 6 and Year 7 Pupils*. London: QCA Publications.

Qualifications and Curriculum Authority (1998/165) *The Long-Term Effects of Two Interventions for Children with Reading Difficulties*. London: QCA Publications.

Qualifications and Curriculum Authority (1998/247) *Analysis of Educational Resources in 1997/8 – Key Stage 2 English Resources and Key Stages 3 and 4 English Course Books*. London: QCA Publications.

Qualifications and Curriculum Authority (1999/282) *Making Use of Optional Tests – English and Mathematics – Report on the Use of Optional Tests with Children in Years 3, 4 and 5 in 1998*. London: QCA Publications.

Qualifications and Curriculum Authority (1999/391) *Teaching, Speaking and Listening in Key Stages 1 and 2*. London: QCA Publications.

Qualifications and Curriculum Authority (1999/392) *Improving Writing in Key Stages 3 and 4*. London: QCA Publications.

Qualifications and Curriculum Authority (1999/418) *Not Whether But How – Teaching Grammar in English at Key Stages 3 and 4*. London: QCA Publications.

Qualifications and Curriculum Authority (2000/584) *A Language in Common: Assessing English as an Additional Language*. London: QCA Publications.

Qualifications and Curriculum Authority (2000/587) *Curriculum Guidance for the Foundation Stage*. London: QCA Publications.

Qualifications and Curriculum Authority (2000/627) *Year 7 Optional Tests in English, Teacher Pack*. London: QCA Publications.

Qualifications and Curriculum Authority (2000/635) *Year 8 Optional Tests in English, Teacher Pack*. London: QCA Publications.

Qualifications and Curriculum Authority (2001) *Working with Gifted and Talented Children: Key Stages 1 and 2 English and Mathematics*. London: QCA Publications.

Randall, J. (2001) 'Wizard Words: The Literary, Latin, and Lexical Origins of Harry Potter's Vocabulary', *Verbatim – The Language Quarterly*, Vol. XXVI, No. 2, Spring 2001, 1–7, Chicago: Word, Inc.

Rees, F. (1996) *The Writing Repertoire – Developing Writing at Key Stage 2*. Slough: National Foundation for Educational Research.

Reid, J.F. and Donaldson, H. (eds.) (1977) *Reading Problems and Practices*. London: Ward Lock Educational.

Robinson, A. (1995) *The Story of Writing*. London: Thames and Hudson.

Rosen, H. (1988) *The Irrepressible Genre*. in Maclure *et al.*, q.v.

Rosen, M. (1998) *Did I Hear You Write?* Nottingham: Five Leaves Publications.

Rudduck, J. (1994) *Developing a Gender Policy in Secondary Schools*. Buckingham: Open University Press.

Rundell, S. (2001) 'How to Improve His Stories', *Times Educational Supplement* (1 June, 2001). London: TSL Educational.

Sampson, G. (1985) *Writing Systems*. London: Hutchinson.

Sapir, E. (1966) *Culture, Language and Personality*. University of California Press.

Sasanuma, S. (1980) 'Acquired dyslexia in Japanese: clinical features and underlying mechanisms', in Coltheart *et al.*, q.v.

Sassoon, R. (1989) *A Quick Look at Handwriting Problems*. Hitchin: Dyspraxia Foundation.

Sassoon, R. (1995) *The Practical Guide to Children's Handwriting*. London: Hodder and Stoughton.

Schonell, F. (1942) *Backwardness in Basic Subjects*. Oliver and Boyd.

School Curriculum and Assessment Authority (1996) *Promoting Continuity Between Key Stage 2 and Key Stage 3*. London: SCAA Publications.

School Curriculum and Assessment Authority (1997) *Making effective use of Key Stage 2 assessments at the transfer between Key Stage 2 and Key Stage 3 to support the teaching of pupils in Year 7*. London: SCAA Publications.

Shakespeare's Globe Theatre (2001) *Globelink*. London: Globe Education.

Sheridan, M.D. (with revision by Frost, M. and Sharma, A.) (1997 edition) *From Birth to Five Years – children's developmental progress*. London: Routledge.

Skottun, B.C. (2000) 'The magnocellular deficit theory of dyslexia: The evidence from contrast sensitivity', mini-review, *Vision Research*. 40: 111–127.

Slobin, D.I. (1971) *Psycholinguistics*. Glenview, Illinois: Scott, Foresman and Co. Hillsdale, NJ: Erlbaum.

Smith, F. (1973) *Psycholinguistics and Reading*. New York: Holt, Rinehart and Winston.

Smith, F. (1978) *Reading*. Cambridge: Cambridge University Press.

Smith, F. (1982) *Writing and the Writer*. London: Heinemann Educational.

Smith, F. (1988) *Understanding Reading*. New York: Holt, Rinehart and Winston.

Smith, L.B. (2001) 'How domain-general processes may create domain-specific specifications', in Bowerman and Levinson, q.v.

Smith, N. (1999) *Chomsky – Ideas and Ideals*. Cambridge: Cambridge University Press.

Smyth, A. (2001) 'On reading, reflex and research', in *The Psychologist*, Vol. 14 No. 2 82–83.

Snowling, M.J. (2000) *Dyslexia*. Oxford: Blackwell Publishers.

Southgate, V., Arnold, H. and Johnson, S. (1981) *Extending Beginning Reading*. London: Heinemann Educational.

Sparks Linfield, R. (1995) 'Marks on the Page: children as editors', in Bearne, q.v.

Spelke, E.S. and Tsivkin, S. (1999) 'Initial knowledge and conceptual change: space and number', in Bowerman and Levinson, q.v.

S.R.A., Text: Blue 2c/15, *The Great Fire of London*, S.R.A.

Stannard, J. (1998) *The National Literacy Strategy Trainer's Cassette 2*. London: Standards and Effectiveness Unit, Department for Education and Employment.

Stein, J. and Walsh, V. (1997) 'To see but not to read; the magnocellular theory of dyslexia', *Trends in Neuroscience*, Vol. 20, No. 4, 147–152.

Stevenson, V. (1999) *The World of Words*. New York: Stirling Publishing.

Stine, R.L. (1994) *Deep Trouble*, Goosebumps Series. London: Scholastic Children's Books.

Stuart, M., (1999) 'Getting ready for reading: early phoneme awareness and phonics teaching improves reading and spelling in inner-city second language learners', in *British Journal of Educational Psychology*, 69:4, 587–585.

Tannen, D. (ed.) (1984) *Coherence in Spoken and Written Discourse*. Norwood, NJ: Ablex.

Taylor, W.L. (1953) 'Cloze Procedure: a new tool for measuring readability', *Journalism Quarterly*, 30: 415–433.

Tomasello, M. (1992) *First Verbs: A case study of early grammatical development*. Cambridge: Cambridge University Press.

Tomasello, M. (2001) 'Perceiving intentions and learning words in the second year of life', in Bowerman and Levinson, q.v.

Tough, J. (1973) *Focus on Meaning*. London: Allen and Unwin.

Tough, J. (1977) *The Development of Meaning*. London: Allen and Unwin.

Voors, R.O. (2000) *Write Dance – Getting Ready for Writing*. Bristol: Lucky Duck Publishing.

Vygotsky, L.S. (1962) *Thought and Language*. Cambridge Mass: MIT Press.

Washtell, A. (1998) 'Routines and Resources', in Graham, J. and Kelly, A. (eds.) *Writing Under Control*. London: David Fulton.

Waxman, S. (1990) 'Linguistic biases and the establishment of conceptual hierarchies: evidence from pre-school children, *Cognitive Development*, 5: 123–124.

Weeks, A. (1992) *Your National Curriculum Planning and Integrating Themes*. London: New Education Press.

Wells, G. (1977) 'Language Use and Educational Success: An Empirical Response to Joan Tough's "The Development of Meaning" ', *Research in Education*, 18: 9–34.

Wells, G. (1981) *Learning Through Interaction – The Study of Language Development*. Cambridge: Cambridge University Press.

Westwood, P. (1999) *Spelling – Approaches to teaching and assessment*. Camberwell, Victoria: ACER Press (The Australian Council for Educational Research).

White, J. (1986) *The Assessment of Writing – Pupils Aged 11–15*. Windsor: Assessment of Performance Unit, Department of Education and Science with National Foundation for Educational Research/Nelson.

Whorf, B.L. (1956) *Language, Thought and Reality*. Cambridge, Mass: MIT Press.

Wilkinson, A.M. (1971) *The Foundations of Language*. Oxford: Oxford University Press.

Wilkinson, A., *et al.* (1980) *Assessing Language Development.* Oxford: Oxford University Press.

Williams, A. (1977) *Reading and the Consumer.* London: Hodder and Stoughton.

Wray, D. and Lewis M. (1997) *Extending Literacy: children's reading and writing non-fiction.* London: Routledge.

Wray, D. and Lewis, M. (2001) 'Developing non-fiction writing: beyond writing frames', in Evans, J., *The Writing Classroom.* London: David Fulton.

Wyse, D. (1998) *Primary Writing.* Buckingham: The Open University Press.

Yarrow, F., and Topping, K.J. (2001) 'Collaborative writing: the effects of metacognitive prompting and structured peer interaction', in *British Journal of Educational Psychology.* 71/2: 261–282.

Yates, I. (1993a) *How to be Brilliant at Making Books.* Leamington Spa: Brilliant Publications.

Yates, I. (1993b) *How to be Brilliant at Writing Poetry.* Leamington Spa: Brilliant Publications.

Yen Mah, A. (2000) *Watching the Tree.* London: Harper Collins.

Young, A.W. (1987) 'Cerebral Hemisphere Differences and Reading', in Beech, J.R. and Colley, A.M., q.v.

Zimet, S.G. (1976) *Print and Prejudice.* London: Hodder and Stoughton.

■ Useful Websites

British Dyslexia Association: *www.bda-dyslexia.org.uk*

Dyspraxia Foundation: *www.embrook.demon.co.uk/dyspraxia*

Globe Education: *www.Shakespeares-globe.org*

National Support Project for Storysacks: *www.storysacks.co.uk*

QCA Marking Guides for Writing: *www.standards.dfes.gov.uk*

|Index of Authors and Sources

Alston, J., 137
Altmann, G.M.T., 22,40
A.M.S. Educational, 151
Arnold, H., 47, 134
Arnold, R., 15
Arnot, M. *et al.*, 12, 13, 14

Baddeley, A.D., 48, 49, 51
Baddeley, A.D. and Hitch, G., 48
Bancroft, D., 17–19, 22–24, 31, 32
Barnes, D., 40
Barnes, D., Britton, J. and Rosen, H., 40
Baron-Cohen, S., 10
Barrett, T.C., 143
Barrs, M. and Cork, V., 144
Barrs, M. and Pidgeon, S., 16
Barrs, M. *et al.*, 49, 83, 107
Bauman, R., 151
B.B.C., 56
B.D.A., 14, 56
Beard, R., 14, 59, 61, 62, 68, 74, 76, 79, 83,
                92 94, 100, 113
Bearne, E., 100, 114, 155
Beech, J. and Colley, A. (eds.), 6, 7, 8, 141
Bereiter, C., 74, 92
Bereiter, C. and Scardamalia, M., 73
Berger, P.L. and Luckman, T., 31
Bernstein, B., 39
Bettelheim, B., 152
Betts, A., 52, 132
Biddulph, S., 12
Bowerman, M. and Levinson, S.C. (eds.), 23, 24,
                32, 33
Bradley, L. and Bryant, P. E., xi, 46, 63
Bremner, J.G., 23
Brierley, J., 1
Bristow, J. *et al.*, 48, 49, 107, 108, 124, 141, 142
Brown, R., 19
Brownjohn, S., 107
Bruner, J.S., 73, 152
Bryant, P., 63
Bryson, B., 34, 35, 36, 38
Byrne, B., 51, 62, 63

Carroll, J.B. and Casagrande, J.B., 31, 33
Carter, R., 5, 6, 9, 10, 13, 18, 39, 47, 48, 49, 55
Chang, G.L. and Wells, G., 156
Chanquoy, L., 115, 117, 124
Clark, E.V., 19, 23
C.L.P.E., 38, 83
Colley, A., 141
Collins, F., 93, 107
Coltheart, M. *et al.* (eds.), 54, 55
Conrad, R., 50
Corden, R., 26, 28, 40–42, 73, 81, 151, 152, 157
Coulson, M., 48, 51
Craik, F.M. and Lockhart, R.S., 49
Crowhurst, M., 99

Crystal, D., 18, 20, 21, 22, 25, 34, 40

Das Gupta, P. and Richardson, K., 23
Davie, R. *et al.*, 8
De La Mare, W., 105
Demb, J.B. *et al.*, 55
Demont, E. and Gombert, J.E., 142
DfEE (1998), 12, 13, 14, 41, 59, 66, 91
DfEE (1999a), 39, 66, 148
DfEE (1999b), 66
DfEE (2000), 39, 66
DfEE (2001, rev.), 18
DfEE (2001/0019), 38, 66, 73, 91, 161
DfEE (2001/0055), 68, 94
DfEE (2001/0107), 94
DfEE (2001/0476), 142
DES (1988), 144
Donaldson, M., 23
Downing, J. and Leong, C.K., xi, 46
Drozd, K.F., 23

Ehri, L., 65, 67
Ellis, A.W., 52
Ellis, S., 107
Engle, R.W. *et al.*, 49
Evans, J. (ed.), 37, 107, 117

Fawcett, A.J. and Nicolson, R.I., 55
Fawcett, A.J. *et al.*, 55
Fernald, G.M., 66
Fifield, P., 155
Fisher, R., 111
Fontana, D. and Evans, M., 49, 51
Frater, G., 163
Frith, U., 47, 60

Gahagan, D.M. and Gahagan, G.A., 151
Gathercole, S.E. and Adams, A.M., 51
Gathercole, S.E. and Pickering, S.J., 51
Gentry, J.R., 64
Gopnik, A., 32, 33
Goswami, U.C. and Bryant, P.E., 47, 63
Graham, J. and Kelly, A. (eds.), 70
Grainger, T., 81, 152, 153
Gravelle, M. (ed.), 38
Gredler, G.R., 61
Greenfield, S.A., 1, 2, 3, 7, 17
Gregory, E., 38
Grugeon, E. *et al.*, 42, 149, 150–52, 157
Gurney, R., 18

Halliday, M.A.K., 25, 26, 27
H.C.C., 56
Henry, J., 12
Hodgson Burnett, F., 102
Hooker, J.T. (ed.), 165
Hulme, C., 6

Hutchcroft, D.M.R., 134
Hutt, C., 8, 9

Johnson, M.H., 2

K.C.C., 98, 115
Kinmont, A., 83, 91, 92, 114, 131
Kipling, R., 132
Kress, G., 93

Lamb, C., 155
Latham, D.S., 49, 51, 142
Laurita, R.E., 64
Lazim, A. and Ellis, S., 142
Lee, V. and Das Gupta, P. (eds.), 17–24, 31, 32,
           47, 48, 51, 60–64, 141
Lennard, J., 107
Lewis, M. and Wray, D., 100
Lyons, J., 23

Maclure, M. et al., 40, 150, 151–153, 156
Mahy, M., 138
Malory, T., 138
Marcel, T., 55
McPhillips, M. et al., 55, 56
Melnik, A. and Merritt, J., 142
Messer, D.J., 24, 64
Messer, D.J. and Millar, S. (eds.), 23, 24, 50, 64, 69
Millard, E., 14
Miller, G.A., 49
Miyake, N. and Shah, P. (eds.), 49, 51
Moffett, J., 92
Moir, A. and Jessel, D., 9, 10, 13
Moline, S., 107
Morwood, J. and Warman, M., 64

N.W.P., 110
Neate, B., 107
Nicolson, R.I., 50, 69
Nicolson, R.I. and Fawcett, A.J., 55, 56

Oakhill, J., 21, 46, 47, 60–64, 141
OFSTED (1999), 39
O'Sullivan, O. and Thomas, A., 61
Ozawa, F. et al., 5

Parker, S., 150, 153
Perera, K., 107
Peters, M.L., 65, 66
Phinn, G., 117
Piaget, J., 23, 25, 31, 32
Pinker, S., 3, 5, 6, 17, 18, 19, 34, 36
Porter, M., 1
Power, R. and Power, E., 168

QCA (1998/052), 80
QCA (1998/081), 11, 12, 13, 100
QCA (1998/144), 160
QCA (1998/247), 142
QCA (1998/165), 56, 63
QCA (1999/282), 75, 76

QCA (1999/392), 73, 75, 82, 115
QCA (1999/418), 75
QCA (2000/587), 149

Randall, J., 64
Rees, F., 87
Reid, J.F. and Donaldson, H. (eds.), 61
Robinson, A., xii, xiii
Rosen, H., 151, 152
Rosen, M., 121, 124
Rudduck, J., 16
Rundell, S., 12

Sampson, G., xi
Sapir, E., 32
Sasanuma, S., 54
Sassoon, R., 71
Schonell, F., 66
Shakespeare's Globe Theatre, 156
Sheridan, M.D., 2, 5
Skottun, B.C., 55
Slobin, D.I., 35, 36
Smith, F., 46, 103
Smith, L.B., 34
Smith, N., 23, 24, 39
Smyth, A., 55
Snowling, M. J., 45, 55, 61, 63
Southgate, V. et al., 133, 134
Sparks Linfield, R., 114
Spelke, E.S. and Tsivkin, S., 24
S.R.A., 140
Stannard, J., 41
Stein, J. and Walsh, V., 55
Stevenson, V., 35
Stine, R.L., 132

Taylor, W.L., 133
Tomasello, M., 33
Tough, J., 26, 27, 28, 39

Vygotsky, L.S., 23, 32, 73

Washtell, A., 70
Waxman, S., 31
Weeks, A., 111
Wells, G., 28, 39, 59
Westwood, P., 71
White, J., 100
Whorf, B.L., 32
Wilkinson, A.M., 45
Wilkinson, A.M. et al., 92
Williams, A., 137
Wray, D. and Lewis, M., 100, 108
Wyse, D., 149

Yates, I., 70
Yen Mah, A., 36, 37
Young, A.W., 7, 8

Zimet, S.G., 137

| Subject Index

accelerated learning, 54
accentual verse, 106
alliteration, 63, 107
alphabet, origin of, xi, xii, xiii
aphasia, 3
appreciative reading, 53
articulatory loop in working memory model, 51
assessment and planning cycle, 159, 160, 163
assessment, criteria for, 76, 82–86, 88, 89, 149
assessment, using for setting challenges for
        progress, 54, 76, 77, 159
associative structure in children's writing, 74, 88
automation, 47, 52, 53, 61, 67–69

basic connectives, 79
basic phonology – acquisition of, 20, 21
Barrett taxonomy of aspects of comprehension,
        143
bias, awareness of, 137, 101
blending, xii, 47, 62, 63, 151
brain, 1–16

categories of writing, 93–111
central executive in working memory model, 48–51
cerebral cortex – part of the brain, 3
chaining, in children's writing, 80, 82, 84, 85
characterization, 53, 156
clause structure, 80, 81, 119, 120
clauses, 22, 79, 84, 85, 86
cloze procedure, 53, 133
coarticulation, 62, 63
coherence, 82, 114, 115
cohesion, 82, 114, 115
collaborative modes of working, 84, 114, 115,
        136, 157, 158
collaborative writing, 74, 114, 115
communicative writing, 88
complex sentences, 21, 79, 80, 81
composition and review, 73, 83, 113, 114
composition, structural development and stages,
        73–87
compound sentences, 21, 79, 85
comprehension, 53, 141–144
conjunctions, 79, 80, 81
connectionism, 24
connectives, 22, 79, 80, 81
connectives, early…., basic…. and sophisticated,
        79, 80
context, 47, 64, 133
co-operative play, 25
corpus callosum – part of brain, 3
criterion-referenced tests, 76
critical periods, 2, 3
cross-curricular action plan, 110
cross-curricular uses of some text-types, 109–111

cross-curricular work, 75, 109–111
cursive handwriting, 68
CVCs, 62, 63

decentring, 91, 92
different writing systems, xi, xii
digraphs, 21, 60
draft, 52, 75, 79, 82, 113, 114
drama, 153, 154
dysgraphia, 54
dyslexia, 6, 54, 55, 56

early brain development, 1–16
early writing – support strategies, 77, 78
echolalia, 17
economy, of expression, 119–120
egocentric play, 25
elaborated code, 39
elaboration in writing, 119–121
ELGs – early learning goals, 27
ellipsis, 46
embedded clause, 80, 81, 120
emergent reading, 89
emergent writing, 77, 88
encoding skills, 60, 61
end-stop rhyming, 106
English as an additional language (EAL),
        teaching pupils with EAL, 37, 38
English language, 34–37
English – social and cultural differences in, 39, 40
enrichment for writing, 115, 123, 124
enrichment through topic approach, 124–129
epistemic stage – Bereiter, 74
exploratory talk, 26, 150, 151
expressive reading, 89

focusing strategy in writing, 115, 121–123

gender differences (brain), 8, 9, 10
gender differences and implications for teaching
        and learning, 14, 15, 162
gender differences in the educational situation,
        11–14, 100
genres, 93
grammar, 21, 22, 35, 36
grapheme, 48, 52, 60, 68
grapheme/phoneme correspondence (GPC),
        60–62, 68

handwriting, 67–70
hemispheres (brain), 3, 5, 7
hemispherical differences and characteristics, 3, 5
high frequency clusters of letters (HFCs), 60
higher level reading skills, 132–144
holophrase, 18

iambic pentameter, 106
icon answers, 78
ideational fluency, 78
improvement in writing – pointers for, 163, 164
inclusion, 162
independent reading, 89
inflections, 19
informative reading, 89
initial-letter shorthand, 78
interactive journal, 78
interpretive reading, 89
insertions, 109, 114
inventive spelling, 78

kanji and *kana*, xii, 54
kenning, 91
kernel sentences, 20, 140
kinaesthetic, 52, 68, 69

language acquisition, 17–29
languages and social and cultural differences, 34–37
language and thinking, 31–43
laterality, 5, 6
left-handedness, 6, 8, 69, 70
LCWC, 65
linguistic relativity hypothesis, 32, 33
literacy, 45, 46
long-term memory, 48

magic line, 78
main clauses, 66, 79
Main Idea Analysis, 139–141
meaning – development of memory span, 51
metalanguage, 66, 73, 80
metalinguistic skills, 66, 73
metaphor, 84, 114, 119
metrical feet, 37, 106
modelled writing, 69, 80, 114
monologue, 24
morphemes, xi, 63
myelinization, 2, 3

normal curve, 76

onset and rime, 63
optic chiasma (brain), 7
optic nerve (brain), 7
oracy, differences between oracy and literacy, 45, 46
oracy, importance of for literacy, 40–42
organization, of writing (composition), 73–87
orthography, 47, 61, 63, 64
over-extensions, 19, 20

P scales, 19, 27
parallel play, 25
performative stage – Bereiter, 74
persuasion in writing, 101, 102, 103, 104, 129, 154
phonemes, 48, 52, 60, 62, 68
phonographic, xi
phonics, 47, 51, 61

phonology, 20, 21, 47
phonological loop in working memory model, 48, 49
phonological training, 51, 63, 67
phrases, 19, 80, 120
pictographic writing systems, xi
pivot grammar, 18, 27, 28
play writing, 77
précis, 139–141
prediction, 53, 135
primary/secondary divide, bridging, 160, 161
production – as in speaking and writing, 45
prosody, 17, 37
purposes, 93, 94

quality, flow, and pace, 159, 160
quantitative verse, 166

reading profile, a, 89
reception, listening and reading, 45
recount, 95
relational structure, 88
relative pronoun, 79
response partners, 114
restricted code, 39
review (composition), 59, 73, 115
rhyme, 63, 106
rime (and onset), 63
role-play, 61, 149, 152, 153
roots (word derivations), 35, 63, 64

Saccades, 50
SATs, 76, 84
scaffolding, 73, 100, 101
scene-setting, 136
SCWC, 66
selective note-making, 139
self-generated writing, 113
semanticity, xi, 20
sentence markers, 77, 85
sequencing (reading), 53
sequencing (writing), 115–118, 135
Shakespeare projects, 155–156
shared writing, 67, 69, 78
short-term memory, 49
similes, 84, 114, 119
simple sentences, 21, 79, 85
skills – developing effective skills in writing and reading, 46, 47, 60–62
skills – encoding, 59–71
speaking and listening, development at different stages, 149–151
spelling, 59–67
spelling strategies, 65, 66
stages of early speech, 17–29
standardized tests, 76
story drama, 153
storytelling, 151, 152
streamers, 78
style and form, 93, 137

subordinate clauses, 79–81, 84–86, 120
syllabification, 63
syllables, 37, 47, 80, 106
syntax, 21, 35, 36, 38

teacher/scribe, 77
telegraphic speech, 19, 27
text types, 91–111
theatre workshops, 153–155
theory theory, the, 33
thinking and feeling, 91–93
transitivity, 33, 34, 35, 147, 148

visual memory span, 51
visuo-spatial scratch-pad, in working memory
 model, 48

unified stage – Bereiter, 74

whole school perspective, 160, 163
word banks, 78
working memory model, 45–56, 67
writing process components, 59, 60
writing profile, a, 88

young children's language uses, 24, 25, 27, 28

zone of proximal development (ZPD), 23, 73, 159